MW00563193

PRAISE FOR *WOMEN LIFERS:*
LIVES BEFORE, BEHIND, AND BEYOND BARS

"In the worlds of academic debate and penal reform much attention is given to the need to provide alternatives to imprisonment for women serving short custodial sentences and to the need to minimise the disruption to their lives that such sentences can entail. *Women Lifers: Lives Before, Behind, and Beyond Bars* takes us into oft-hidden territory: the reasons for the increase in the number of female lifers, and more particularly, how women find themselves in the predicament of long-term imprisonment and what it is like for them. The book presents us with compelling and moving stories from women lifers, focusing on their pathways in to prison, their lives in prison and how they have adjusted, and then on expectations, hopes, and for those eligible, preparation for release. The authors have made women lifers and the issues which pervade their lives both visible and memorable through sensitive and nuanced research. This is a very important, lucid and thought-provoking book which deserves wide readership." —**Loraine Gelsthorpe**, Institute of Criminology, University of Cambridge, United Kingdom

"The authors provide all the necessary background and contextual information about women and crime for any reader to understand and appreciate the punitiveness of lifer policies in the United States. At the same time, through extensive interviewing, the authors brilliantly disabuse lifers as violent bloodthirsty criminals. Instead, they vividly document how an abusive partner, a sub-par education, or a dead-end job can collide into the unthinkable—life behind bars." —**Miriam Northcutt Bohmert**, Indiana University–Bloomington

Women Lifers

Lives before, behind, and beyond Bars

Meredith Huey Dye and Ronald H. Aday

ROWMAN & LITTLEFIELD
Lanham • Boulder • New York • London

Published by Rowman & Littlefield
An imprint of The Rowman & Littlefield Publishing Group, Inc.
4501 Forbes Boulevard, Suite 200, Lanham, Maryland 20706
www.rowman.com

6 Tinworth Street, London SE11 5AL, United Kingdom

British Library Cataloguing in Publication Information Available

Library of Congress Cataloging-in-Publication Data Available

ISBN 978-1-5381-1302-8 (cloth: alk. paper)
ISBN 978-1-5381-1303-5 (electronic)

∞™ The paper used in this publication meets the minimum requirements of
American National Standard for Information Sciences—Permanence of Paper
for Printed Library Materials, ANSI/NISO Z39.48-1992.

Printed in the United States of America

To the women living life behind bars
Thank you for sharing your stories.

Contents

List of Tables and Figures

List of Case Histories

Acknowledgments

We are extremely grateful to the amazing women whose stories are shared within these pages. Without your openness and willingness to give voice, this written work would not be what it is. We hope that we retold your experiences in a way that reflects who you are as people and so that you no longer feel as forgotten or invisible.

All of the women are (or were) incarcerated within the Georgia Department of Corrections (GA DOC), who approved the project and facilitated our visits with these women. We must thank Lisa Haughey, especially, for leading and supporting us. We could not have completed this project without you creating a pathway into prison for us. Thank you for your constant commitment and encouragement.

As full-time faculty at Middle Tennessee State University, we could not have completed this project without the support for data collection from the Department of Sociology and Anthropology. Both Ron and I received financial awards and course release time from the Faculty Research and Creative Activity Awards and Non-instructional Assignment Grants. We also had support from colleagues and numerous graduate research assistants over the years including Deann Lamb Rizziere, Amanda Kaiser, Jordan Raley, Lori Farney, Victoria Ong, Nicole Cook, Mary De La Torre, Huey Davis, and Alicia Wray.

We also acknowledge the endless support from our families who allowed us time to travel and write, and who listened to our ideas and the women's stories. In many ways, you have helped share the stories and experiences of these women lifers with us.

Chapter 1

Introduction to the Lives of Women Lifers

UNDERSTANDING WOMEN IN THE CRIMINAL JUSTICE SYSTEM

Crime and criminal justice are most often thought of as men's domain, and the numbers support this conclusion. According to the Uniform Crime Report, in 2017, approximately 10,000 homicides were committed by men compared to just over 1,400 by women.[1] Similar trends are evident for other violent and property crimes with only a few exceptions (e.g., embezzlement). When women do commit crime, especially violent ones, their behaviors, actions, and motives are sensationalized by the media and misrepresented to the uncritical public and policy makers. However, until recently, women in the criminal justice system have been invisible to the public, policy makers, and researchers.[2] In part because of this invisibility, the number of women in U.S. prisons has increased dramatically since the 1980s, and has in rate outpaced that of men's incarceration.[3] In 1980, about 13,000 women were incarcerated in state and federal prisons. At year-end, 2016, females made up about 7 percent of the 1.5 million prison population, equivalent to roughly 112,000 women in state and federal prisons in the United States.[4] While mass incarceration has certainly affected men, these figures represent a more than 700 percent increase in the incarceration rate for women over this time frame. At the time, almost no one noticed or cared to notice the problems of "mass incarceration."[5] Some celebrated these increasing numbers as a positive outcome of the "war on crime" and evidence that the criminal justice system's "get tough" approach to crime was working. Others were engineering and benefiting from a profitable business that is now known as the prison industrial complex.[6]

Although media representations would suggest differently, these increases have not corresponded to an increase in women's crime or violence. Overall, crime rates have declined markedly since the 1990s and these declines actually preceded the rise in incarceration rates.[7] In addition, compared to men, women are more likely to be arrested and imprisoned for property and drug offenses than violent crimes (see table 1.1).[8]

Instead, the increase in women in the criminal justice system reflects an "equality movement" where women are treated the same as men when it comes to arrest, conviction, sentencing, and imprisonment based on the idea that in the past women have been treated too leniently (i.e., "chivalry hypothesis").[9] As a form of vengeful equity,[10] this trend reflects a backlash to the women's equality movement of the 1970s and 1980s as well as perceptions of girls' and women's increasing criminality and, in response, the need for harsher penalties. Women are considered "doubly deviant" defying both gender and legal norms, and according to the "evil woman hypothesis," are treated more harshly by the criminal justice system as a result.[11] For the

Table 1.1. Percentage of sentenced men and women under the jurisdiction of State and Federal Correctional Authority, by Most Serious Offense, December 31, 2015

State:			
Most serious offense	All	Male	Female
Violent	54.5	55.9	37.0
Murder or manslaughter	15.0	15.1	14.0
Property	18.0	17.3	26.9
Drug	15.2	14.4	24.9
Public Order	11.6	11.7	10.2
Other	0.7	0.7	1.0
Total Number of state prisoners (sentenced)	1,298,159	1,204,799	93,360
Federal:			
Most serious offense	All	Male	Female
Violent	7.7	8.0	4.5
Murder or manslaughter	1.6	1.6	1.4
Property	6.1	5.2	18.6
Drug	47.5	46.8	56.4
Public Order	38.2	39.5	19.7
Other	0.5	0.5	0.7
Total Number of federal prisoners (sentenced)	172,554	161,332	11,222

Source: Carson, E. Ann. *Prisoners in 2016*. Washington, DC: US Department of Justice, Office of Justice Programs, 2018. https://www.bjs.gov/content/pub/pdf/p16.pdf

public and those policy makers who are far removed from the realities of the criminal justice system, offenders are "monsters" and "evil," are never victims themselves, and deserve to pay for their crimes. This public sentiment and outcry fueled the incarceration binge where more people were sentenced to prison and for longer periods of time; yet this fury failed to consider the consequences for those incarcerated and their disrupted communities.[12] Women especially were an afterthought in the male-dominated system. When women's needs were considered, they received "special" programs that were "gender-specific." While intentions were noble, these programs and this "special" attention to women's crime and incarceration was typically to the detriment of women and their families,[13] and resulted in greater numbers of women in the criminal justice system, for longer sentences, but continued invisibility and mischaracterization of their experiences.[14]

GROWTH OF THE U.S. LIFER POPULATION

These trends and the reasons behind these trends hold true for the imposition of life sentences as well, which saw a fivefold increase from 1984 to 2016.[15] Currently, there are over 206,000 lifers in U.S. state and federal prisons; one in seven people in prison are lifers (see figure 1.1).[16] While the vast majority of lifers are men, over 6,700 women are currently serving life, life without parole, or virtual life (50+ years). Over 70 percent will be eligible for parole after serving a set number of years (e.g., fifteen or twenty years), which varies by state and has varied over time, becoming increasingly longer and more punitive. In the state of Georgia, for example, a person with a life sentence is not eligible for parole until after serving thirty years. Some life sentences are solely symbolic and retributive, and equate to death sentences, as they reach upward of 600 or 999 years of stacked charges, convictions, and sentences.[17] According to the Sentencing Project, sentences of "life without parole" are used almost every state, but are disproportionately used in Florida, Pennsylvania, Louisiana, California, and Michigan.[18]

Despite these numbers, incarcerated women, and women lifers specifically, represent a relatively small percentage of the overall correctional (about 7 percent) and lifer populations (about 4 percent). Within each state system, as few as 100–500 women are incarcerated for life. Compared to men and other women in the system, women lifer's invisibility is obvious—it is easy to overlook, discount, diminish, and forget such a small group. These are those whom we "lock up" and "throw away the key."

This invisibility is evident not only in allocations of money, time, and attention within the criminal justice system, but also within research literature.

Much of the literature on lifers focuses on men with life sentences.[19] While a growing body of literature focuses on women offenders/prisoners, relatively few focus specifically on those serving life sentences. With the exception of a few research articles,[20] a recent ethnography,[21] and Lempert's 2016 qualitative study of women lifers in Michigan,[22] much of the extant literature on female lifers is dated (1990s) and consists of small samples from prisons in California,[23] Ohio,[24] the United Kingdom,[25] and Canada.[26] Differences in samples and locations as well as the research methodologies limit the generalizability to the overall population of women lifers in the United States.

Women serving life sentences tend to be older women (average age is forty), with children, serving a sentence for a violent offense (primarily murder) perpetuated against a known victim (who may also be a domestic abuser). The vast majority of women lifers have no prior prison history, but extensive histories of physical and sexual victimization.[27] Despite the term "lifer," many of these women will be released from prison after serving long sentences. Beyond this basic profile, there is much more to learn and share about the lives of women lifers.

Figure 1.1.   Growth of Life Sentences, 1984–2016

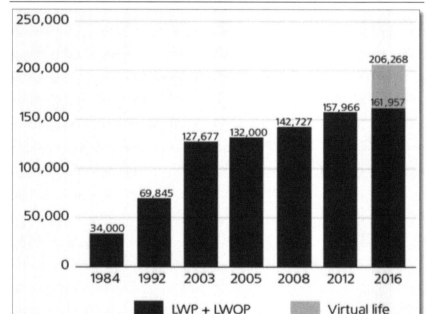

Source: Nellis, Ashley. *Still Life: America's Increasing Use of Life and Long-Term Sentences*. Washington, D.C.: The Sentencing Project, 2017. http://www.sentencingproject.org/publications/still-life-americas-increasing-use-life-long-term-sentences/

While we focus on the trends in crime and incarceration and reasons behind the trends, we fail to hear or listen to the stories of these women's lives. Who are the women serving life in prison? How did they find themselves there? How have they coped with their new lives and how have their lives changed with the passage of time? What are their expectations and hopes for after serving their time in prison? This book is intended to trace women's lives before, during, and following a life sentence. In particular, we seek to give voice to those who are silenced, misrepresented, and made invisible. As one of the women we interviewed shared:

> Lifers are in some sense stereotypes. Not everybody is a cold-blooded murder. Some people just got caught up and a lot of women are in here behind a man. I think people need to study women's cases more and read in between the lines for more details and truth. I think they should have more programs for lifers to learn skills and to use outside of prison. They seem discriminated against at times. If a lifer has no purpose or nothing to do that's when they tend to act out. I think judging by inmate's character and conduct some lifer's should be given the chance to go home. A lot of these women would not come back or commit more crimes.

In this book, we expand on each of these concerns, and others, voiced by the women we met. We agree with Lora Bex Lempert, who writes:

> When the focus is on the deed, or on the woman's flaws and weaknesses, and not on the social forces that underscore the crime, women who kill become the monsters of popular lore. However, when their deeds are contextualized and the criminal sanctions are demystified by an understanding of the details of their lives (e.g., disorganized childhoods, inadequate educations, sexual abuse and physical trauma, limited employment opportunities, delinquent peers, violent relationships), they lose the sensational qualities and much of the onus shifts to society's failure to provide relief to women trapped in intolerable situations.[28]

STUDYING WOMEN LIFERS

The very invisibility that allows the public and policy makers to ignore and stereotype women in prison also hinders researchers' abilities to attempt to understand women's incarcerated lives, making them even more invisible. Gaining entry and access to conduct prison research is difficult especially for an outside academic/researcher, and once permission is approved, women may be skeptical or reluctant to share their stories. For women lifers, some do not like talking about their sentence, try to stay to themselves, or are in denial that they have a life sentence. As one woman lifer shared with us:

Everyone handles doing this time differently. I haven't had the opportunity to sit and talk with other lifers because most of the ladies surviving a life sentence do not like talking about the fact they are lifers. Serving a life sentence is very, very difficult and extremely sensitive subject that is usually never discussed.

Another woman shared:

I don't spiritually or mentally receive the sentence than man put on me because I am not guilty. I have never spoken the sentence out of my mouth, so believe me its hard to sit here since I have never acknowledged it.

We relied on previous experience working with and conducting research in prisons throughout the southern United States. Like others,[29] we formed collaborative partnerships with those working in the prisons and the women serving lengthy amounts of time in these prisons. Using key gatekeepers, we worked to gain trust and build rapport. For these reasons, it is very much a privilege to share these women's voices and experiences. We take serious the task so that these women become and feel visible.

We administered a structured survey questionnaire in three women's prisons in the state of Georgia between January and June 2010, and a similar follow-up questionnaire in two of the prisons in June 2018. One of the prisons was located in the capital, a metropolitan area of the state (closed at follow-up), while the other two women's prisons are located in rather rural, remote areas at opposite ends of the state (north and south), approximately two hundred miles apart. Over time, most of the women, at some point, had served portions of their sentence in all of these women's prisons in the state, from diagnostic and reception to long-term confinement, being transferred between prisons by request or with little choice in the administrative decisions regarding their housing.

We followed standard procedures for conducting research in prisons, including receiving approval from our university's institutional review board and the state department of corrections. Using the online department of corrections inmate search options, we identified all women with life sentences in the state. We provided this list to each prison, and on the days of on-site visits, we met the women in cafeterias and other visitation settings. We described the nature of the project and provided consent forms and questionnaires to all who were willing to participate. Some chose not to participate for personal reasons, and some were unable to participate due to work conflicts or administrative reasons (e.g., mental/physical health, or medical appointments). However, very few women refused to participate. The majority of women we met agreed to participate, and did so enthusiastically. They were eager to share their experiences and have someone listen to them.

We did not collect names or prison-issued inmate numbers with the survey questions to ensure the confidentiality of those who participated. Some women included this information in order to stay connected with us and to provide a name and face for the responses they gave. We followed up via mail correspondence with all of the women, sending them an aggregate report of the findings, and individually with those who were especially willing to share their thoughts and experiences on serving a life sentence. To ensure confidentiality and to limit the likelihood that any single individual's words or specific cases would be identified, we do not use actual names. With 214 women, we chose not to assign pseudonyms for women lifers, except for selected case histories included in each chapter. However, we are mindful of how terms and labels such as "murderer," "offender," and "inmate" are used to refer to women in prison and those with life sentences, and avoid using them. Although we did not assign names, we do provide a descriptive context for their voices (i.e., age, amount of time served, motherhood status, health, etc.) and make deliberate efforts to emphasize the woman lifer as a person, not a number or a crime.

Of the 303 women serving life sentences in the state at the time of the first survey, 214 participated (71 percent). They represented the variety of women serving life, and were representative of the entire women lifer population in the state. At follow-up, of the women who were still incarcerated and had served fifteen years or more of their sentence, 94 were available and agreed to complete the follow-up survey questionnaire. Some of these women were nearing parole or had parole review dates. Currently, over 400 women are serving life sentences in the state of Georgia, a state which incarcerates over fifty thousand people, about 17 percent of whom have life sentences. The vast majority of the lifers in this state are men (95 percent), and most do have the possibility of parole (75 percent).

SURVEY QUESTIONS

In addition to demographic profile questions, the survey questionnaire consisted of both closed and open-ended questions regarding self-reported physical and mental health conditions and healthcare services in prison; the Hopkins Symptom Checklist;[30] prison adjustment scale;[31] prison supports and activities; family supports; questions specific to coping with a life sentence; and Templar's Death Anxiety Scale.[32] For those who indicated a history of abuse, we asked additional questions about their victimization, including an intimate partner violence inventory which measured incidents of physical, verbal, social, and sexual abuse, and controlling threats. The follow-up survey focused specifically on women lifers who had served fifteen or more years of their sentence, and included questions pertaining to release and re-entry expectations.

The initial questionnaire was lengthy—eight pages with forty-two questions for all women and an additional three pages with thirteen questions for women with histories of abuse. All questions were worded at an eighth-grade reading level using everyday, jargon-free terms. We read the survey questions to women who needed assistance due to language barriers (e.g., Spanish speakers) and reading and writing difficulties, especially those who were older with visual impairments and limited use of hands due to arthritis. We transcribed these responses onto the paper survey. Although we anticipated that some women with visual problems or who were unable to physically provide written responses might need assistance, all the remaining women who agreed to participate did so without our help. Using open-ended prompts provided in the questionnaire, women wrote extensively on their experiences with initial adjustment and coping with a life sentence, changes in adjustment over time, unique experiences as a women lifer, family connections, religious beliefs, and victimization by and violence toward an abuser. Likewise, women were given space to voice expectations and concerns about getting out of prison. In addition, after completing the paper surveys, we listened to individual women who shared their experiences and concerns with us informally through personal communications, and later via mail. Each of these methods helped to inform the conclusions we present about the lives of women lifers.

SAMPLE PROFILE

In her description of women serving life in Michigan, Lempert writes: "The act of killing is extraordinary, but most women who kill are in every other way ordinary."[33] While 93 percent of women lifers in the state we profile were convicted of murder charges, the vast majority have no prior prison history. Thus, for about 95 percent of the women, their life sentence is their first time incarcerated. Other than murder, women in this state can also be sentenced to life on a "two strikes" policy including drug felonies, and for being a party to the crime of murder, or one of the "seven deadly sins" outlined by the state including robbery, rape, or kidnapping. Women referred to the "party to a crime" laws in the state time and again. As this woman told us:

> There are a lot of women in prison that didn't actually commit the crime of murdering another human being. We are doing life sentences for being around the people that actually did the crime.

As shown in table 1.2, our sample profile is consistent with the lifer population in the state and other "ordinary women" with regards to age, race, marital status, and educational level. The average current age is 41 years, and ranges from the youngest being 19 and the oldest being 78. At follow-up, the oldest woman lifer was 86 years old. On average, the women began their life sentenced at age 30 (range 14–70 years), and had served an average of 12 years (range < 1–35 years) at the time of the initial survey. About 16 percent of the women were sentenced to life as juveniles (< 18 years old), with the youngest sentenced in 1999 at the age of 14.

Like much of the criminal justice system, the women lifers in this sample are disproportionately nonwhite (> 50 percent). Whether obtained prior to or during their sentence, about three-quarters of the women have at least a high school degree/GED. Only about 25 percent do not have a high school diploma or GED, while about 11 percent hold a college degree. A little over half are or have been married; most have living family members including parents (70 percent), siblings (87 percent), children (70 percent), and grandchildren (35 percent).

In the initial survey, over 83 percent of the women in the sample indicated a history of abuse as an adult and/or child. This included physical, sexual, and/or emotional abuse. As described more fully in later chapters, these abuse histories were often lengthy, violent, injurious, and concentrated in a specific part of life course (e.g., early childhood or during key relationships). The effects of these experiences compounded over time and greatly impact pre-incarceration lives, pathways to prison, and current adjustment to a life sentence. For about 62 percent of these women with abuse histories, abuse played a factor in their life sentence. Abuse began as early as age 2, or as late as 52 years (average age 19 years). As their stories tell, and others have concluded, these women are "more vulnerable than violent."[34]

BOOK OVERVIEW

This book is organized along three stages in the lives of women lifers. The first follows women's pathways to prison (entry) and includes descriptions of their lives before their life sentence. Chapter 2 describes their pre-prison characteristics such as drug and alcohol problems, mental health conditions, and overall demographic profiles as well as the patterns in their criminal histories, crimes, and convictions. Chapter 3 details the most typical pathway to prison for women serving life sentences: histories of abuse in childhood and/ or adult intimate partner violence. Many of the women lifers in this sample killed abusive partners. One of the most common questions directed toward women who kill abusive partners is, "Why didn't she just leave?" Based on prior research,[35] we know that women's ability to leave is complex. The women lifers in this sample describe the consequences of their abuse; the measures they took to stop the abuse such as leaving (multiple times), calling the police, and getting restraining orders; and the way their abuse experiences influence their lives today, in prison.

Table 1.2. Sample Profile for Women Lifers in Georgia

	Initial Survey, 2010 (n=214)		Follow-up Survey, 2018 (n=94)*	
	Average or %	Range	Average or %	Range
Age (years)	41.43	19–78	51.43	34–86
Age at First Prison Sentence (years)	29.28	14–70	28.82	14–68
Juvenile Lifer (<18 years of age at sentence)	16.4%		15.1%	
Time Served (years)	11.99	<1–35	21.63	15–38
Prior Prison History (% yes)	5.14%		8.6%	
Race:				
Nonblack	54.79%		46.8%	
Black	45.21%		53.2%	
Education:				
Less than HS	25.5%		14.9%	
HS education or GED	37.0%		42.5%	
Some college higher	37.5%		42.5%	
Marital Status:				
Never Married	42.9%		42.4%	
Ever Married (includes divorced, separated, or widowed)	56.1%		57.6%	
Living Family Members (% with):				
Parents	69.3%		49.5%	
Siblings	86.9%		78.0%	
Children	70.6%		70.3%	
Grandchildren	34.9%		50.5%	
Abuse History (% yes)	83.7%		77.2%	
Abuse a Factor in Incarceration (% yes)	62.0%		49.4%	

*Follow-up sample consisted of women lifers with fifteen or more years served of their life sentence.

The next part of the book focuses on women's lives while serving a life sentence and how women adjust to a life in prison. Chapter 4 examines overall adjustment including initial reactions to receiving their life sentence, and adjustment over time. "Adjustment" includes living and getting along with other women "offenders"; dealing with prison staff; feeling disconnected from the outside; loss of freedom, privacy, and comfort; being bored; and worries about becoming institutionalized. Women lifers cope with their life sentence individually and personally (e.g., religious/spiritual means) and through prison supports including activities, programs, and friendships.

Maintaining connections with family members on the outside is a salient concern for women lifers who worry about being forgotten with the passage of long stretches of time. These concerns make up a large part of "doing time" for women lifers and their families. In chapter 5, we describe the ways women lifers maintain contact with family, the importance of family, and their involvement in parenting/grandparenting from prison. We describe their barriers to maintaining contact and satisfaction with family relationships as well as issues with reconnecting with family after release from prison (chapter 9).

Chapter 6 provides an overview of the current physical and mental health problems that women lifers face. There are three unique factors that affect women lifer's health: (1) Women serving life arrive at prison later in life than other incarcerated women, bringing with them age-related health issues; (2) typically, incarcerated women, including women lifers, are physically older than their actual age (by about ten years older) due to both pre-prison lives and prison deprivations; and (3) women lifers suffer both physically and mentally from injuries sustained as a result of trauma and abuse histories. In light of these factors, we describe women's healthcare utilization, reliance on medications, costs and copays, health deterioration, and concerns about getting sick in prison and staying healthy while in prison. Specific health-related concerns for women lifers involve their nutrition, diets, and available foods (i.e., junk foods versus fresh fruits and vegetables); dental care; and the physical pains of aging behind bars.

In terms of mental health, we report their self-reported levels of current depression, anxiety, interpersonal sensitivity, and somatization. We also examine specific indicators of Post-Traumatic Stress Disorder (PTSD) related to both pre-prison abuse histories and experiences adjusting to living in prison. When women begin their life sentences, they report feeling that their lives are over and they "just wanted to die." Although incarcerated men and women think about, attempt, and complete suicide at any time during their imprisonment, we look at initial and current thoughts of suicide and hopelessness about the future as additional indicators of mental health and prison adjustment.

For some women lifers, their sentence is a death sentence; they will not leave prison alive and their only escape will be through death. Some deaths are chosen (i.e., suicide) while most are health and age-related, many dying much younger than the norm for those not incarcerated. Women lifers worry about dying in prison and experience the deaths of loved ones on the outside as well as those of important friendships made on the inside. Chapter 7 details these losses, fears, and how women lifers cope with the losses of living in prison as well as those of dying in prison.

Chapter 8 focuses specifically on the role that religious supports play in the lives of life-sentenced women. While some come to prison with strong religious backgrounds and convictions, others "find" religion within the prison walls as they cope with losses and adjust to their lives in prison. Among the vast majority of women lifers, religion touches nearly every aspect and experience of life behind bars, including dealing with the loss of freedom, health issues, disconnections from family, and the ups and downs of the parole process.

Women lifers are forgotten by society in the haste to punish; they serve out their life sentences, changing themselves in the process, and for most eventually realizing the reality of release from prison. Chapter 9 focuses on women's expectations and preparations for parole, release from prison, and reentry into the larger society, and society's and their unpreparedness for this phase of their life sentence. While most women lifers maintain hope for release from the beginning, this hope may diminish over time. As parole dates approach, hope may swell only to be crushed with denials. For those who are granted a release date, those hopes for release become reality, and for many, turn to anxieties about living outside of prison, including reconnecting with family, supporting themselves financially, dealing with a changed world, and confronting the stigma of being a formerly incarcerated person/lifer/ murderer. Few programs are available for women serving life; vocational and reentry programs are reserved for those with less than two years to serve before release. Lifers do not qualify because they have an indeterminate number of years to serve (e.g., twenty years to life) and do not know when they will be released. The invisibility and throw-away-the-key mentality surrounding women lifers, thus, also has consequences for successful reentry. However, persons serving life sentences have been ignored even as policy and research has shifted focus to concerns about prisoner reentry.[36]

We conclude the book with a call for more research and policy attention to the forgotten population of women (and men) lifers in U.S. prisons. Chapter 10 summarizes the overall takeaways from these women lifers' experiences, and outlines why they (should) matter to everyone. Excessive punitive practices within a system of penal harm mark their experiences. Although we do not deny or seek to diminish the pain suffered by victims and their families, we argue that the lives of women lifers and their families are also important. They are more than their crimes and have also felt victimized by others and the entire system. From them, we can learn reasons why we should challenge penal harm as well as how we can move forward in criminal justice reforms to a system that is framed by human justice.

SUMMARY

Throughout each of the chapters in the book, we find several reoccurring themes among women lifers and point to how these experiences shape their pathways to prison, their adjustment to life behind bars, and their expectations for getting out of prison. The first focuses on women lifers' histories of abuse, trauma, and mental health problems. The effects of these experiences are felt (and often ignored) as the women live their lives behind bars. The second theme concerns women's family relationships and supports, and worries about maintaining some bond with their family members and reconnecting with family after serving their life sentence. A third theme is their reliance on religious supports during their time in prison as a way to cope with their sentence, and a buffer against fears, anxieties, and hopelessness. A final theme involves the processes of aging and maturing for women lifers, along with their efforts toward self-improvement and education. In all of these areas, women lifers deal with stigma, loss, and maintaining hope.

What is inspiring, though, is how, on balance, most women lifers find strength and courage to make a life and seek to redeem themselves even as they are cut off from the rest of society. They act as mentors and role-models for other women including young lifers or "short-timers"; provide a stability to the ever-changing, yet structured prison environment; and garner some respect for these positive positions from staff and other inmates. Even still, women lifers face barriers to "success" within and outside of prison. They are denied programs because of their long sentences, denied parole multiple times after serving lengthy amounts of time because of the circumstances of their crimes, and face stigma from staff and other inmates who "throw their time" at them and tell them they are never getting out of prison. As they age, these taunts become more believable. The Pardon and Paroles Board also sends this message to them through repeated parole denials and lack of transparency with the process. The following chapters in this book include direct quotes and stories shared by the women and several case histories which give voice and context to these women's lives.[37] In all of these we expand on and explore the experiences that women lifers confront while serving life behind bars.

NOTES

1. "Crime in the United States," Federal Bureau of Investigation, 2017. https:// ucr.fbi.gov/crime-in-the-u.s/2017/crime-in-the-u.s.-2017

2. Belknap, *The Invisible Woman: Gender, Crime, and Justice.*

3. The Sentencing Project, "Women in the Justice System." http://www.sentenc ingproject.org/template/page.cfm?id=138

4. Carson, *Prisoners in 2016.* https://www.bjs.gov/content/pub/pdf/p16.pdf

5. Chesney-Lind, "Patriarchy, Crime and Justice."

6. Carceral, *Prison, Inc.*

7. Mauer, *Race to Incarcerate.*

8. Carson, *Prisoners in 2016.*

9. Belknap, *The Invisible Woman,* 173.

10. Chesney-Lind, "Patriarchy, Crime and Justice."

11. Belknap, *The Invisible Woman,* 173.

12. Mauer and Chesney-Lind, *Invisible Punishment.*

13. Solinger, Johnson, Raimon, Reynolds, and Tapia, *Interrupted Life.*

14. For a more humanistic perspective on women in a Georgia prison, see the photo journalism project by Jan Banning, *Pulaski Women's Prison, 2013.* http:// www.janbanning.com/pulaski/

15. Nellis, "Throw Away the Key."

16. Nellis, *Still Life.*

17. Aday and Krabill, *Women Aging in Prison.* See also George, *A Woman Doing Life.*

18. Nellis, *Life Goes On.*

19. Leigey, *The Forgotten Men.* See also Kazemian and Travis, "Imperative for Inclusion of Long Termers and Lifers in Research and Policy," and Liem, *After Life Imprisonment.*

20. Dye and Aday. "'I Just Wanted to Die.'" See also Leigey and Reed, "A Women's Life before Serving Life," and Fedock, "Life before 'I Killed the Man That Raped Me.'"

21. George, *A Woman Doing Life.*

22. Lempert, *Women Doing Life.*

23. Owen, *"In the Mix."*

24. Roscher, "The Development of Coping Strategies in Female Inmates with Life Sentences."

25. Genders and Player, "Women Lifers: Assessing the Experience."

26. Jose-Kamper, "Coming to Terms with Existential Death."

27. Leigey and Reed, "A Woman's Life before Serving Life."

28. Lempert, *Women Doing Life,* 14.

29. Quina et al., "Through the Bullet-Proof Glass."

30. Derogatis, *Brief Symptom Inventory (BSI).*

31. Zamble and Porporino, *Coping, Behavior, and Adaptation in Prison Inmates.*

32. Templer, "The Construction and Validation of a Death Anxiety Scale."

33. Lempert, *Women Doing Life,* 14.

34. Mauer, King, and Young, *The Meaning of Life: Long Prison Sentences in Context*, 2.

35. Leonard, *Convicted Survivors*.

36. Kazemian, and Travis, "Imperative for Inclusion of Long Termers and Lifers in Research and Policy."

37. We chose to use italics for all quotes taken directly from the women's words in their surveys, letters, and personal conversations in order to highlight them and make sure they are heard.

Chapter 2

Life before a Life Sentence

"Not everybody is a cold-blooded murderer. Some people just got caught up and a lot of women are in here behind a man."

"Circumstantially, we have almost walked the same journey, being abused and/or manipulated, faced with a situation that we either felt trapped [in] or done so in the name of love."

"Women are just sentences, courts don't look at what some for us went thru by our spouse or friend. They only look at . . . hey she killed a man."

Women's lives before prison are often marked by histories of physical, sexual, and emotional abuse, traumatic experiences, poverty, and mental health problems including suicide attempts and drug use. These experiences provide a context for women's "pathways" to crime, convictions, and sentences. As described in one quote above, women's lives are often reduced to their crime by the police, courts, and even their families. The context surrounding their involvement in the commission of a crime, which for women lifers typically is a murder, is also stripped down, identified only by numbers and offenses such as "murder" or "cruelty to children." Without further examination, many assume this is the whole story of these women's lives and pathways to prison. But there is more we can and need to learn about who is sentenced to life in prison and why.

In 1994, Kathleen Daly identified five pathways to women's involvement in the criminal justice system—street women, harmed and harming women, drug-connected women, battered women, and other women.[1] These pathways, or similar groupings, have been substantiated within a variety of different samples of women in the U.S. criminal justice system as well as women in European prisons.[2] Apart from "street women," the pathways proposed by Daly and others involve physical and/or sexual abuse during childhood, intimate partner violence, or drug use. For some of the women, their victimization is directly linked to crimes of violence which are committed in acts of self-defense and retaliation against abusers. Other direct links are evident in cases where women resort to crime or criminal lifestyles—prostitution, theft, drug sales—as a means of survival. More indirect links between victimization and crime result from efforts to confront mental health issues primarily through the use of drugs as a coping mechanism, escape, or a part of their physical/sexual abuse. A cycle or pattern of crime and addiction develops, interrupted briefly by jail/prison time, and without other interventions, continues unaddressed. Notably, these experiences are either not evident, not recognized, or not as prevalent in men's pathways to prison.[3] Available research on women lifers suggests that their pathways to prison are unique compared to men, and to women serving shorter sentences.[4] Women lifers report more extensive histories of abuse/trauma as children and adults, parental drug use and incarceration, suicide attempts, and PTSD.[5]

Despite these pre-incarceration histories, many women serving life sentences have atypical pathways to prison in comparison.[6] To those outside of their homes, their lives before prison in many ways seemed ordinary, normal, and a portrait of the American Dream. Referring to seven years of emotional and sexual abuse, a twenty-seven-year-old mother who killed her husband, said: *"I did not want anyone to know my life wasn't perfect."* As An Nuytiens and Jenneke Christiaens describe of their sample, "These women are considered atypical in pathways perspective because their pathways are not characterized by risk factors. They do not have addictions, did not grow up in a damaging environment, or had not been arrested before . . . [they] had committed only one serious offence, such as homicide, arson, or drug smuggling."[7] These women lifers enter prison older, without criminal histories or prior incarceration, and thus, the existing profiles of women serving life sentences resemble most closely Daly's pathways for "battered" and "other" women.

However, women lifers do not represent a homogeneous group. Pathways to a life sentence, for women at least, vary by criminal/prison history, presence of mental health and/or drug and alcohol problems, and victimization/abuse histories as well age at sentence. Most of the women in our sample came to prison later in life (over the age of thirty) with no prior prison experience, but with extensive histories of abuse, mental health problems, suicide ideation, and to a lesser extent drug and alcohol problems, all of which they may not have reported, or were either not recognized by others or ignored. Another distinct group of women lifers are those who were sentenced as juveniles (eighteen years old or younger) and those in their early twenties. Their pathways are also marked by histories of abuse, family traumas, drug use, mental health problems, and suicide attempts.

In this chapter, we provide a portrait of the women lifers' pre-prison lives, and how they arrived in prison serving a life sentence, including their direct and indirect pathways. We add to this portrait a description of the unique, less common pathways some women lifers take to prison including those with prior histories of incarceration (less than 5 percent of the women), those sentenced as juveniles (about 16 percent), and those without abuse histories. As these stories reveal, some women it seems were set up from birth for prison, while others never could have imagined a life behind bars.

FAMILY, CHILDHOOD, AND PRE-INCARCERATION BACKGROUNDS

According to official reports complied by Georgia Department of Corrections (GA DOC),[8] 46 percent of the women serving life in the state had lived with both their mother and father growing up. Another 40 percent lived with their mother only, with 35 percent reporting absent fathers. For 10 percent of the women, they lived with their grandparents during their childhood, and the remaining 4 percent lived with others (i.e., foster care, father only, or other relatives). About 10 percent reported absent mothers.

These living arrangements were characterized by poverty, crime, alcohol/drugs, and abuse. About 18 percent reported frequent beatings growing up; their experiences with abuse are detailed more fully later in this chapter and in chapter 3. In addition, 35 percent of the women lifers reported criminality in their families; for some, their parents were incarcerated. For example, one woman shared: *"My father was abusive to my mom and to me. He also went to prison for shooting her."* For 27 percent of the women, alcoholism was reportedly in their families with 20 percent also reporting family member's drug abuse.

All of these experiences affected not only the women's direct paths to crime but also their ability to achieve an education. For example, at age forty-one one woman explains: *"I know my decisions in life led to my conviction. I had no education hardly"* [twenty-two years old at the time of her sentence]. She received her GED during the first few months of her incarceration. While most people take education for granted, approximately 54 percent of the women serving life had not completed high school, either because they had dropped out or because of their conviction as a juvenile. Prior to prison, only 26 percent had a high school diploma or equivalent (GED); 17 percent had some college; and 3 percent had a college degree or higher. Eighteen percent had never worked or were incapable of working, and about 45 percent were unemployed at the time of their crime. Only about 10 percent indicated they were on welfare prior to coming to prison, and about 30 percent worked full time. An additional 4 percent worked part time, while 2 percent were students prior to their crime and incarceration.

PRIOR PRISON HISTORY

What is particularly unique among women serving life sentences is that unlike many women incarcerated in jails and prisons in the United States, the vast majority of women serving life sentences have no criminal record or experience with incarceration. Although there were a variety of circumstances surrounding their crimes and convictions, and many of the women held very marginal statuses, for 95 percent, their very serious offenses resulted in their first time in prison. A fifty-seven-year-old woman who killed her husband said: *"I didn't even knowingly know a single felon before my arrest"* even though she had been a victim of family violence as a child and adult. Only eleven women in this sample reported having served time in prison before their life sentence. Among these women, seven had never been married and four were widowed. Three of the women received their life sentences in their forties, and for two of them, their prison histories also began later in life, just before they received their life sentence. The remaining eight women were between the ages of twelve and twenty-four the first time they were incarcerated; for five of these women, their life sentences followed their first incarceration within six years. As such, their age at their life sentence was also relatively young including three juvenile lifers (< eighteen years old).

CASE HISTORY 2.1: I'M STILL NOT SURE WHY

At age fifty-two, Linda fatally shot her husband. From all outward appearances her life was normal. She had a college degree and went to work early every day. *"I had a good job and my family always loved me."* Her life was busy and revolved around her home and husband, but she was isolated from family and friends for her entire twenty-five years of marriage. She had no issues with drugs or alcohol, no treatment for mental health problems, or thoughts of suicide prior to prison. However, she pled guilty but mentally ill to his murder, and all involved in her case agreed. For her entire marriage what no one saw or cared to see was how being dominated and controlled by him and fearful of his physical violence, Linda's goal was to please him and be a better wife. Even today, she still blames herself for everything. She says, *"I'm guilty. I think he'd still be alive, and I'd still be married. I went crazy. The only bad guy in this marriage was me."*

CRIMES AND CONVICTIONS:
"CAUGHT UP" AND *"BEHIND A MAN"*

For 93 percent of the women serving life sentences, their crime of conviction is listed on their DOC record as murder. While there are a variety of male homicide offenders, in nearly all the cases, the murder victims among the women lifers were known to the women and included family members, spouses, children, friends, or neighbors.[9] Only the few exceptional cases such as robbery and motor vehicle theft involved strangers. The remaining women were charged, convicted, and sentenced to life in prison for crimes of kidnapping (3 percent), robbery (3 percent), rape (1 percent), and drug convictions (1 percent).

By listening to the women's stories and reading about their cases in court documents, however, we learned that the processes and context surrounding their convictions were not as straightforward as their official records or as malicious as the sensationalized media accounts suggest. In addition to murders described by the women lifers as "self-defense" and justified based on battering experiences, victimization, survival, and escape (detailed in chapter 3), women lifers explained: *"There are a lot of women in prison that didn't actually commit the crime of murdering another human being. We are doing life sentences for being around the people that actually did the crime."* Women emphasized how they were not "cold-blooded murderers," and how *they* did not kill anyone. This twenty-one-year-old woman described women lifers in this way: *"Not everybody is a cold-blooded murderer. Some people just got caught up and a lot of women are in here behind a man."* Another woman, who was seventeen at the time of her sentence in 1994, added how her experience "behind a man" explained her part in a crime that led to her life sentence.

> I didn't commit the act, a friend did, but it wasn't a malice and intent on his part. It wasn't planned but they [prosecutors] acted like we were cold, but yet we were charged with felony murder, which means a felony was in process and murder happen by mistake.

Most of the women acknowledged their part in a crime—few maintained their "actual innocence"—but many expressed their views of themselves as "not a murderer." For example, *"My charge is murder and I didn't kill anyone, though I am guilty of driving the car that transported the others"* [eighteen years old when sentenced in 2001]; *"I didn't commit a murder. Yes, I did fight those that ganged me but I never shot my best friend that was killed"* [thirty-three years old when sentenced in 2001].

As these women's explanations show, their direct pathways to a life sentence largely depended on state laws and policies at the time—in particular, the "get-tough" period of the mid- to late 1990s with mandatory sentences and two-strikes laws for the "seven deadly sins" in this state. In the examples cited above and several others later in this chapter, women were charged and convicted according to Georgia code §16-2-20[10] as "parties to the crime." Instead of a lesser sentence, "every person concerned in the commission of a crime" that led to murder may be charged, convicted, and sentenced to life, regardless of their role in the actual murder, as parties to the crimes. A policy that has especially affected women, we find numerous examples among women lifers in this state where a murder occurred during the commission of a felony. When the woman took part in the felony, or had knowledge of the crime whether before or after the fact, she also received the same charge and conviction as the primary male perpetrator. According to Lempert's study of women doing life in Michigan, 60 percent were convicted for aiding and abetting a male perpetrator in a felony.[11]

The same party to the crime policy was applied to crimes of kidnapping, rape, robbery, and crimes against children. For example, one woman serving life was convicted and sentenced for attempted rape and cruelty to children. She took her underage daughter to the doctor where she discovered that her live-in boyfriend had molested and impregnated her daughter. While she did not commit the rape, the state charged her because of her alleged knowledge of the rape, and her argued lack of intervention. At trial and on appeal, she argued a battered woman's defense which was quickly denied by the court. At the time of our interview as well as at follow-up, she had no other avenues to pursue with the courts except to serve her time behind bars—fourteen years now and counting. Although convictions based on party to the crime of rape were rare among women lifers, a more common story was shared by women whose live-in boyfriends or husbands physically abused them and their children. In cases where their children died from injuries sustained as a result of the abuse, the mothers were also charged and convicted of murder due to their knowledge of the abuse or lack of intervention.

Whether intentionally or through negligence, but in relatively few cases, mothers have killed their children.[12] Media accounts such as those of Susan Smith or Andrea Yates frame public views of "mothers who kill." But for women serving life sentences for murder and cruelty to children, we found that many of the cases involved the death of the women's children were a direct result of "discipline" or "beatings" by a husband or live-in boyfriend, and represent another path where women come to prison "behind a man."

Women lifers who were sentenced as a party to murder of their own child were more accepting of their sentence than women charged as parties to felony murder (e.g., during a robbery). They felt guilt and shame, blamed themselves, and many are still grieving the loss of their child even more so than the loss of their freedom. However, courts and parole boards are especially tough on women when their crimes involve children.

They seem to just look at "the crime" not the person behind it or circumstances. My boyfriend murdered my daughter while babysitting her. I have been denied parole 5 times while the man who murdered my daughter is at home. I'm being considered again now and I'm terrified they'll just say no again without considering any facts or all I've accomplished while incarcerated 26 years.

The primary argument is that mothers should protect their children. When mothers fail to do so by staying with controlling and abusive partners and/ or failing to seek medical care for an injured or sick child, their actions are viewed as worse than those of a violent or abusive male partner. Regarding the death of her daughter, this woman stated: *"I was away from home (to the store) and my child was murdered."* According to court transcripts, her live-in boyfriend had admittedly kicked the child in the abdomen which caused internal bleeding and led to her death three days later. She confessed that she was afraid to take her daughter to the hospital because of the abuse and the courts ruled that this indicated malice on her part, not simply negligence. She explained: *"It was said that I knew about it after the fact, and 19 years later because I have no financial means for an attorney—I'm still here. Long story short. He only did eight years because his charges were overturned to involuntary manslaughter."*

CASE HISTORY 2.2: THE MOST DEVASTATING EXPERIENCE OF ALL

At thirty-two, Bonnie was single mother of three young boys (ages two, four, and six). After divorcing from her alcoholic husband of ten years, she moved in with a man, David, she had known for about three months. A father of three girls, Bonnie trusted him enough to move in with him, and he often watched her boys while she was working second shift as a nursing assistant. Within two months, her youngest son was dead. Both Bonnie and David made statements to police that attributed his injuries to the actions of her older sons (which was not likely). However, of the injuries to her son, Bonnie said, *"it was strange that every time I got home, there was something else* [another injury]." On the night of the fatal injuries, David told Bonnie her son had fallen from the back porch. *"By the time I got home and found out about it he was doing fine, no other injuries I could tell of, but he had a headache. I gave him children's Tylenol. The night after he had fallen, he'd thrown up in his sleep and stopped breathing. I rushed him to the hospital where he was pronounced dead."* Despite the fact that she was not home at the time of the fatal injury, both she and David were charged and convicted of murder, cruelty to children, and failing to seek proper medical treatment for her son's injuries. Processing her grief from behind bars has been extremely difficult—*"I block it as not real"*—but she says, *"My child was murdered and I am still in therapy about that."*

JUVENILE LIFERS

Partly due to recent Supreme Court rulings regarding juveniles, fewer juveniles are sentenced to life in prison in the state today.[13] Currently, only one female, age eighteen, is in an adult state correctional facility for women in Georgia. However, among the women we interviewed, 16 percent were sentenced to life in prison when they were juveniles (n = 34). Twenty-two of these women were seventeen and eighteen years old at the time of their sentence. The youngest was fourteen at the time, and the remaining eleven were fifteen and sixteen years old. Among the juvenile lifers in our sample, a number of high-profile cases of girls who committed murders had been covered extensively and sensationalized by the media. For example:

- With supportive, yet strict grandparents whom she lived with during her mother's incarceration, one juvenile reported sexual, physical, and emotional abuse during her childhood as well as drug and alcohol use, mental health treatment, and suicide attempts. At age fifteen she and another teen killed her grandparents, stole the grandparent's car, and ran. Once caught, they pled guilty to the murders and received life sentences.
- A similar story provides the context for a fourteen-year-old who shot and killed her great-aunt after an argument over the family car. Evidence of mental illness, a "deprived childhood," and child abuse were well known to her. At the advice of her public defender, and lacking financial, educational, and family resources, she pled guilty to murder and received life in prison.
- A traumatic upbringing, which by her account did not end when she was adopted at eleven years old and brought to the United States, a fifteen-year-old and her sister were found guilty and sentenced to life in prison in their adoptive mother's death. She reported experiencing all forms of abuse growing up, as well as mental health problems and suicide attempts with some time in a mental hospital as a child. On more than one occasion she and her sister ran away from home alleging abuse from their adoptive mother. No one intervened, and although she argued self-defense at trial, she and her sister were found guilty and sentenced to life in prison. Other than her sister, she has no family for support.
- Unlike these girls, another had a juvenile record that dated to age twelve, and her childhood arguably set her up for a path to prison. Although her juvenile crimes were not discussed, she is currently serving life for armed robbery and two counts of murder she committed at the age of fifteen along with another female juvenile. In her account, she said *"I was being raped and I took the life of the men who were raping me."* The state and media accounts, however, describe the fifteen-year-old as a "cold-blooded

murderer" who targeted two men, asking them for a ride and luring them to a motel under the premise of sex, but with the real intention to rob them. The state argued that they methodically shot and killed "execution-style" the two men at a hotel and took $200 from them. Despite her account, she pled guilty at the advice of her public defender. Already by age fifteen she had a history of drug use, mental health problems, suicidal thoughts, and all types of sexual, physical, and emotional abuse. She had very little education, lacked resources, and had absolutely no family support. Not a single family member was present at her court appearances.

- Similarly, with a childhood that was described in court as "horrific," another teen left home—a home that was characterized by a drug-abusing father—as a high school dropout and entered nude dancing and prostitution. The victim of pimps and drug pushers, she, along with a female codefendant, was charged and convicted of three counts of robbery and murder. She was age nineteen by the time of the murders.

In each of these cases, the girls were the primary perpetrators of the killings—most often of a family member and/or abuser. Only four of the juvenile lifers (17 percent) reported no history of abuse, and among those with histories of physical, sexual, and emotional abuse, 90 percent indicated abuse played a factor in their crime and incarceration. What is clear from the accounts of these juveniles serving life sentences is that their pre-incarceration childhoods were characterized by concentrated traumas early in their lives, deprivation, a lack of support from family, teachers, and their communities, and a legal system with very little leniency given their ages and background experiences. In several of the cases described above, the prosecutors were quoted in media and court records stating that they were not allowed by law to seek the death penalty "because they were juveniles" implying that if not for the law, they would consider the death penalty. Jan Buttrum's story, detailed in a book written by Jodi Lowry,[14] provides an extended picture of a juvenile lifer whose pathway to prison can be traced from birth. She was the youngest female sentenced to death in the state of Georgia. Her sentence was commuted to life in prison in 1991 because she was a juvenile at the time of the murder. She will be eligible for parole in 2019 after serving over thirty years in prison.

Among juvenile and early onset lifers—those in their early twenties—the cases described above are the exceptions. Many more women sentenced to life in prison before the age of eighteen as well as those in their early twenties were convicted on charges of felony murder as a party to the crime of murder. Of these women, most had completed their high school degree or were doing fairly well in school, and they had at least some family support, although most all were never married or mothers. Poverty, abuse, and, in some cases, drug use was reported. As their accounts demonstrate, these women lifers were also "caught up" or came to prison "behind a man." Their life sentences can be directly attributed to policies at the time of their crimes—all occurred during the 1990s' "get tough" era of criminal justice and "superpredator panic"—and nearly all of these women are still behind bars. Just a few of these women's accounts demonstrate the patterns in their cases:

- At the age of fifteen, she was convicted of being a party to the crimes of murder, robbery, and motor vehicle theft. She, along with her twenty-two-year-old boyfriend and another male accomplice, shot a couple and stole their car. People testified at her trial that her boyfriend controlled her with a gun.
- Similarly, a seventeen-year-old, was with her twenty-two-year-old boyfriend when he shot his dad's live-in girlfriend and stole her truck. She is still in prison at age forty-one and has served nearly twenty-five years of a life sentence.
- Another, at age sixteen, was sentenced to life for being a party to the crimes of armed robbery and kidnapping. Although no one was murdered, she, along with four men and one other woman, were characterized and convicted as "gang-related" offenders.
- Age eighteen at the time, one young woman was convicted as a party to the crimes of robbery and murder. Her boyfriend and a male who testified against her in court had bound a seventy-one-year-old man with duct tape, beat him, and robbed him. Later that evening, her boyfriend and another male robbed him a second time (without her). The victim died of a heart attack as a result of the trauma. She is serving a life sentence for murder because she was driving the car at the time the men committed the first robbery and had knowledge of the crime.
- Another young woman (age nineteen) and her husband along with two other men robbed and killed a man. They took his truck and $31. She argued a coercion defense and stated *"I didn't kill him, my batterer did."* But the prosecutors described her as "enticing the victim to a trailer home" and the couple as "natural born killers" based on the popular movie at the time. After the jury watched the film in its entirety as evidence in the trial, she and her codefendants were found guilty and sentenced to life in prison.

Georgia lawyer and blogger, Jeffrey Johnston, stated of these parties to a crime cases: "Being in the wrong place, at the wrong time and with the wrong people could cost you your freedom!"[15] Every woman lifer has a unique story, the details of which are often lost or packaged by the media and courts as one-sided. The similarities in the stories, though, are difficult to overlook, and are about more than the "wrong" place, time, or crowd. Even in cases where coercion was presented (and established) as a defense, the young women's roles in the crimes were portrayed by the courts and the media as manipulative and evil-minded; they "baited," "enticed," or otherwise "lured" a victim to their robbery and death at the hands of an older, male accomplice, typically her boyfriend. Their roles in a murder arguably involved their knowledge of the potential crime and lack of intervention. In many of these cases, women had no power or feared for their lives if they had tried to intervene. Eighteen at the time of the crime, one lifer said: *"My boyfriend is one of my co-defendants. If I left he may have killed me next. He beat my unborn baby out of me because he wasn't ready to be a daddy."* The women lifers we interviewed who were directly affected by these policies had a difficult time understanding why they were serving a life sentence. They acknowledged (as do we) the pain and loss experienced by victim's families but feel (or have felt) injustice over the court's overly harsh reaction their specific role in the crime. While most of the younger lifers did not kill abusive partners, the effects of abuse and trauma in their early life-course ultimately did have an impact on their pathways to crime and time behind bars. Now in their late thirties and forties, these women have served a range of sixteen to twenty-five years of their life sentences.

WOMEN WHO KILL IN SELF-DEFENSE

According to Elizabeth Leonard, while men are more likely to kill out of aggression and jealousy, women are more likely to kill in self-defense after a history of battering.[16] Three out of four women charged with killing their abusive partners accept a plea or are convicted and often receive lengthy prison

---

CASE HISTORY 2.3: WILL I EVER HAVE A LIFE BEYOND THESE WALLS? [JUVENILE LIFER IN HER OWN WORDS]

"I was only 15 when I got incarcerated and before that time I saw my life as that of any typical teenager. I was rebellious and hung around the wrong crowd, but I was at that age when I wanted to fit in a be accepted. Of course, at the time nobody could tell me that because I was young and naïve and just thought I had everything figured out. I also had a lot of problems at home with my mother. She was a single parent trying to raise me and the financial struggle was always apparent. I had some emotional problems due to the death of my father at age 5. I acted out and did things like underage drinking and smoking weed. I met this boy when I was fairly young, and first love became a real concept to me. I ended up leaving home to follow him, not knowing that my life would be drastically altered from that point on. I had a love for dancing and always dreamed of becoming one since I was little girl. I have always regretted not pursuing it because instead I ruined my life from any chance of achieving those dreams."

sentences. Attorneys who represent battered women who kill may have little understanding of the dynamics of abuse and its psychological responses. Or, these lawyers may be reticent in admitting abuse records into evidence for fear that the prosecution will turn them into a motive for a crime of revenge. Additionally, a contributing factor to outcomes in these cases is that the majority of battered women who kill cannot afford the services of a private attorney at the time of their arrest, and they are frequently assigned public criminal defense representatives who are overworked and underskilled.[17]

Among the women lifers we interviewed who had killed abusers in self-defense, most were trying to end the relationship or leave the relationship when the violence occurred. For other women, at the time of the homicide, "nothing different or new" was going on, but were circumstances where violence escalated. Typically, these homicides were not planned.

> Many women kill their abusers because it is either their life, the abusers or their children's. Sometimes it's a conscious choice, but most times its an immediate action taken only to save yourself. Georgia didn't believe in self-defense, so here we all sit.

As one example, referring to her husband, this twenty-one-year-old woman lifer said, *"I wanted him to leave my home. I stabbed him accidentally one time and he died. Last time* [I left] *he found me the next day and beat me."* Of her experience, another woman said, *"It* [knife] *hit him one time and he died from a single stab wound."* In many of these situations, women were fighting for their lives:

> I believe if I hadn't ended up here [prison] for fighting for my life that day and killing my boyfriend I would probably be dead or still enduring the abuse. [twenty-two years old age sentenced, in abusive relationship for four years]

After experiencing ten years of severe abuse, a forty-two-year-old woman shared a similar kill-or-be-killed situation: *"I had to defend myself against my husband to keep him from killing me. I was sentenced to murder."* Length of the abusive relationship was not a determining factor for most women lifers. As described by this woman lifer, who was a police officer at the time of the homicide, she was forty-two years old and had suffered about four months of abuse. *"After my house burned, my husband became crazy abusive. He raped me and beat me one night and I grabbed my service weapon to defend myself. He jerked the gun out of my hand and it went off killing him."*

Women who kill intimate partners receive a disproportionate amount of media attention compared to men who kill their wives or girlfriends. Unfortunately, this leaves the public with the message that wives are trying to get away with murdering their husbands. Labeled as "black widows," scorned women, or women who snapped, it remains the case that when women kill, even in self-defense, they are no longer viewed as a victim. In sharing the stories of women lifers, we focus almost exclusively on women who kill. Summaries of their pathways, crimes, and convictions are retold in this chapter and detailed even further in chapter 3. However, it is important to emphasize that the vast majority of homicide offenders are men.[18] Furthermore, husbands and boyfriends are more likely to kill their wives or girlfriends than the reverse, and this fact is often masked by not only the unbalanced media attention but also the marked declines in homicide over the past thirty years.[19] Three of the most important trends in intimate partner homicide include: (1) over 40 percent of female homicide victims in the United States are killed by an intimate partner compared to 5 percent of male homicide victims; (2) the rate at which females are killed by intimate partners is twice that of males; and (3) the gender gaps in victimization have widened over time. All of these trends mean that women are less likely to kill intimate partners today than in past decades, but the rate at which men kill their wives and girlfriends has remained relatively stable. In fact, today female homicide victims are more likely to be killed by an intimate partner than other family members or strangers compared to any time in the past three decades. The implication of these statistics is that while policies and programs may have assisted battered women so that many can now "just leave" an abusive relationship before having to "resort" to killing an abuser, women in abusive relationships also remain at a high risk of homicide at the hands of their abusers.

DRUG AND ALCOHOL USE, MENTAL HEALTH PROBLEMS, AND SUICIDE IDEATION

While the overwhelming majority of women with life sentences in our sample reported experiencing physical, sexual, and emotional abuse as children and/ or adults, over 50 percent of them reported no problems with drugs or alcohol prior to their incarceration. As a whole, then, drug use among women lifers was not as prevalent compared to other women involved with the criminal justice system.[20] Evident in this forty-eight-year-old woman's statement—*"I was fearful and didn't fit into those who used drugs, etc."*—is her inexperience with drugs. In similar cases, women who were incarcerated later in life (over the age of thirty) with no histories of drug use, found their pathway to crime and a life sentence shocking and made statements such as, *"How could this have happened to me?"* and *"I never dreamed or could have imagined this happening to me."*

At the time of our initial survey, four women in the state had been sentenced to life in prison for drug crimes including trafficking and sales of cocaine or meth-amphetamine. Thus, for these women, drugs in the form of sales were a direct pathway to crime along with a variety of early marginal life experiences. Eleven women in the sample of 214 reported pathways that were solely drug connected (no abuse histories). These cases typically involved felony murder convictions where women were accomplices or a party to the crime. Nearly all of the felony murders were during the course of a robbery, involved the use of a gun, resulted in a shooting death, and were committed with/by a male perpetrator.

While 30 percent of the women lifers reported only drug problems and 13 percent reported both drug and alcohol problems, only 1 percent indicated a drug addiction. About 6 percent described their alcohol use as "alcoholism." As such, of those who had ever used drugs or alcohol, the majority indicated abuse or ex-perimentation. More common, though, were women lifers who reported drug use as a way to escape their traumas of physical, sexual, and/or emotional abuse and cope with mental health problems (about 45 percent). When asked what other factors contributed to her violent offense, one woman explained: *"Depression, smoked crack to control my feelings and thoughts."* She was under the influence of cocaine at the time of her crime. Other lifers also indicated that alcohol and drugs impaired their thinking at the time of the crime. Within women's accounts of their crimes and pathways to prison were very clear evidence that alcohol and drug use was common among their abusive spouses and boyfriends, contributing to the violence and trauma they experienced as victims and survivors.

Use of illegal drugs such as cocaine was not as common among women lifers as was those who used prescription drugs to treat depression, especially among many of the women lifers who lived with and ultimately killed abu-sive spouses. After twenty-five years of abuse, a fifty-year-old woman who shot her husband said she took prescription drugs for depression, and to deal with the abuse she experienced *"having to get prescription drugs to try to live with my husband day by day."* Age thirty-one at the time of her sentence, a woman who killed her husband talked about how her mental health problems and reliance on prescription drugs contributed to her crime.

> My daughter died May 11, 1986 of SIDS. I never dealt with that issue then. It was still an issue in May 1997 when my crime occurred. I was heavily medi-cated (prescription) to ease this and not aware of my surroundings or I would have prevented it.

Speaking directly about her crime, another woman in her fifties said:

> I was taking Xanax for depression and I've often wondered if that contributed to my behavior in grabbing the gun to begin with. I do not believe in violence and that was the first time I had defended myself.

More than 65 percent of the women reported treatment for mental health problems, and for a little over 32 percent of the women, these problems tended to co-occur with drug and alcohol problems and abuse histories. In fact, mental health problems were significantly more common among women with abuse histories and drug use (75 percent report mental health problems) than those with no abuse histories (37 percent report mental health problems) or those with no drug problems (65 percent report mental health problems). Another indication of mental distress, over 45 percent of the women reported suicide ideation prior to their incarceration. Abused physically and verbally by her mother most of her childhood, an eighteen-year-old lifer said: *"I was in such a blackhole emotionally all I wanted to do was die."*

For younger women, drugs and abuse came early in their lives and for some was often accompanied by sexual abuse, prostitution, or involvement in crimes with older boyfriends. For other women lifers, both their abuse experiences and their drug use were long-term, in excess of twenty years, and played a role in the crime. For example, one woman described her history of abuse from childhood, and how at the time of her crime she was *"having flashbacks of past abuse and rape."*

Women with lengthy abuse histories, typically those who were relatively older at the time of their sentence and defined as "battered women," were less likely to report problems with drugs or alcohol than other women (38 percent). For about 70 percent of women with histories of physical, sexual, or emotional abuse, they reported no treatment for mental health problems or suicide ideation. Instead, they kept their abuse hidden from family and friends, even accepting the abuse as a part of their life. Abuse factored into about 62 percent of these women's direct pathways to crime and a life sentence. Indeed, the most common pathway for women sentenced to life after the age of thirty (later onset), was to either shoot or stab their current or ex-husband/boyfriend. As described above, childhood and early adult experiences with abuse as directly or indirectly related to their crimes and incarceration were common pathways. Chapter 3 details the physical, sexual, and emotional abuse experiences among the women lifers we surveyed.

A small portion of the women lifers (thirty-four women) reported no abuse history. Underreported abuse is possible as some women did not feel comfortable discussing their abuse, and/or did not view themselves as victims of abuse. For instance, several women lifers who killed their boyfriends or husbands fit the pattern of women who kill abusers, yet they reported no abuse history. A few distinct patterns were evident among women lifers without histories of abuse. First, black women were overrepresented (65 percent of those who reported no abuse) compared to the overall sample. Second, proportionately, these women were more than twice as likely to have a prior prison history (12 percent). Third, they were more likely to involve drug or drug-connected crimes and convictions, self-described altercations/accidents which led to someone's death, or parties to crimes such as robbery where motives were money or drugs.

SUMMARY

Women lifers' lives before their life sentences resembled a variety of well-known pathways to crime and prison, yet their personal accounts and stories revealed a range of experiences with abuse, trauma, and life circumstances. However, some of the women had histories of poverty and childhood traumas that impacted their pathways, while others lived rather "ordinary" lives in terms of education, careers, and children. Most of the victims in their cases were known to the women, whether husbands and boyfriends or their own children, but a sizable portion of the women lifers were convicted as parties to the crime in the murder of acquaintances or strangers. One distinct path to prison described by the women was "behind a man" who was often the primary perpetrator, their abuser, or both.

Women lifers do feel guilt and remorse over their life choices and the consequences of those choices for their families, the victims, and their victims' families; but they tell a story which emphasizes how they are not "cold-blooded murderers." One woman summed up their pathways: *"Most of us are here for the same thing, abusive relationships and poor representation from public defenders."* Many women lifers were abused and battered by those who were supposed to love them; some were coerced and fearful during the commission of the crime as well as during the prosecution/trial; they often coped with these traumas and mental distress alone and with drugs and alcohol. Although abuse and mental health issues were also common factors in women lifers' pathways, drug addiction and drug crimes were not a prevalent, primary pathway to prison.

While the stories of women's lives prior to prison provide a context to their lives—not an excuse for their crimes—they also point to the pathways and traumas which women bring with them into prison, which if ignored or exacerbated during confinement, affect adjustment to life behind bars and have important implications for women lifers' reentry following their life sentence. After describing in more detail the ways women experienced abuse and its consequences throughout their life-course, and the methods they attempted to stop the abuse, we examine the way they describe their lives in prison.

NOTES

1. Daly, *Gender, Crime, and Punishment.*
2. Lempert, *Women Doing Life.* See also research by Brennen, Breitenbach, Dieterich, Salisbury, and Van Voorhis, "Women's Pathways to Serious and Habitual Crime: A Person-Centered Analysis Incorporating Gender Responsive Factors"; DeHart, "Pathways to Prison: Impact of Victimization in the Lives of Incarcerated Women"; Dye and Aday, "I Just Wanted To Die"; and Fedock, "Life before 'I Killed the Man That Raped Me.'"
3. Leigey and Reed, "A Women's Life before Serving Life."
4. Chesney-Lind and Rodriguez, "Women under Lock and Key: A View from the Inside."
5. Leigey and Reed, "A Women's Life before Serving Life."
6. Nuytiens and Christiaens, "Female Pathways to Crime and Prison: Challenging the (US) Gendered Pathways Perspective."
7. Nuytiens and Christiaens, "Female Pathways," 208.
8. *Inmate Statistical Profile: Active Lifers,* Georgia Department of Corrections, July 2010. http://www.dcor.state.ga.us/sites/all/files/pdf/Research/Monthly/Profile_lifers_2010_06.pdf
9. Fox and Fridel, "Gender Differences in Patterns and Trends in U.S. Homicide, 1976–2015."
10. A complete description of the Georgia "party to the crime" criminal code can be found at https://law.justia.com/codes/georgia/2010/title-16/chapter-2/article-2/16-2-20/.
11. Lempert, *Women Doing Life,* 13.
12. Meyer and Oberman, *Mothers Who Kill Their Children*; Whiteley, "'I Am More Than a Crime': Interviews with Women Who Kill."
13. See *Roper v. Simmons, 2005*; *Graham v. Florida, 2010*; *Miller v. Alabama, 2012*; and *Montgomery v. Louisiana, 2016.* A description and links to these court rulings can be found at http://www.pbs.org/pov/15tolife/supreme-court-cases/ and http://www.sentencingproject.org/publications/juvenile-life-without-parole/
14. McDaniel Lowry, *Jan: The Youngest Woman Sentenced to Georgia's Death Row.*
15. Jeffrey Johnston, "Party to the Crime: Don't Be Caught with the Wrong Crowd." https://www.jeffreyjohnstonlaw.com/blog/2014/10/party-to-a-crime.shtml
16. Leonard, *Convicted Survivors.*
17. Labelle and Kubiak, "Balancing Gender Equity for Women Prisoners."
18. FBI, *Crime in the U.S.* https://ucr.fbi.gov/crime-in-the-u.s/2017/crime-in-the-u.s.-2017.
19. Fox and Fridel, "Gender Differences in Patterns and Trends in U.S. Homicide, 1976–2015."
20. Bronson, Stroop, Zimmer, and Berzofsky, *Drug Use, Dependence, and Abuse among State Prisoners and Jail Inmates, 2007–2009.* https://www.bjs.gov/content/pub/pdf/dudaspji0709.

Chapter 3

Bullied, Bruised, and Battered

"Bitch, I'm gonna kill you tonight. . . . One of us ain't gonna live."

"He set me on fire, stalked me from state-to-state."

"He abused me in every way possible: physical, mental, verbal, sexual, and emotional."

 "I still cry in the shower and scrub my body as if I can scrub the filth and shame away."

In the chapter on pathways to prison, we discussed the important role that past abusive histories play in leading to lengthy prison sentences. It is well documented that incarcerated women report a much higher incidence of victimization than those in the general population. A total of 83 percent of the women in our study indicated they had suffered from either emotional, sexual, or physical abuse prior to incarceration. Two-thirds reported being victims of physical and/or sexual abuse, with three out of four stating they were also victims of various forms of emotional and verbal abuse. The typical victim of domestic abuse was twenty-one years of age (range fifteen to fifty-two) when the abuse started, and the mean number of years these incarcerated women reported being in an abusive adult relationship prior to incarceration was eight years. We explore in this chapter the onset of abuse, illustrations of a full range of abusive situations, and the types of actions and strategies taken to bring a halt to the abuse. Compelling narratives are disclosed about the types of injuries the women sustained, traumatic events that occurred as the women sought help from families and criminal justice agencies, the challenges faced in leaving a toxic abusive relationship, and the lingering long-term consequences.

Interested researchers have attempted to identify the individual and social factors that show why women are more susceptible to victimization than are men. Sociological, biological, and psychological perspectives have been introduced as possible explanations for abusive interrelationships. Social theories have linked domestic violence to the social structures and cultural norms that legitimize abusive behavior. The culture of violence implies that the approval for violence in our society is reinforced by the frequent use of physical violence to settle family disagreements. Another explanation includes the notion that violence is learned, handed down from generation to generation. Others have championed the feminist view where wife battering and other controlling behaviors can be traced to male privilege.[1] Still others accept that a significant number of domestic perpetrators exhibit behaviors associated with personality disorders, mental illness, self-esteem problems, magnified by stressful situations.[2] Those holding this view argue that violence is more likely to occur when individuals have difficulty maintaining self-control or have the need to control others. When coupled with the presence of alcohol and drugs, this frequently leads to highly volatile situations, putting women at risk of abuse. Certainly, many of these indicators were present in the stories of victimization shared by these women serving life sentences.

EARLY CHILDHOOD EXPERIENCES

While our questions focused more on abusive relationships during adulthood, numerous women also shared detailed accounts of victimization they encountered during childhood. The unfavorable impact abusive behaviors directed toward children cannot be overstated and so documenting these experiences are important when assessing trauma over the life course. Child therapists have found that exposure to extremely abusive situations over a longer duration damages the chemistry and structure of the brain, adversely affecting thinking, memory, and emotions.[3] For the women in our sample, harsh and unusually cruel childhood episodes of physical, emotional, and sexual abuse were frequently mentioned, with the majority of incidences occurring within their own families of origin. For example, one woman shared the pains of emotional abuse encountered when her parents gave her and her three sisters away to different family members. This feeling of abandonment is reinforced by abusive statements such as, *"My mom called us all kinds of names and said we would never amount to nothing. They never said they loved us, never hugged us, or did anything with us and acted like were we a nobody to them."*

Childhood sexual abuse is frequently mentioned as the most emotionally charged form of abuse; therefore, the most difficult to acknowledge. Of course, when the identity of the offender is known and personally close to the victim (i.e., family member) the trauma appears to be even greater. This betrayal of trust can have an enormous negative effect especially on small children who look to their parents as someone who will watch over and protect them.[4] Feelings of vulnerability, helplessness, and perceived inability to escape from abuse were frequently expressed by the women lifers. One woman, still exhibiting symptoms of PTSD, shared how she was raped by her stepbrothers and father at a very young age:

> The abuse started when I was only six. My two older brothers and my father raped me till I ran away at age 12 because I had no one I could turn to. I ran to a Seventh Day Adventist school and they took me in. The preacher there took me to a hospital and I was so torn up on the inside that they paid the bill and kept me in the hospital. No charges were filed against my brothers or father because my dad was friends with the judge and the sheriff. I could never have children as a result of my injuries.

Another older black woman acknowledged, *"I was sexually abused from age 9–13 by my father. I was told by him that if I said anything he would kill my mother. This experience resulted in my being very depressed and eventually I became hooked on prescription drugs."* Another child victim of physical and emotional abuse shared extensive information about her long history of abuse early in her life.

> I was insulted and felt worthless. I was physically abused when my sister messed up. I was verbally abused to the point my mind was programmed to hate myself. When I sought help from my teachers, my mom would convince them everything was okay and then beat me. What hurt the most was when my mom kicked me out because of her boyfriend and then married him. A few weeks before I attempted suicide I was released from the hospital for slicing my wrists because my mother verbally disowned me.

Other victims reported feelings of guilt and shame as a result of the trauma. As one woman stated, *"This abuse made me feel dirty and alone and it made me not trust people."* Another said, *"Until I came to prison, I thought I deserved punishment. I figured I wasn't a good person."* These feelings of self-blame were linked with guilty feelings and reactions to abuse later in life. As one childhood sexual abuse survivor mentioned, *"Later, when I was raped, I felt that it was my fault and therefore didn't even report it to the police or anyone else."* It is understandable that victims of childhood abuse would be anxious to leave home as soon as possible, and this could have created haste in finding a boyfriend or husband. Several of the women mentioned running away from an abusive home environment only to find themselves drawn into one abusive encounter after another. For example, one victim who was isolated and abused emotionally and physically by her father revealed that she

"jumped into abusive relationships one after another, was always so easy to manipulate, and scared, due to zero self-esteem."
Many of those women who discussed their abuse in childhood often found the abuse following them into adulthood. One woman indicated her abusive life began at five years of age:

> My dad and mom beat me all my life until I was 16 years old when I left home to escape the abuse. I married and still got beaten by my husband. After I divorced him I stayed depressed and married again and tried to kill myself because I kept getting beat up. All in all, I was in abusive relationships for over 15 years.

INTIMATE PARTNER ABUSE

As we have already learned, many of the women who found themselves in various forms of domestic violence and abusive relationship as adults had already been introduced to an abusive lifestyle as young children. Over fifty women in our sample revealed that their initial encounter with domestic abuse started during their early dating years as a teen between the ages of fifteen and nineteen. Often these various forms of abuse took place concurrently as described by a twenty-seven-year-old lifer who suffered through an abusive lifestyle starting at age nineteen and lasting for eight tumultuous years.

> He alienated me from everybody. He abused me in every way possible: physical, mental, verbal, sexual, and emotional. I just accepted it as my life. I didn't know what to do without it. He made me feel so awful, like a dog at times and all I could think was—this is my life—this is what it is. I was in prison then too.

Regardless of the length of time in an abusive relationship, two-thirds of the women felt their abuse histories often played an important role in their current incarceration.

Physical Abuse

Physical abuse is any intentional act causing injury or trauma to another person. The use of force may result in bodily injury either internal or external. As one woman mentioned, *"My ex never left marks that could be seen. He preferred kidney punches, shoves and threats of death."* One of the most obvious effects of domestic violence is the permanent physical damage that frequently occurs when women are battered over a prolonged period of time. The overwhelming majority of the women lifers indicated they were fre-

---

CASE HISTORY 3.1: IF I DIDN'T DO AS TOLD, HE WOULD BEAT ME

Jane's abusive relationship began at the age of sixteen and lasted six years. Her abuser was her baby daddy who would also constantly threaten her family and loved ones. Battered extensively over an extended period of time, Jane tried to curb the abusive behavior by calling the police on several occasions. However, in doing so, she was only beaten later even more severely. Jane was battered excessively suffering from numerous broken bones, scratches, teeth knocked out, being knocked unconscious, multiple bruises, black eyes, cuts, and welts. She constantly experienced emotional abuse, was terrorized and screamed at, threatened with a weapon, bullied, and verbally put down. Beatings would take place should she leave the house without permission, receive a cell phone call from anyone besides a family member or the abuser or if she missed one of her abuser's calls. In her words: *"If I didn't do as he told me I'll get beaten in front of our kids and the children became as traumatized by those events."* Always in fear for her and her family's life, Jane eventually made the decision to leave the relationship for good. Looking back Jane realizes she may never fully recover from the abuse she experienced at such an early age. *"I still have frequent flashbacks and suffer from some of the physical injuries."*

---

quently pushed, grabbed, shoved, hit with a fist or slapped around the face, and choked. Approximately one-half (47 percent) of the women reported being trapped in extreme battering situations ranging from black eyes, numerous cuts, welts, and bruises to being knocked unconscious. As the case history in textbox 3.1 illustrates, the use of physical force often resulted in a variety of internal injuries (40 percent) along with a substantial number reporting broken bones (26 percent), teeth knocked out or chipped (11 percent), and knife or other stab wounds (16 percent). Approximately 5 percent admitted they had been wounded from a gunshot.

As a result of the abusive encounters, one-half of the women reported that they made frequent trips to the emergency room or the doctor for medical help. One woman who sustained extensive physical damage shared, *"He set me on fire, stalked me from state-to-state and I am still having surgeries to repair back damage from years back. I still have night tremors, am hyperalert and easily startled."* Another stated, *"He used a taser on me and threw my baby against the wall because of his jealously towards the baby. One of the last things he did was running me down with his car."* One older woman now in her sixties summed up the exhaustive experience of living the life of a victim:

I married early at age 20 and the abuse just continued from my childhood. My first husband used to shoot in the house or hold a knife to my throat or a gun to my head. I was told not to scream and not to breathe. Every husband I've had, has beaten, stabbed or done something violent to me. It's been a life of abuse for too many years.

Sexual Abuse

Research has shown that roughly 50 percent of women experiencing physical assault by an intimate partner will also experience sexual assault by that same person.[5] Self-reports from the women lifers suggest that to be the case here. Several women had the courage to describe violent and degrading encounters, with either their spouses or boyfriends, that frequently led to multiple forms of abuse simultaneously. Two-thirds of the women indicated they were frequently made to perform sexual acts such as anal or oral sex against their wishes. One woman, who had been raped multiple times, described her sexually abusive past and destructive consequences.

> My boyfriend would get mad at me if I didn't want to have sex so he would rape me. My husband liked to sodomize me. I think they just like me for sex and it made me feel insecure about myself. I didn't forgive my abusers and when I got angry, it just came out in a violent rage.

While some of the sexual victims described force as the only type of rape—*I was held down and taken by force*—others defined their victimization in more extreme terms such as co-occurring with a battering or sadistic experience. One out of four reported having a foreign object used on them in a sexual way. One woman who eventually killed her abusive husband talked about the multiple forms of abuse she encountered almost every day: *"Everyday driving home after working 10 hours to be screamed at, and being physically, mentally and sexually abused. It was terrible having objects being forced on you to have sex."* Another described that her husband occasionally spit in her face and pulled her hair so hard it caused whiplash and she also revealed to us how she, *"was tied up and anal raped and then my husband burnt my bottom with cigarettes while calling me a dirty cunt."* One older lifer who was the victim of incest at an early age and who came to prison thinking she deserved punishment described one of her abusive episodes:

> The physical abuse was daily. I'd get things thrown in my face if I wasn't being slapped. I've been in the shower only to have an AK47 pointed at my face and told I was going to die. I was held there for hours, raped by the gun and not knowing if he would shoot or not. I was a nothing who deserved what I was getting because I'm also an incest survivor.

Other women described being raped in front of their children as a form of punishment and control. For example, one woman was raped the day she filed for divorce and another was raped when she returned home from the hospital after a miscarriage. Regardless, the women often described a perpetrator who felt entitled to sex or was using sexual violence as a way to punish or exert power in a personalized, degrading manner.

By the time I divorced, I felt ugly, worthless and broken. The sexual abuse was the worst and was what finally pushed me strong enough to say "no more." When my 4-year-old daughter told me "we could find a daddy that doesn't make you cry" I realized she could see what I thought was well hidden.

Emotional Abuse

When sharing the pervasive context of domestic violence among these marginal women, it should be acknowledged that psychological or emotional vulnerability is a normal occurrence when encountering physical or sexual abuse. Emotional abuse, like physical abuse, is used to control, demean, harm, or punish. Many people assume that emotional abuse is not as severe or harmful as physical abuse, but most women victims disagree. We found that one of the biggest problems emotionally abused women faced was getting others to take this type of invisible abuse seriously. Numerous women complained that family members didn't understand the true impact of this type of abuse. In fact, the presence of emotional abuse is the greatest risk factor and predictor of physical abuse, especially when a woman is called names and ridiculed in front of others. Emotional abuse, like any other form of abuse, is about power. Men often use this type of abuse to threaten, intimidate, harass, or punish a woman in order to get her to comply with his abusive demands.

Like other forms of abuse, we found that various forms of verbal put-downs and total lack of respect had a devastating effect. About 90 percent of the women reported their partner frequently made verbal insults toward them on a frequent basis. The overwhelming majority (85 percent) of the women said their partner showed total disrespect by frequently swearing at them, telling them they were ugly and unattractive, screaming and yelling as well as other insults often in front of children and others. Such criticisms, especially if they are frequent and toxic, can have far-reaching consequences for victims often leaving permanent scars. As one lifer recalled, *"I was constantly ridiculed by my husband and just being told you are worthless especially when you grew up poor and don't believe you're worth much anyway can be devastating."* Another stated that after years of verbal and emotional abuse she attempted suicide.

The most devastating thing for me was finally getting it that I was truly not valued. After my suicide attempt, he [husband] said we should have just kept the police and paramedics out of the house. And then he never bothered to come to the hospital to visit me. I realized that was the beginning of the end for us.

Women in our sample also mentioned emotional abuse that can primarily take the form of humiliation which often destroys the person's sense of self-worth and the ability to overcome further acts of control. One woman shared, *"I was so humiliated in front of other people like when I was raped and beaten in front of my young sons. The abuse is still alive and well in my life, because of being abused."* Another woman who suffered from an emotional abuser indicated he used a steady stream of low-level emotional assaults followed by verbal threats and other acts of violence that can do great psychological harm:

> What bothered me most was that my ex was very well perceived in public. His verbal abuse was very quiet, calm, and controlled. Behind closed doors he threatened me with a gun, forced me to have sex and mentally twisted things around where I thought I was wrong and he was right.

Controlling Threats

The types of abuse and threats used to control victims often varies across relationships. The onset of physical aggression is preceded by nonviolent verbal abuse and behavioral restrictions. Early on in the relationships, the abuser may present himself to be a very attentive and loving person. The desire to know the whereabouts of a woman's activities at all times may at first make the woman feel valued. Women in our sample discussed that they were stalked, received frequent phone calls for reassurance, and were questioned about daily activities. As one young twenty-three-year-old victim who was living with her abuser stated, *"He was very controlling and would time me in the shower or how long I was gone to the store."* Another shared, *"I was totally under his thumb and to this day have never had a driver's license."* Four out of five of the abused women in our sample complained that their partner/spouse didn't want them to socialize with friends and if the friends got in the way they were often threatened. This controlling act is described by the following, *"He would go to work and take my keys to the car, the cord from the phone and I was not allowed to go anywhere except to meet the kids at the school bus stop. I was not allowed to have friends."*

The overwhelming majority (over 80 percent) reported that the abuser used controlling tactics such as anger and temper tantrums when she disagreed with the abuser's point of view, bullying tendencies, threats to use a weapon, or simply ordering the women around. This power-over model often just became a way of life as one woman noted. *"I didn't know how to exist without the abuse and fear in my life. This was my reality."* Extreme jealousy was also frequently mentioned (82 percent) as a recurring theme for the male abuser of low self-esteem who often became violent. About the same number of women (78 percent) indicated that their abuser frequently acted as if they would like to kill them. This behavior, the jealousy and anger often endured from maliciously controlling men, was revealed when we asked the abused women if they ever received any damage to personal property stemming from their violent relationship. Over 80 percent of those responding shared a variety of volatile reactions coming from their abusers. These fits of temper included clothes being ripped off, burned, or thrown away; TVs destroyed; holes punched in the walls; phone lines being cut; furniture broken and destroyed; dishes broken; windows smashed in. Destruction of personal and/ or sentimental items such as pictures and jewelry was also a common occurrence. Such fits of rage were illustrated thus: *"My ex once burned all my clothes and he also burned my kid's clothes at the same time. He shot at my car and totally damaged our home. Yes, he tried to destroy everything that meant anything to me."*

Other controlling behaviors mentioned by our sample included partners who exhibited jealousy and possessiveness and frequently attempted to isolate the victim. We found from the women's accounts that perpetrators often invent or exaggerate the victim's attention to and from other men. Insecure batterers may also be jealous of attention that victims receive from friends, family, and coworkers, or in some cases family pets. As one lifer remarked, *"My boyfriend was jealous of my pet bird and he threw it outside because he didn't want to share my attention."* Another individual mentioned having her puppy shot right in front of her. This can be particularly damaging when used in conjunction with other fear tactics. As one woman who suffered from extreme emotional abuse stated, *"He intimidated and threatened me with a weapon as a tactic to keep me away from my friends. I was fearful he would hurt me or my family."* An older woman who had been in an emotionally abusive relationship for twenty-six years by a stalking, overly jealous and controlling spouse shared the following:

> I was constantly being accused of being with someone else if I was just a few minutes late. He also accused me of having sex with someone else. I became alienated from my daughter, family and friends because I couldn't go anywhere without him wanting to be with me. He checked my odometer and tire tracks to see if I had been anywhere. He checked my pager and answering machine and had me change my phone number to keep old boyfriends from calling. He had me destroy photos of ex-boyfriends. He called my job and came to my worksite often.

Although this individual was not a recipient of sexual or physical abuse or injured in any way, her narrative demonstrates the traumatic emotional damage that living in a prolonged controlled state of existence can have, especially with little evidence of respect or trust exhibited. Such a state promotes a feeling of helplessness and hopelessness and eventually takes a toll on the psychological well-being of the emotionally battered victim. For example, one fifty-one-year-old woman who had been frequently put down, screamed and yelled at, ordered around, and bullied by a jealous and controlling abuser for twenty-five years eventually snapped, taking her abuser's life.

> He completely dominated me, but I let him and never walked away. He screamed at me about 3 weeks after we were married. He punched a hole in the wall, locked me in the bathroom and said he was leaving. He came back after a few hours and said he felt really bad but it was my fault. So, after that, to please him was my goal. But remember I never walked away.

The responses we received indicated that verbal abuse and controlling threats played an important role in reinforcing the "sense of entitlement" common in traditional male abusers. Due to the constant threats and injuries, it is obvious that many of the abused women and their families lived in constant fear of their lives. Men prone to be abusive feel they have the right to "dominate" and will use any means necessary to control their victims. By instilling controlling measures such as anger outbursts, verbal threats, or the use of a weapon or other bullying tactics, victims often become fearful and feel they are at the mercy of these coercive acts. While the emotional abuse leaves no physical scars, it serves to bind the intimate partner to the abuser as effectively as chains or ropes.[6] With a lack of resources, battered women often become isolated, entrapped, and cannot envision a way out. Learned helplessness often becomes her way of life as she simply becomes resigned to her fate in life. Unfortunately, women who are emotionally abused often find that their experiences are minimized or misunderstood by those they turn to for help.

PLEASE STOP THE ABUSE

People have a remarkable ability to adapt to adverse conditions across the life course, including domestic disputes. It is a common occurrence for abused women to express conflicted feelings about how best to settle an abusive relationship that has gradually deteriorated over time. Battered women too often become ensnared into an ongoing forceful relationship due to the many conflicting dynamics. For most victims of domestic abuse, the initial preference is to develop a strategy to end or reduce the significance of the abuse. Victims face difficult decisions as they, over an extended period of time, come to grips with the best way to proceed. Of course, they are especially concerned about engaging in intervention behaviors that might escalate the abuse, bringing heightened fear for the safety of their children and for themselves. In chaotic unstable relationships there may be specific stressful events

CASE HISTORY 3.2: GOING TO THE LAW WOULD BE A WASTE OF TIME

Sarah is a sixty-seven-year-old who has been a victim of sexual and physical abuse practically all of her life. As she states, *"I have been in lots of bad relationships and I feel like this may be why I'm in prison. No one really knows how bad things have been all my life—nothing I could talk about because I knew my life would be in danger."* The sexual abuse started when she was four or five years of age. When the victimization started, Sarah's father told her that he would beat her to death if she ever told anyone about the abuse. Although Sarah did eventually have the courage to tell her mother the liberties her father was taking, her threatened mother was too afraid to attempt an intervention. Told constantly that she was no good, Sarah was not allowed to make new friends, and when she did attempt to meet other men, her father would beat her due to his jealous anger. Sarah's father and every other man who abused her told her that going to the law would be a waste of time because if she did pursue legal action she would be killed. Eventually turning to alcohol, Sarah on two occasions considered taking her own life.

that can "push people over the edge" and toward a help-seeking pattern to do whatever it takes to end the abuse. While women through "learned helplessness" have been socialized to remain in abusive relationships at all costs, the proverbial straw that breaks the camel's back—the final horrendous incident —literally forces them to consider a significant life change.

After overcoming the fear to act, women in abusive relationships may lack the necessary social support or financial means to engage in a proactive intervention. Two-thirds of the women indicated that as the abusive situation evolved, they initially sought help from family and friends, whose support was not always there. Some of the women mentioned being talked into remaining in an abusive relationship by family members with statements such as, *"They begged me not to divorce," "They didn't believe me," "You made the mistake, you live with it,"* or *"My mother talked me into going back to him."* Along a similar line, another compelling story from a sixty-year-old lifer reveals the frustration many of the women feel when trying to escape their toxic abusive life.

I was forced to stay with my husband because my family does not believe in divorce. I once left him and took the children and he called family and threatened to kill himself. I had to return to that hell. And once I divorced him due to his sexually molesting one of our children, I was forced to remarry him because my family disowned me. This merely added an approval for him to continue the abuse.

Others felt they had just worn out their welcome where friends and family were concerned. In the words of one woman, *"My family and friends are just sick and tired of being pulled into our situation."* In some situations, the violence was so volatile that family and friends were too scared to get involved since they also received threats on their lives from the abuser. Threats like, *"He told me if I left him he would kill me and my whole family," "My spouse threatened to set my friend's house on fire if I didn't come out and leave with him,"* and *"He terrorized my family members, and I went back to him in order to protect them"* were common responses from the women seeking a solution to the abuse. Other women indicated they just didn't have any family or friends they could rely on for support and assistance. For instance, one individual who was attempting to take out a warrant changed her mind due to being heavily influenced by her mother-in-law. After receiving knife wounds and being knocked unconscious, this same woman was trying to end the relationship when she was told, *"Bitch I'm gonna kill you tonight."*

Victims often turn to a variety of community supports such as faith leaders or other counseling services (20 percent) or, if available, a women's shelter (11 percent) to seek safety and personal resolve. Often domestic violence shelters are not readily available particularly in rural areas or in some cases may not accept certain victims due to organizational guidelines. For example, one woman who had tried numerous avenues seeking support singled out the fact that *"Abuse shelters wouldn't take me because I had a 13-year-old son."* Her family also lived far away, so finding sources of support was difficult. This victim's abusive spouse agreed to see a counselor, but wouldn't return after their initial visit. Others indicated that they tried relying on their faith, and some acknowledged talking to their ministers about the abuse. We have already mentioned that some families were dead set against separation or divorce and even demanded that the victim remain in the destructive relationship. This notion that sometimes the church can also make matters worse by using prayer as an answer to control the abuser's temper or help the woman become a better wife reinforces this dilemma.[7] While religious groups can be an important foundation of emotional support and pragmatic assistance, they may also tend to remain silent when it comes to male aggression. While an overwhelming number of church leaders thought that perpetrators must assume responsibility for their actions, the same number also felt that victims must bear some of the blame.[8]

Several women mentioned the fact that family members sometimes simply deny the abuse, or blame the victim for their abusive situation, or were unsupportive to the idea of leaving a contentious relationship filled with violence and turmoil. Additional research which argued that "the family ought to be preserved at whatever cost" has infiltrated the teachings of various religious institutions.[9] This notion has led to inconsistent responses to domestic violence, if not substantial support for patriarchy and violence against women. As one victim recalled, *"My family told me to go back and obey my hus-*

band." With an emotional commitment to the relationship, abused women are likely to incorporate techniques of rationalization whereby they accept excuses by abusers and deny the seriousness of the victimization. As these tendencies continue, they become intertwined with the women's diminishing sense of self-worth.[10]

The criminal justice system is one of first places victims go to restore order in a volatile relationship. It should be mentioned that many of the women in our sample were incarcerated during a prior era when intimate partner violence was considered a family problem. Although there was a lack of consensus about how the police should respond to domestic violence, almost half (46 percent) made their abusive relationship public by calling the police to intervene, frequently to no avail. For example, *"The police I contacted said they couldn't do anything without bloodshed. The times he broke my bones or caused stitches he was briefly apprehended. He didn't do significant time until he shot me."* Another older lifer who was incarcerated for more than two decades, shared her experience with the police when her marriage suddenly turned abusive after more than twenty years of marriage.

I went to them for help even writing a statement that I was afraid for my life. They told me if he hadn't put me in the hospital there was nothing they could do. They told me he had a right to tear up anything in the house he wanted to. In the state of Georgia, the only choice a woman has against defending herself against her spouse is death or life in prison.

Some of the women shared positive accounts of their abusive situation. As one recalled, *"I called 911 and the police came, saw the bruises and arrested him."* This victim acknowledged that after calling the police she often did not follow through, *"I would call the police but couldn't bring myself to press charges. I would try to leave or leave him alone but he would come back because I didn't know how to function outside of the abuse anymore."* Another woman who had been in three abusive relationships over a seventeen-year period voiced her frustrations on the ineffectiveness of the criminal justice system in upholding the restraining order.

Restraining orders are only paper and not a deterrent of abuse. I was raped and beaten in front of my children when I filed for divorce. I was robbed numerous times. Charges were always reduced for a plea to something not close to the experience.

Lack of an adherence to a restraining order can prove detrimental for a vulnerable victim as the abuser may often seek retaliation after procuring police involvement. Additionally, women who have negative, ineffective experiences with police or hold cultural norms avoiding police were less likely to call for police help during episodes of violence. *"I was taught that you don't deal with the police unless you have to"* or *"The thought of calling the police never entered my mind"* serve as barriers to involve the police.[11] Or in some cases the threats may be so severe that the risk to call the police is just too great. As one woman explained, *"After being beaten almost to death and stabbed with a knife and warned about what would happen if police were called again, I was literally too afraid to call."*

Several of the women and their abusers quickly learned that when their calls for police protection were ignored, the more likely their abusers would continue the abusive tactics without any major repercussions. One physically abused young woman, after calling the police, found herself to be under arrest as well. In her words, *"They told my parents and then me that I should obey my husband."* Frequently, intervention through the criminal justice system, such as the filing of restraining orders or filing for separation, only increases the anger and aggression of the batterer. As one lifer recalled, *"I often kept my mother on the phone to avoid being abused and so I would have a phone contact witness to call 911. I often drove to my mothers' house to get away or ran to a neighbor's house to avoid being killed."* Even today, with mandatory laws requiring officers to make an arrest when called to a domestic violence scene, some police officers would rather not get involved in a domestic matter. While some of the women reported that police intervention was effective in immediately stopping the violence, other respondents consistently reported mixed or negative experiences dealing with the police or the legal system. As one woman vowed, *"I had called the police so many times before. I knew I was wasting my time."* In a similar situation where the police had been summoned, another person said, *"I let the cop talk me out of having him arrested."*

The battered women acknowledged that they used a variety of other alternatives in attempting to sway their abuser to stop the violent attacks. Although we made no attempt to seek information that would have provided answers about the order of such strategies, it is obvious that the majority of victimized women went to great lengths to reduce the violent relationship or to totally escape the situation altogether. The most universal method (78 percent) was trying to hide, leave, or run away. For example, *"I often ran and hid from him until things calmed down"* was a common statement many of the women uttered when trying to stay alive. Another 72 percent said they tried moving out of the home only to often return on their own or in some cases after being threatened by the abusive boyfriend or spouse. In other situations, 42 percent of the women indicated that they were at least temporarily able to get the perpetrator to leave the home. In extreme cases, about one-third of the women with abuse histories filed for divorce. While most of those followed through with the divorce, several remained in the relationship. As one young lifer who had very frequently suffered from emotional and sexual abuse shared:

> I filed for divorce and when he said he would change I dropped the divorce. When the abuse continued, I filed again about a year later and this time I went through with the divorce. I tried to move out and hide from him but I had to go to work and ended up going back home. I just didn't want anyone to know that my life wasn't perfect.

THE STRUGGLE TO LEAVE

As the previous section suggests, many of the abused women made multiple attempts to seek assistance in what often became futile efforts to end their violent relationships. While some just wanted the abuse to stop, others were eventually able to summon the courage to permanently leave the relationship. Women stay in battering relationships for a number of reasons ranging from love to religious beliefs to financial reasons to fear. While battered women may be very determined to leave, it normally takes anywhere from five to seven attempts to successfully accomplish such a move.[12] One young woman who later got a divorce after calling 911 and taking out a restraining order recalled, *"He went to counseling for help and we tried reconciliation. It worked for a while, but we finally went separate ways."* However, physically separating from the abuser is not always a successful strategy, and numerous women described overwhelming difficulty in leaving their violent relationships.

CASE HISTORY 3.3: THE POLICE TOLD ME TO TAKE HIM HOME FROM JAIL

Sandy is a forty-three-year-old lifer serving time for the death of her husband. Her abusive relationship began when she was nineteen years old, and the battering continued for another twenty-two years. She was abused in almost every way possible including sexually, physically, and mentally. *"He took all my money and I had to provide receipts for everything."* Sandy was beaten so badly that both feet were broken resulting in permanent nerve damage to her right foot. She was knifed, knocked unconscious, and suffered a variety of bruises along with a broken nose. Although Sandy was beaten badly, she was not permitted to seek medical help. As a means of punishment, her angry husband poured dirty motor oil all over her clothes and broke other household possessions. Sandy made numerous attempts to stop the abuse by calling 911. After receiving a restraining order her husband threatened to burn her and her son alive. After another arrest for abuse and violation of the restraining order, *"the police told me to take him home from jail."* That very night Sandy chose the only option that she felt would keep her and her son safe; that choice was to take the life of her abuser.

Some victims may make the decision to accept or adapt to the violence and begin to reintegrate their personalities to accommodate the abusive situation. Among others, decisions to leave or stay are influenced by the strength of the relationship, how extreme the abuse becomes, maintaining hope that a partner will change, or some cataclysmic event such as children being severely beaten or threatened with a weapon. As one woman expressed:

> I had left but was talked to and promised the abuse would never happen again! The million-dollar statement. Please give me another chance. You are made to feel it is your fault so you listen to your family and give in.

Women often stated that despite a volatile domestic relationship, they remained in love with their abuser. These feelings of love and commitment can serve to prompt them to accept apologies and believe in promises to change like, *"Their behavior got better for a minute, then went back to the same old, same old."* Another noted, *"I loved him and I did not want to accept reality—that this was a deadly relationship. I still wanted to believe it was going to change, because he could be so nice."*

The cycle of violence, which includes shifts between violence and acts of loving contrition, may further cause confused emotions in abused women. Abusers often emotionally entrap victims by manipulating their self-esteem—telling them that they are loved or that they brought the abuse upon themselves. For example, *"He would always come back and say he loved me and he was sorry and that he would never do it again."* One victim recalled, *"I went back with him because he used drugs to lure me and the attention that he gave me."* Another stated, *"He came and cried and begged me to come back and I did. I wish I'd never ever stayed after he started hitting me, but I had no place to go with my children."* In particular, deciding to leave can be difficult for women who have been in long-term relationships. Having so many years invested in a relationship even if it is an abusive one can make the decision to leave even more difficult. One woman in her sixties who was in an abusive relationship for eighteen years illustrates this dilemma by sharing that *"a woman will continue believing that the man is going to change and keep going back like I did. He would come around and tell me he wouldn't hit me any more if I would only give him another chance."* The presence of children can also complicate the decision-to-leave process:

> He decided after we had our first child together that he wanted to hang out with his friends all night and then come home drunk or high and wanted to have sex. It was just crazy and ridiculous. I tried to make it work for our child's sake and I still have a lot of love for him to this day.

This comment reflects how the feelings of love and commitment versus the feelings of fear and pain remain a constant point of contention as victims struggle with the dynamics of an abusive relationship. Often these torn feelings remain a constant across decades of bruises, broken bones, and emotional abuse.

Repeatedly, the women shared their struggles when an extremely possessive intimate partner often simply refused to let the relationship end. As one woman shared, *"People who have never been there talk about just walking away, but it's not always that easy. They come after you."* Another woman who, over a period of eight years of battering, had suffered broken bones, teeth being knocked out, and numerous other bruises and cuts revealed, *"When I would try to leave, he would just track me down and drag me back home."* Other women described situations where their tires were slashed, wires ripped out under the hood, car windows broken out, and even cars completely destroyed in order to stop the victim and often her children from leaving. In light of such controlling behaviors, making the decision to leave, or more importantly being able to leave, is no easy task. Sometimes it's a conscious choice, but most times for battered women it's an immediate action taken in a fleeting moment in an attempt to save their own or their children's lives. The notion of kill or be killed becomes a true reality, and we found in some cases that that decision had to be made in the spur of the moment when threats become imminent.

It is well documented that a woman is most susceptible to becoming a homicide victim when she is attempting to leave an abusive relationship. We found that the stories of numerous lifers indicated that the violence and controlling behavior generally escalated when the victims were attempting to leave. Threats from the abuser to kill the victim or family and friends were common during scenes when attempts were being made to physically leave. The following death threats illustrate some of the personal accounts described by abused women trying to escape their violence situation:

My husband came after me and tried to run my car into a ditch and threatened to kill me.

He came looking for me and followed me wherever I was or went. And he threatened to kill me if I didn't come back to him.

When I tried to leave, he pulled a gun on me and put it in my face. When I did leave, he found me and came and got me.

When I tried to leave, he threatened my family members, and I went back to protect them.

I was choked until I greyed out and then he beat me.

Approximately one-half of the women who responded indicated that they were charged with homicide, which ultimately ended the violence directed toward them. The overwhelming majority were either already separated or divorced, trying to leave or end the relationship when the deadly event took place. Battered women who strike back in a deadly fashion toward their abusers experience more severe trauma than other abused women.[13] Usually, those who respond with force have extensive abuse histories of incest and physical abuse as children as well as sexual and physical torture by their husband.[14] For example, one young lifer who became an abuse victim at age sixteen and after two years of intense suffering decided to sever the relationship. Her abuser, who was very controlling and extremely jealous, constantly screamed and yelled at her, frequently stalked, bullied, and extensively sexually and physically abused her. In her words, *"I was trying to get away and I was scared and afraid so I stabbed him once and he bleed to death. He was stalking me at the time and jumped out of the bushes."* An older lifer also shared her marital experiences with an abusive drug addict whom she had reported to the police over twenty times.

> Nothing worked and no one except my lawyers and the police would help. The police couldn't catch him so they told me to do whatever I had to do. They knew I had a permit to carry a gun. They also knew all the charges on him. He didn't want to do any time so he said it was either me or him that dies.

One of the major differences between battered women who kill and those who do not is the fact that they are able to successfully escape and move on with their lives. In fact, one-third of the abused lifers were able to get a divorce. However, we found several cases where even after divorce the violence and terrorist acts continued, leading to a fatal ending.

> My husband had gotten on drugs really bad and started taking money from our businesses and our bank account. We had been together for 10 years before the abuse began and it lasted 2 years before we were finally divorced. But the abuse didn't stop. After getting a restraining order and eventually a divorce, he found me in San Diego. So, for the children's sake, I ended up moving back with him but living in separate houses. The last words I heard him say, "one of us ain't gonna live!" I had heard I'll kill you over and over, but I always brushed it off. But this time I knew he meant these words when I saw the look in his eyes this time.

THE LINGERING EFFECTS

Domestic violence can have a far-reaching impact on its victims and society as a whole. Of course, physical injury is one of the most obvious consequences suffered by victims. Immediate injuries include bruises, contusions, cuts, and broken bones. These injuries generally heal rather quickly and are not perceived as highly serious by most people. However, some domestic violence victims face more serious consequences as a result of these types of injuries. Also, injuries that leave visible scars—such as facial disfigurations; loss of teeth, fingers, or toes; or scars on the neck, arms, or legs—can have a detrimental effect on the victim. Gunshot wounds, stabbing wounds, burns, and trauma to the head are also excessive injuries which may affect the long-term quality of life of certain victims. Some injuries may prove significant enough that they result in loss of mobility due to an incomplete healing process.

In addition to various types of physical injuries suffered by victims of violent crime, victims of sexual assault endure extreme trauma leading to a variety of medical issues. We found that the abused women were more likely to suffer from chronic physical health problems than those women without an abusive past. Gastrointestinal problems, stomach ulcers, and migraine headaches were common problems. In addition, some of the women suffered additional health problems as a result of severe cases of abuse such as undiagnosed hearing loss and vision problems, dizziness, and concentration issues. A few of the lifers are still having surgeries to repair damages done due to excessive battering while others are missing teeth and are living with broken bones often unattended when the abuse occurred. Some still continue to suffer from chronic head or other internal injuries that are common reminders of near-death experiences prior to incarceration. In addition, women with histories of abuse frequently turn to drugs or alcohol as a means of coping with an abusive relationship or to numb the pain.

Based on measures from the Hopkins Symptom Checklist, we found that women lifers reporting sexual abuse as a child or adult were significantly more likely to report higher levels of depression, somatization, interpersonal sensitivity, anxiety, and disciplinary infractions when compared to those women who reported no abusive histories. The abused women were also more likely to experience suicidal thoughts as well as attempting suicide. It is not surprising that high rates of mental illness have been found among incarcerated women suffering from extensive victimization. A frequent consequence of violence against women is post-traumatic stress disorder (PTSD), characterized by intrusive thoughts, nightmares, and flashbacks. As one physically and emotionally scarred woman reminded us:

> My abusive past has left me with low self-esteem and very hard to trust. It has been humiliating and a life time of scars inside, especially bad dreams. It made me feel unworthy for years. I still sometimes cry in the shower and scrub my body as if I can scrub the filth and shame away.

Decades later several of the abused women were still complaining of the flashbacks related to previous abuse and rape situations. Although we failed to ask for particular indicators of PTSD, numerous women volunteered that they suffered from hypervigilance or from being easily startled as they continue to reexperience traumatic events from the past. Estrangement from the ability to form and maintain relationships is also considered a symptom of PTSD. Since numerous women had transitioned from an abusive childhood into multiple abusive relationships as adults, they tended to question their ability to select men who would treat them with respect. As one lifer recalled, *"I thought I had found Mr. Right, but it was another Mr. Wrong."* One option mentioned by numerous women was to refrain completely from getting involved in any future relationship with men. This point is reinforced by the following narratives showing the far-reaching consequences of a trauma filled past:

I do not ever want to have another relationship with anyone. I will never trust a man again. I can never be alone with a man again because now that I've been convicted of a felony a man can tell lies and I would be locked up. It's true you will go to jail then you have to prove you are innocent and with a criminal record I would come back to prison.

As I look back over my life and my relationships with men I now realize I never picked a man that didn't abuse me in some way. From all that I have read and heard from other women, it makes me think that a good man is hard to find. At the age I am now I believe that I will be better off by myself.

For the many women who suffered from a history of sexual abuse, a woman's experience of being strip-searched can reactivate the trauma that prior abuse has created. It provides feelings of degradation by having to expose herself to people who exercise power over her daily existence and serves as a reminder of her abuse history. This intrusive mandatory practice often results in flashbacks, humiliation, and emotional numbing. As one lifer asserted, *"The memories just never go away, because it's a life I just can't fix."* One older woman discussed her memories of humiliation imported to prison:

I was so humiliated when my husband would abuse me in front of other people by slamming me down and ripping my clothes off. Now, every time I am taken somewhere in handcuffs and shackles for another man's crime I feel equally as humiliated and embarrassed. The abuse is still alive and well in my life. Only the judicial system is the perpetrator. It's sad.

Higher levels of anxiety are reported for older women who were abused across a lifetime, and individuals who experienced multiple traumas are at particularly high risk for symptoms of distress.[15] This is the case for many of the lifers in our study who had spent most of their adult lives in abusive relationships, which left permanent emotional scars.

Despite the long-term consequences of abuse and the toll it has taken on the battered women in our sample, we found a glimmer of hope for some of the women going forward as they reconcile the negative outcomes of an abusive past. However, this can be a slow, tedious process as these women work through a vast range of emotions and trauma accumulated from childhood. As one woman acknowledged, *"The abuse really hurt my way of thinking. It has taken a long time to retrain my own mind and see how bad things really were for me."* It must be remembered that many of the women are not only dealing with victimization, but also social/emotional constraints and other indicators of social marginalization prior to incarceration. For example, the following account describes the important progress being made by a woman who survived a battered past, which started when the victim was in her early twenties and continued for twenty-seven long years:

> I just completed a residential substance abuse treatment program where I learned how to handle my feelings, situations, and to detach from relationships. I have learned to be my own person and to identify the difference between healthy and unhealthy relationships. I have to start with setting boundaries and exercising my rights as a person.

Another woman talked about the realization that despite enduring a tumultuous past, she now possesses a sense of maturity and personal growth as they reminisce about their ability to move forward with their lives. For example, *"I've had 20 years of self-help and therapy. Through emotional maturity, growth and healing, I now have a successful life and a very healthy personal perception of myself."* A woman who had to defend herself at an early age offered another positive view of her time in prison, *"In a way I'm thankful for what happened to me and the time I've spent in here learning about what life is all about and how it should have been and not been."* Despite the breadth of negative outcomes associated with violent and prolonged victimization, there is some evidence that many of the women are making the effort to cope with their abusive past.

SUMMARY

This chapter documented that violence across their life span for women serving life sentences has been pervasive and severe. For many, the abuse started during childhood and only ended when victims were forced to defend their lives. Males exerting power and control were a common theme as these women were exposed to almost every form of abuse imaginable. We learned that the abused women went to great lengths to escape their abusers, but often were hindered from a reluctant criminal justice system and, in some cases, a lack of family support. We heard firsthand accounts as to why so many women struggle when attempting to leave an abusive situation. Our findings provide a vivid account of what the word "trapped" means for women with no place to go, and how leaving only makes matters worse. Today these women are permanently damaged and continue to suffer from the long-term effects of emotional, sexual, and physical abuse, and interventions and programs designed for survivors of domestic violence are needed now more than ever. Not only would this improve the potential for prison adjustment, it would also increase the chances of successful reintegration back into the community. The courage these women showed in sharing their histories of abuse and to give support and voice to other women currently in battering relationships is remarkable.

NOTES

1. Zosky, "The Application of Object Relations Theory to Domestic Violence."
2. Dutton, *The Abusive Personality: Violence and Control in Intimate Relationships*.
3. Conklin, *Criminology*.
4. Wallace and Roberson, *Family Violence*.
5. Aday and Krabill, *Women Aging in Prison*.
6. Wallace and Roberson, *Family Violence*, 72.
7. Tracy, "Patriarchy and Domestic Violence: Challenging Common Misconceptions."
8. Levitt and Ware, "Religious Leaders' Perspectives on Marriage, Divorce, and Intimate Partner Violence."
9. Nash and Hesterberg, "Biblical Framings of and Responses to Spousal Violence in the Narratives of Abused Christian Women."
10. Ferraro, "Battered Women: Strategies for Survival."
11. Wolf, Ly, Hobart, and Kernic, "Barriers to Seeking Police Help for Intimate Partner Violence."
12. Wallace and Roberson, *Family Violence*.
13. Bright and Bowland, "Assessing Interpersonal Trauma in Older Adult Women."
14. Beattie and Shaughnessy, *Sisters in Pain: Battered Women Fight Back*.
15. Aday and Krabill, *Women Aging in Prison*.

Chapter 4

Life behind Bars

Living with a Life Sentence

"This will never be a home away from home but I have found some family in here. I've had to make a life in this place and even a few, very few staff has helped."

"Now I just live 'this' life the best I can and just try to stay positive. Nothing really changes but your attitude."

"Adjustment" to life in prison is a nebulous concept with a variety of meanings. Typically, these include overall measures of adjustment to environmental conditions of the prison, interactions with staff and other inmates, and disconnections from the outside world;[1] emotional/mental health conditions such as depression, anxiety, and anger;[2] and disciplinary infractions/misconduct.[3] Contemporary approaches to understanding "adjustment" to prison point to multidimensional forms of adjustment, especially for women in prison.[4]

A substantial body of literature has examined the relationship between imported, pre-prison factors and adjustment to prison deprivations among both men and women living behind bars.[5] The victimization-to-offending trajectory and the mental health and substance abuse histories that many of these women bring to prison, along with the depriving conditions of prison, have important implications for women's overall adjustment to a long-term prison sentence. Most men and women serving life sentences eventually "maturely cope" with prison.[6] Women lifers navigate "the mix,"[7] and according to Lempert[8] and George,[9] within six to seven years establish a substantive life for themselves within prison—including educational improvements, service contributions to the prison and others both within and outside the prison, self-actualization and awareness, relationships with prisoners and staff, religious engagement, and re-establishing bonds with family. However, initial adjustment to a life sentence is marked by shock, numbness, and despair, which continues for some women lifers.[10] The women's voices included in this chapter take us from their initial reactions to their life sentence, early adjustments, adjustments over time, and how women lifers "do time" with one another, prison staff, without their families, and with or without the hope for parole/going home.

INITIAL REACTIONS TO RECEIVING A LIFE SENTENCE

When we asked the women in our sample about their initial thoughts and feelings upon receiving their life sentence, they related to us a set of common emotional responses including shock, disbelief, numbness, and denial. Feelings of numbness, fear, and shock make sense given that 95 percent of the women lifers were in prison for their first time. As a couple of women shared: *"It was a surreal experience. I felt that it was a mistake and this couldn't be happening to me,"* and *"I couldn't believe this was happening to me. I thought I was dreaming."* These emotions were felt regardless of the age at which they were sentenced. A woman just starting her sentence at age forty-five said: *"I couldn't believe it was really happening to me. I still don't believe it."* A woman sentenced at age seventeen and who had served sixteen years of her sentence shared a similar experience: *"I was numb and I didn't accept my sentence in the beginning. It was unrealistic to me."*

For these women who had very little experience as offenders within the criminal justice system or with incarceration, the initial reaction was a culture shock, or "prison shock." Taking a completely foreign and unexpected trajectory, women lifers had to adjust to being incarcerated, and being incarcerated for the rest of their lives. A thirty-year-old, college-educated lifer said: *"In comparison, my whole world was catapulted into another dimension, the people, ideals, morals, and behavior was culture shock."* Another woman with a similar background coming into prison agreed: *"It was like I had entered the Twilight Zone."*

Most of the women lifers indicated they felt devastated and hopeless; some were scared; others were angry; and a few felt relief when they received their sentence of "life." The reactions to these emotions and the reasons behind these emotions followed a few overlapping patterns, which for some changed with time, as evident in the voices above, and for others played out as a tug-of-war, pulling them in conflicting emotional directions (e.g., hopeless to hopeful; denial to acceptance; and death to life). For example, this woman felt that her life was over, but she also had reason to live:

> I believed God would turn it around at the same time I felt like my life was over and I wanted to die but I didn't kill myself because it would hurt my mom and dad. Since I'm alive I can still be a part of their life even in prison.

Her response also demonstrates two key themes for women lifers and their adjustment: God and family. Women relied on God (or were angry with God) and emphasized the effects of their sentence on their families—this life sentence was not only happening to them but also to their families. Responses like these came with passionate and powerful recollections of their sentencing and incarceration, their own traumas, and feelings of hopelessness and injustice. In contrast, some women could offer only a few words to describe their thoughts and feelings, while others could not remember their experiences. Either actual loss of memory due to trauma or because they were medicated for mental health reasons, women simply stated: *"Don't remember, I was severely mental health at that time"* and *"I was heavy medicated and don't remember to be honest."* Another woman recalled a bit more about her initial reaction to her life sentence:

I couldn't believe it because back then I didn't think innocent people went to prison. To be honest, I had a "blackout" of sorts. I recall being sentenced. I remember giving my jewelry to my attorney. The next thing I recall was being led into the county jail. No idea how much time lapsed.

By far the most common response, primarily to feelings of hopelessness, were thoughts that their lives were over, that they would never get out of prison (i.e., "see daylight"), and that they would die in prison. Many held general notions of wanting to die because they were scared, hopeless, or overwhelmed by the thought of so much time in prison and away from their families. We heard repeatedly from the women the reactions:

I couldn't do this. I wanted to die.

I can't do this. I'm so scared. I want to die.

That I wish I were dead.

I wanted to die.

I wanted to die. I just knew I could not make it.

My heart stopped and time stood still. I could not wrap my mind around life without my children. I thought I'd rather die if they had to grow up without me.

Discussions of eventual death (*"That I will die in here"*) and symbolic forms of death through losses (*"My life is over,"* *"How can I do this,"* and *"How can I live without my children"*) were also common reactions (these losses are discussed more fully in chapter 7). For example, family is life for many of these women, and their life sentences equated to a loss of that life/their family. As these women told us:

> I was going to die here and that I may never get out to see my daughter grow up to be there for her and my family.

> I would die in here (hell). That I had lost my family.

> My life was over and I lost my family and kids.

The reactions of hopelessness and unwillingness to accept a life in prison without family are clearly heard in these voices. However, even when women did not mention losses of family or wishes that their life was over, the sentence of life in prison meant, for them, that their lives were finished whether physically or mentally, and that that they would not make it inside or out of prison.

> My life was pretty much over and I was scared. [Another shared the same thoughts, but said she was "numb."]

> I felt like I was finished, like life was done and I'd never get out.

> How can I do this and stay sane? Will I ever have a life beyond these walls again? Am I strong enough?

Hopeless, and not willing to accept a life in prison, women also shared specific thoughts of ending their own lives and actual suicide attempts as well as preferences for lethal injection/death penalty. Actual and immediate death was preferable to them at the time they began their incarceration. Those who were very open about their thoughts of suicide shared: *"My thoughts at first was killing myself and my feelings was I had no hope on nothing anymore"* and *"My thoughts were to kill myself because I am here for nothing."*

Preferable to killing oneself, a few women mentioned that the death penalty would be better than a life in prison and they wished to receive lethal injection, or at least be given the option of death rather than life/death in prison. For example, *"Give me the lethal injection please. Just end my life now. Don't wait and let me die in prison"* and *"I was afraid of prison and asked for lethal injection. When I got to prison I realized it was worth dying to avoid it."* One woman whose original sentence by the state was death offered this contrast: *"My original sentence was death. So that was a terrifying moment. The life sentence meant that I could help people."*

Along with thinking that their lives were over, a second distinct reaction to the emotions of confusion, disbelief, and powerlessness surrounding the receipt of their life sentences concerned religious meanings and interpretations of their lives (reliance on religion is discussed more fully in chapter 8).

Larger-than-themselves plans and purposes gave women a reason to live, a hope for getting out one day, and a desire to "be there" for others. Although religious beliefs sustained women throughout their time in prison, some women's only responses to their life sentence was to rely on God. They felt hopeless and that their lives were out of their control. By placing the outcome of their lives with God, women believed *"God would turn it around"* or if not, *"God will see me through this. This is not the end of my life."* For these women and others, their sentence was a part of God's plan or will for them. As described by these women:

> I was in a state of shock at first but yet I was still calm. I was a Christian before my incarceration and I believe that God has a plan and purpose for my life and this sad to say was a part of it all.

> When I was first sentenced to life, I was in denial, but when I realized it was true. I handed the situation over to God. And God has done every step of this sentence with me.

They also placed their families in God's control, emphasizing how He would protect them and their families. Given women lifers' pathways to prison, concerns for their family's safety and health were prominent. Since they were no longer there to "protect" their parents, children, and siblings, they placed their fears and concerns about their families with God.

> My thoughts and feelings were to have a wonderful relationship with God and let him take control and sense [*sic*] I couldn't do anything about it to put my whole family in his hand and let God bless us all and stay in the will of God. God would see me through it and protect my family and myself.

Belief in God or some larger purpose (e.g., "truth") balanced their feelings of hopelessness and loss of control in their lives, protected their thoughts and hopes, and helped them adjust to their life in prison.

> My adjustment was based on the belief that the truth would be revealed if I just hold on another day—I'll get to return to my family. Truly, to this day I still feel if I can hold on another day tomorrow could be the day of my deliverance. If I ever let go of that hope, I find I want my life to end.

As the quote above suggests, for many women, their initial thoughts and feelings were based on ideas of "innocence." In addition to disbelief that they received a life sentence for a crime they committed or played a part in, some women maintained a sense of innocence and that at some point and somehow the truth about what happened in their case would be revealed—*"I knew that I was innocent and I will be free someday."*

Feelings such as these coincided with feelings of hope for some; others felt a sense of "injustice" either because they were innocent or because they felt their sentence was based on poor representation, bad evidence, or in some way not fair. Anger was the most common emotion among these women, and they directed their anger at God, the judicial system, and anyone who had let them down including those who gave false testimony or who they argue actually committed the crime. Anger toward God is evident in the following quotes:

> How could this happen to me! I was mad as hell at God because he knows the whole of it all. Why would he let this happen to my children and me.

> I wanted to kill myself because I thought that God had turned his back on me. Because he knows that I am truly innocent and he allowed this to happen to me anyway.

> [I was] bitter, pissed off. I know, I'm innocent, God knows, I'm innocent. I don't have the money to pay a good lawyer, I'm fucked without a kiss or a hug or an orgasm.

Women also directed their anger outward to the judicial system and argued that their cases were "political" and influenced by larger system factors such as election years and laws aimed at "gang-related" crimes (e.g., accomplice, or party to the crime, laws).

> I was angry at the system, the county. I was a political case. If they convicted me then elections would run a certain way.

> ANGER! I was convicted on a lie. I was found guilty under the Party to a crime law. It was testified that I didn't kill [him] but a co-defendant said it was my idea.

> Injustice. I am a victim of §16-2-20, my charge is murder and I didn't kill any-one, though I am guilty of driving the car that transported the others.

Women convicted of murder under "party to a crime" laws felt strongly their sentence was unfair and too harsh. They were confused and made comments such as *"How can 4 people kill?"* and *"I always thought a person got a life for killing someone on purpose."* Others felt tricked by the state—some took pleas out of fear of no parole or harsher sentences. Further, in a state without self-defense laws, women who tried to protect or defend themselves against victimization and abuse were left with a life sentence, and anger: *"I was mad as hell because I was being raped and I took the life of the man who was raping me. The state paid me back by taking my life away."* Another woman echoed each of these thoughts and experiences from her case:

I knew immediately the feelings of injustice by them having false witnesses the prosecutors got so they could get a feather in their hat. I've been used as an example that the courts are fair to men of abuse even though I was the one being abused and defending myself.

Knowing that their actions were self-defense also gave some women the will to keep pursuing appeals and a change in their sentence. Relying on God and her innocence, this woman said: *"I knew God was with me and I would keep fighting to get out. I was innocent of the charges and had acted in self-defense."*

Given the overwhelming sense of devastation among most women in the sample, and likely how most of us might expect to feel if we were sentenced to life in prison, it was not as common for women to report feeling relief. A few did, and one woman, incarcerated as a juvenile, explained that she had waited two years through her trial and spent that time in solitary confinement at the county jail. She responded that her initial reaction was *"Relief to get it over with. I had waited two years for my trial."* She added, *"I never thought I'd still be locked up 14 years later."* Avoiding trials by taking pleas, other women felt relief that their case was settled, accepted their sentence, and started a new life behind bars.

In addition to relief, some accepted their sentence and their responsibility, but did not give up hope regardless of whether they would never get out or were just there "for now." These women shared these similar thoughts on acceptance:

I have probably been more accepting of my sentence as I know the crime I committed in deserving of a hard sentence. My incarceration is my fault.

Lord, I'm never getting out of prison, but I accept full responsibility of my actions. I made a bad mistake.

For women who experienced physical, sexual, and/or emotional abuse, most felt justified for their actions of self-defense, accepted their sentence even if it was deemed too harsh/lengthy, but also expressed a relief or feeling of safety after receiving their sentence. Within their initial reactions and reflections on adjustment we heard women say: *"I would rather do life than to be in the house with that man."* Referring to eight years of abuse by her husband, one said: *"I was in prison then, too."*

Along with acceptance, though, came feelings of guilt; they were sorry for what they had done, but also about leaving behind family/children, and they blamed themselves for failing their children. One woman's initial reaction was: *"That I was a failure as a mother."* Another recalled not thinking about herself at the time, but of her children and what would happen to them. Other women shared similar thoughts and experiences, and frequently pointed to

CASE HISTORY 4.1: THE EVENTS THAT BROUGHT ME TO PRISON

Since 2001, the year her husband was killed, Martha, age sixty-eight, focuses on how her experience in court brought her to prison. She said, *"I did NOT enter a plea. I turned it down and went to trial."* At jury trial she had a court-appointed attorney who did not call witnesses or expert testimony, but the state did. *"I am not angry with the jury because they never received my defense."* Evidence of abuse and circumstances of the crime including her husband's attack on her, knocking out her front teeth, while he was under the influence of cocaine were not introduced. Martha admits that she did not want to take the stand because *"I too am a mother and I did not want to say anything negative about my husband, because his mother was there or my family."* Convinced by her attorney to testify *"if you want to go home,"* Martha said, *"this was all a set-up because when I took the stand the DA attacked me without any objection from my lawyer. The events that brought me to prison."*

the effects of their sentence on their families. This woman's thoughts accurately sum up the experiences of many:

> Wow! I've never been in trouble and I thought what will happen to my kids. I was pregnant, what would happen to my child. How can I tell my kids this, where did I go wrong?

Being a mother as well as having a history of abuse influenced the way women lifers reacted to their life sentences initially. As shown in the quotes above, one of the biggest concerns over their sentence involved "losing" their families. Despite different ages at their sentence, current ages, time served, and prior prison history, women reported similar thoughts and feelings when they received their sentence of life in prison. They were in denial and disbelief, felt hopeless of ever getting out/dying in prison, and anger over perceived injustice. For others, they looked to their faith and God's purpose, maintained hope for release, and accepted their sentence with time.

EARLY ADJUSTMENT EXPERIENCES

Women lifers had a variety of early adjustment experiences which they vividly recalled. According to one lifer, *"The adjustment was horrible. Something I'll never forget."* They spoke specifically of the noise, lack of privacy, being uncomfortable and anxious in the prison environment, learning all of the rules/changing rules, and the loss of freedom. Prisons as institutions are built on rules and structure, but despite the controlled environment, life is characterized by uncertainly and change. Paradoxically, women must deal with the boredom and routine of doing time. To avoid boredom, some keep busy, while others deteriorate in their mental health. Operating behind the boredom/anxiety paradox is a loss of freedom and control. Speaking about their early adjustment experiences, women lifers reflected on the "craziness" of those first days, months, and, for some, years. As these women explained, they had a lot to "get use to":

> My initial adjustment was crazy. Had to get use to a lot of different ways of living. In time, I've learned to accept change because it's an everyday occurrence in prison. It's not new anymore or surprising.

> My adjustment I'm still working on it. It's kind of hard right now because it's my first time and a lot of things that go on I'm not use to.

A lack of experience with the prison environment and naiveté about who is in prison framed women's early experiences in their sentence. Some spoke about not knowing *"how people are in prison"* and *"what to expect from people."* According to one woman, who was like most who had never been in prison, the environment was nothing like she saw in movies or on TV.

For another woman, who was thirty-five years old when she was sentenced to life, the loss of freedom was the hardest:

> I did not adjust well. The first year was the hardest because I am a very outdoors person. I felt like an animal confined in a cage like the animals in the zoo that seem to be in a zone. I have learned to adjust by looking for positive things to do.

Her analogy to the caged animal coincides with other women's early adjustments to the lack of privacy. Women are constantly under surveillance by staff and other inmates. One of the juvenile lifers explained: *"At first it didn't seem real to me and I didn't know what to think. It was hard getting use to the people and the lack of privacy."* This lack of privacy also made some fearful because they did not know what to expect. A couple of women shared their experiences with the unfamiliar prison structure and rules, and staff: *"My initial adjustment was fear of the unknown, being around strangers and how I would be treated by the other inmates and staff."* Another *"had difficulty in adjusting to prison rules and staff reactions to inmates."* A third woman who had served six years at fifty-four years of age summarized her experience as: *"I hate it here. The staff yells at you, curses you and are very rude. This has not changed with time. I hate it still."* Interactions with staff are a reminder, too, of their loss of freedom and identity. According to one lifer, *"they* [staff] *strip us of who we are constantly,"* while others point out that most staff *"treats us like animals,"* and *"treat all inmates like bad children."*

In addition to anxieties about the unknown and unexpected, women experienced physical discomforts of being in prison, including poor appetite, inability to sleep, and digestive problems. One lifer in her mid-thirties spoke specifically about adjusting to the noise, while two of the women lifers—one age twenty-three and the other fifty-two—provide a picture of these early experiences as well as how they responded over time:

> Initially, after the horror of diagnostic when I didn't have a bowel movement for 9 days, I adjusted surprisingly easy. . . . However, now that the initial adjustment is over, the rest of my life stretches out with appalling length. [age fifty-two at sentence]

> At first I used to cry all [of] the time. I didn't want to eat. All I would do was talk on the phone and shower. I hardly ever got that much sleep until I had gotten on medication. But I got back into my word (the Bible) and God gave me the strength to go forward. So I slowly came off my meds, didn't cry that much and I eat more now. Now my time isn't that hard for me [like] it was. And it was hard at first because I made it hard. [age twenty-three at sentence]

Dealing with the loss of freedom, lack of privacy, interactions with staff and other inmates, the physical discomforts, and general "craziness" of the unfamiliar prison, especially for those with prior mental health problems and abuse histories, exacerbated mental health problems for some women. Speaking about other women lifers' adjustments, the twenty-three-year-old lifer quoted above continued by saying:

> Well a lot of them act out, cut themselves, and things like that. But I don't try to harm myself or act out. I tried to kill myself way before I had come to prison. They make their time hard and the officers are always getting on to them. As for me, I just do what I'm supposed to do and ask God to lead me daily.

Her quote once again reflects the reliance on God to lead them in their adjustment to life in prison.

CASE HISTORY 4.2: DISPLAYED ON A BIG BILLBOARD

Now in her forties, Pam talks honestly about her initial days in court and through her sentencing. *"I was running through life so fast that I didn't know how to live it. From my pains and hurts, I numbed it with the use of crack cocaine. I was rescued through my sentence."* Despite her rescue she says, *"but yes, I was charged and sentenced under the party to the crime law. I was charged with murder and robbery, malice murder and felony murder . . . only one of the above I was guilty."* At the time of her trial she was *"heavily medicated"* and *"couldn't assist my attorney in no way at all."* Working against her also were the politics and policies of the time. *"The district attorney on my case had on display a big billboard during my trial."* Today she says, *"Time was not wasted. I'm not who I used to be. I've learned its not just about 'me'. When I got sentenced they [her family] did too. I ask them to forgive me for anything I caused them to hurt."*

What we did not hear from women regarding their early adjustment was reference to their families and children. Although these loved ones filled their initial reactions to their sentence, most were so focused on survival inside of prison that their families outside were likely intentionally left out of these experiences, which for some were traumatic. As a total institution, this pattern is consistent with how being in prison "cuts" one off from everything else outside the prison walls.[11] However, because over 90 percent of the women were often or always worried about being separated from their families, this was not an aspect of prison where they were able adjust, and likely why they did not mention family matters in reference to how they did adjust.

Since very few of the women had prior incarceration experiences, there were very little differences in their early adjustment based on prior prison history. However, these experiences depended tremendously on age at incarceration. Juvenile lifers (< eighteen years at time of sentence) and some of the younger women (< thirty years) held an *"I don't care attitude,"* and told us so. Of their initial reactions to prison, one woman incarcerated at age seventeen said, *"Fuck the world."* As a result, some of the older women viewed younger lifers as rebellious: *"They aren't trying to better themselves because they're young and have an 'I don't care' attitude"* and *"I see the younger ones rebelling. They have to grow and adjust as I did."* Women who were relatively younger at their sentence indicated that they were rebellious, disruptive, and received disciplinary reports (D.R.) for fighting and not following prison rules. A woman who had served eighteen years of her sentenced noticed how *"for people in my age group at the time of incarceration,* [they were] *very similar in the anger and acting out."*

Initially, these young lifers reported an "easy adjustment" to the prison culture and "the mix."[12] A woman who was incarcerated at age fifteen and had served fourteen years of her sentence shared this:

> Adjusting became easy on a more "I don't have anything to care about" attitude but overtime I grew to change my thinking and wanted to make the best of this experience and not conform to the environment and its negativity.

Real and meaningful adjustment to serving their sentence came with time, growing up, maturity, becoming wiser to prison life and life in general, finding out what really matters to them, and drawing on faith in God—which some did not mention initially. A woman sentenced at age twenty-two and having served nine years said:

> I was wild, fighting, getting into trouble all of the time. I was in denial. My adjustment has changed for the better. First I know who I am in Christ. I've matured now and I know that my God has the first and last say so.

Even the woman who told us she felt like *"Fuck the world"* stated of her adjustment over thirteen years: *"I was rebellious til I realized this time will make you or break you and I just come to the realization that it is only what you make of it."* Making the most of it meant getting involved in programs, following the rules, and looking toward parole. As this woman shared: *"At first I was very disruptive. I got in trouble a lot. Now, I am 11 years D.R. free. I live in the Honor Unit. I work in the library."*

There were exceptions to this pattern. For example, a few women sentenced in their early to mid-twenties reported being "loners" and basically staying to themselves. They described not fitting in with other women lifers who were their age. In another example, a Hispanic woman, incarcerated at age twenty-one said: *"I care about going home. I feel I don't belong here so I try to follow most of the rules and stay out of trouble. Others tend to not care about anything. I want to go home."* She felt she was not represented well by her attorney, agreed to a guilty plea, and felt tricked. She had also experienced eight years in an abusive marriage. Unlike some of the younger women lifers who did not have children, she was a single mother, and her children consumed her thoughts and her hopes for getting out of prison.

Although over 60 percent of the women lifers reported receiving a D.R. at some point in their time behind bars, women who were older at their sentence (> thirty years of age) recounted a very different perspective on their adjustment compared to younger women. One of the older lifers could understand their feelings, though. She replied: *"I'm guilty—many of the others are not. I can't very well be angry. Also I was 52 when sentenced so I've had more of a good life than the younger ones will ever have."*

While most of their initial thoughts and feelings at receiving their life sentence were similar to younger women, older women reported a "hard" time early on adjusting to prison life. They were scared and uncomfortable with both the environment and other women. Older women also indicated that they were "not trouble makers," and followed the rules. They did not feel that they "fit in" with other women in prison, especially the younger women lifers and short-timers. For example, an older woman stated: *"I would say that for the most part they seem to be having a good old time while I can't seem to fit in."* Once again referring to "the mix," a couple of the older women lifers acknowledged:

> It was hard. But I didn't cause any problems, and I still don't. I learned to pray, got a close relationship with God, I mind my business. Don't get caught up in Drama. [age forty-eight at sentence with ten years behind her]

> I do my best to only be there physically and not get involved in prison politics. Most people tell me they're surprised I have a life sentence because I don't act like other lifers.

While younger women lifers referred generally to "trouble," and more specifically to not following the rules and fighting, none discussed drugs, lesbian relationships, or prison politics—common topics in media depictions of women in prison. Only among statements by older women lifers do we find these themes. Given their ages, life experiences, and preference for "staying out of trouble," their early adjustment experiences focused on their fears of those who did in engage in these forms of prison adjustment/culture. Two women spoke specifically about homosexuality and "bulldaggers":[13]

I was disgusted with the horrible homosexuality and ugliness about 60% of the predominately younger women were engaged in and still are. [fifty-five years old, incarcerated at age forty-seven]

My worst fear in prison is who they will put in my room. I dislike having to be around difficult, bullying, brutish people or bulldaggers—I don't judge their lifestyle, I just don't want to live with it. [fifty-seven years old, incarcerated at age forty-seven]

Another older woman lifer (forty-eight years old) said: *"I was fearful and didn't fit into those who used drugs, etc. I was called 'square.' In time I've been accepted and respected as a leader and a confidante."* She would not/ could not even say the word homosexuality/lesbian.

Older women lifers could understand the anger some of the younger women felt and tried to be a mentor and encourage them in their adjustment process. According to the woman quoted above, eventually, older women are accepted and become someone whom others look to with respect. They try to mentor younger women and encourage them. As these older women lifers described: *"You talk to younger inmates to encourage them that aren't as strong; pray for them"* and *"I feel as though I can connect with some of them. I mostly try to encourage them."*

Like all lifers, though, older women also were frustrated by women serving "life on the installment plan" (i.e., short-timers who get out of prison only to come back). Lifers who hold onto hope for release or who feel they may never get out of prison look upon these women with confusion. Of these women, one lifer said: *"Most of the people coming into the prison thinks it is a joke. There's some that keeps coming back 6 and 7 times."* Another added: *"We can do a lot for someone that doesn't have life sentence. We wish we had a short period of time and never come back."*

ADJUSTING WITH TIME

For most of the women lifers, prison was a sharp learning curve. With time, they learned what to expect from the prison structure, staff, and other women, and they adjusted in ways beyond their initial reactions to their sentence and their early experiences. According to their responses to twenty-one adjustment items (shown in table 4.1), the women were able to adjust to life inside prison, but were still bothered most by the ways they are "cut off" from society. In terms of outside deprivation factors, they were most concerned with being separated from family members (92 percent often/always bothered) and not knowing where they stand with parole (78 percent often/always bothered). They also were often/always bothered by their loss of freedom (77 percent) and missing their friends and social life (71 percent). About half of the sample was bothered by not having privacy and quiet, along with staff not listening to grievances. Only about 23 percent of the women lifers worry about feeling physically safe in prison, or becoming institutionalized. The vast majority have goals or ambitions, and do not worry about their relationships with the staff or getting along with other inmates, their job assignments, or prison policies/rules—all deprivations within the "total institution." Regarding "the rules," these women, who had all served seventeen to eighteen years, described their adjustment over time:

> I now have accepted the rules and obey them as much as possible and am more understanding and accepting of staff reactions. [age thirty at sentence, served eighteen years]

> If you follow the rules and do as you are told it would make your time a lot better. . . . Keep your head up at all times and don't focus on your time. Do your time don't let the time do you. [age twenty-six at sentence, served eighteen years]

> I didn't like being in prison but I'm not a troublemaker so I found some friends and they and I started doing Bible studies and that helped me a lot. I haven't changed much. I still try to do the right thing for them and me and also to follow the rules. [age forty-four at sentence, served seventeen years]

In addition to the rules, women adjusted to the environment—lack of privacy, noise, feeling safe. Although some preferred to be loners, most learned to live with and draw support from other women in similar positions and with similar experiences. Equally or more important, women adjusted in the way they interacted with and viewed prison staff. However, the largest determinant of adjustment for women lifers was time, or in their words, taking *"one day at a time."*

What Adjustment Means to Women Lifers

We identified three categories of women lifers' adjustment over time: (1) those relatively new to prison ("newbies") who still had not adjusted along with those with years behind them who said they would never adjust; (2) those who "just adjusted" or adapted to prison; and (3) those who described how prison changed them for the better. For the third group, they were the best adjusted to life in prison, had served the most time of their sentence; they had not only accepted their lives in prison, but also their lives in general and their selves. They maintained positive outlooks, stayed optimistic, and worked to improve themselves through programs and education.

Roughly 5 to 10 percent of the women explicitly stated that they had not adjusted to prison or their life sentence; some indicated that they never will. One of the relatively new women told us: *"I'm still not so adjusted to prison.*

Table 4.1 Indicators of Prison Adjustment (% bothered)

	Never/Rarely	Sometimes	Often/Always
Being Separated from Family	2.4	4.8	92.8
Standing with Parole	9.0	12.8	78.2
Loss of Freedom	4.3	18.3	77.4
Missing Friends and Outside Social Life	13.9	14.8	71.3
Worried of Getting Sick in Prison	13.8	19.0	67.1
Feeling Out of Touch with World	13.0	26.6	60.4
Privacy and Quiet	14.8	27.6	57.6
Family Members Who Have Forgotten You	16.6	26.8	56.5
Staff Not Listening to Grievances	24.5	22.6	52.8
Being Bored/Idle Time	37.1	24.8	38.1
Feeling Comfortable in Prison Quarters	31.0	34.3	34.8
Afraid of Going Crazy	50.0	20.2	29.8
Getting Annoyed or Irritated	26.3	46.9	26.8
No Goals or Ambitions	52.7	21.5	25.8
Physical Safety	52.4	24.0	23.6
Institutionalization	61.6	17.5	20.9
Relationship with Prison Staff	50.2	38.4	11.4
Not Fitting in with Other Inmates	73.5	15.2	11.3
Relationship with Other Inmates	53.3	37.7	9.0
Job Assignments	83.7	12.0	4.3
Prison Policies/Rules	78.8	17.8	3.4

These past 2 years have been hard not just on me but my kids as well as [my] *family."* A woman with years also had still not adjusted and thought she never would:

> I still have not adjusted. I probably never totally will. I can't get used to this lifestyle. I'm very, very uncomfortable. The adjustment has not changed with time as of yet, even after almost 7 years of incarceration.

Another woman, who had served twelve years, was clear in this: *"I will never adjust to this lifestyle. I will be obedient to do what the people tell me to do. But I will never be comfortable with this situation."* As heard here, women were not comfortable, or would not allow themselves to be comfortable with *"this kind of life"* and, therefore, they recognized how they could not adjust *"to prison fully."* Thus, along with worries about their families, those who had the most difficulty adjusting either had not had enough time to reach the turning point of adjustment or they never would. Many still had anger toward others or self-blame. In some ways their self-blame was a form of punishment they continued to place on themselves.

For all of these women and many others, prison was described as "hard," and they did not want to adjust to life in prison because they desired more to be out of prison with their families, receive a new trial, or be granted an appeal. We heard this from a woman with only two years served. She said: *"It's hard. I'm not trying to adjust for the sake my new trial is coming very soon."* Another said that she was not adjusting because, *"I'm not going to be here long. I still believe I'm leaving soon."*

Another 5 to 10 percent of the women had *"just adjusted"* or *"adapted."* They held a common view of prison and their lives that *"it is what it is"* and *"it is crap."* In their own words, they had not *"really adjusted,"* but they did what they had to in order to make it easier on themselves. Even though she thought she had not really adjusted, one woman said: *"It's just something I've got to deal with. Therefore I just do it."* Another woman described her adjustment in terms of adapting. She said: *"I really didn't adjust. As with my childhood I adapted and became a product of my environment."* While some women learned to cope by going through the motions, others dealt with the same losses of freedom, family, and love by pretending *"this isn't real."* They turned the sense of disbelief they felt when they first received their sentence into a reality for themselves. Others indicated that they adjusted pretty well to anything: *"I've adjusted pretty quick, but it's a place I don't want to feel adjusted to"* [served less than one year at time of initial survey]. In other words, adjusting is something she does not want to feel, but she just does it because the alternative would be worse for her. For those women, they described themselves as *"hard"* and *"complacent."*

The last and larger adjustment group represented those who said prison changed them (or they had changed themselves for the better). According to a couple of the women:

> Prison has changed me for the better. I have more responsibility, more dedication, more determination along with being a mentor with positive things to say to help people and increase their inability to grow. I also had an opportunity to increase my vocational education.

> I adjust one day at a time. It changed me for the better by getting into things like church and daily Bible study.

It is among this group of women lifers where it is clear how women, as they say, *"do your time"* and *"don't let the time do you."* In no particular order, these women lifers described their positive attitudes, and the way they accepted who and where they are in life; their reliance on friendships and getting involved/staying busy with programs, work detail, and pursuing their education; and their faith as a way to cope with their life sentence.

Doing Time

As a woman quoted earlier concluded—*"nothing really changes but your attitude."* The way they view the world is the only thing women lifers can control. After that, their goals and ambitions focus on *"something better"* whether *"in here or out there."* To do so, most women adjust or "do time" by getting involved with prison programs and activities. A woman who felt like she was in the Twilight Zone when she first arrived at prison said: *"I try not to spend more than 5 min. a day without occupying my mind with something."* Women also stay busy, positive, and make their time easier with their "detail" or work assignments as well as educational, vocational, and faith-based programs. Many simply focus on "staying busy." After eighteen years in prison, a woman who said her initial reaction to her sentence was "depression," described specifically how she adjusted through staying busy with programs. She said:

> When I first came . . . in 1995 I asked to enter . . . a 9-month program on recovery, life skills. I got my G.E.D. in 1996 and have worked in the greenhouse for 15 years. Got a trade in Horticulture, greenhouse management, commercial green housing, landscaping, business technology. . . . I am 6 weeks from graduating a[n] 18-month program in Faith and Character Base Programming. I have taken every mandated group they have to offer. . . . I have stayed busy, staff and inmates respect me. Everything is the same with time. Time moves on and I continue to do the same.

When we asked the women about how they passed their time, the largest percentage mentioned engaging in solitary activities such as reading (86 percent), listening to music (77 percent), and writing letters (72 percent). About 60 percent also said they do their time by "just being alone." Work details are often solitary activities as well, and for 62 percent of the women they engage in work assignments to pass the time. "Leisure" activities and hobbies help fill the time with 46 percent in engaging in card/other games, 55 percent in watching TV, and 31 percent in arts/crafts. While these may be solitary activities and hobbies, many enjoy spending time in conversation with others and over 85 percent indicated that they have "fellow inmates who enjoy similar social activities as I do" and "fellow inmates share my interests and concerns."

Among women lifers who have "changed for the better," participation in programs and "staying busy" was a key factor in their adjustment. Despite this pattern, only about one-quarter to one-third of women lifers (are eligible to) participate in educational (34 percent) and vocational programs (23 percent). Even fewer are in therapy programs (13 percent) such as anger management, drug and alcohol recovery, and dealing with domestic/family violence. Although women lifer's pathways to prison indicate that they could benefit from these programs, these are reserved for women with shorter sentences— *"We are regarded as the waiters. No matter what is offered lifers can wait. Hey we got time, right?"* This restriction is one of the main ways women lifers see themselves as treated differently than other women in prison.

Inasmuch as women lifers want to be treated like other women in prison— access to education and vocational programs—they also desire to be treated different because of their sentence. In particular, there are *"not enough groups designed especially for the lifers,"* including *"programs for the ones just starting their life sentences (access to those who have 'been there, done that')."* Other women lifers told us:

> There is NO lifer's support group. They [staff] tell them [lifers] that they are never going home, and negative stuff like that. No type of special groups to help them deal and cope with life in here, or anything that will prepare them for their release.

At the state level, a program is available for lifers and long-term offenders. STAND, "Sisters Taking Action for a New Destiny," is designed as a residential program for women lifers and those serving long sentences. Like most all other programs available, this group has restrictions. Women apply for the program and are selected for participation (i.e., a reward). Women are eligible after ten years served of life sentence, which provides no help for dealing with initial adjustment and is too far removed from their unknown, actual release date. For most women lifers, ten years is closer to the midpoint of life sentence than their reentry. After graduating from the statewide program, some women lifers form informal support groups where they mentor others. For women lifers who had participated in a lifer's support group they described the program as *"excellent"* and are grateful for the experience.

Considering that only one program exists for lifers and long-term inmates at the state level (since 2016), not all women lifers have the support they need to adjust initially, throughout their many years behind bars, or as they near parole. In addition, these groups within the prison depend on willing and interested staff and volunteers. For example: *"Our warden here, Ms. K, which I am in her lifers group she treats us with all due respect. I am very thankful to have her on our team."* When these individuals, like the warden, are no longer employed at the prison, the programs are often interrupted, dismantled, or viewed as less successful.

As described in more detail in chapter 8, because of restricted access to these programs, women lifers instead tend to rely much more on their participation in spiritual or religious programs as they adjust to their life sentence. Numerous voices demonstrate the power of religious beliefs and faith for adjustment, but one woman sums up many of the ways women rely on their religious beliefs and activities to cope/adjust:

My belief and faith is vital in my life because there are days when everything begins to crash down on you in one day in this place. Sometimes, things are so stressful in here. I don't know which way to turn but except for God and His Word. People may misunderstand me or even don't want to have anything to do with me because of what I am in prison for, but God will never leave me or forsake me . . . He gives me peace that surpasses all understanding in midst of confusion and turmoil.

Home Away from Home

When women lifers use the word "home," they more often than not are referring to their family home. Within this context, many made specific references to getting out of prison and "going home" to be with/there for their families. One woman who admitted she had not adjusted to life in prison said: *"I'm just here until God sees me home."* She emphasized that prison is "just here" not her home. Instead, home is with family. Women held hope for returning home one day.

Prison is not comfortable like a home. Among women with family support and who had maintained contact with families and "homes," this was the most common meaning of "home." While women who may have experienced traumatic and chaotic family backgrounds had very different notions of about what it means to be at "home," most do not view prison as a "home away from home." Representing many of their voices, one woman said: *"This place, prison, is never home . . . Every day is about survival, existing and staying sane."* Another woman added:

> I do my time and stay in my own world because it is a safe place and follow rules to the utmost as they come . . . I'd just like to go home. I'm not trying to earn brownie points. I just want to work frequently so I do not think of the hurt from being "locked up" and I make my time very useful.

After twenty-eight years behind bars (recently released), this seventy-year-old woman lifer said:

> All programs have had a positive influence, causing me to grow and had been a helping hand. However, in this environment and atmosphere nothing has brought me to the point of entertaining this place as a home away from home.

Nevertheless, in order to do their time, "just adjust," or be "just here" "in this place," women lifers—especially among those who had served lengthy amounts of their sentence—engage in everyday routines and perform "home-like" functions which allow them to create a "home away from home." This includes making coffee each morning; cooking for themselves and others; washing or ironing their clothes; going to work or school; doing crafts and art projects to "decorate" the institution and help others; and enjoying a glimpse of the surrounding landscape. About the positive routines that helped her create a home in prison, one woman said: *"I collect recipes and do homework. I clean the dorm every morning before school."* Another made a similar comment: *"I clean and wash clothes and check on my neighbors. I stay very busy."* A noticeable number of women cited cleaning the dorm each day as an important routine. Although keeping a clean dorm or presentable attire is central to following prison rules, avoiding discipline reports, and staying busy, women also took pride in these routines and roles as accomplishments. One woman described being *"blessed by God with the gift of cleaning."* Another spoke of her work assignment in the prison: *"My detail—I work up front and maintain the front lawn . . . and have found one of my true talents is landscaping/gardening. I find real pleasure in this and peace."* Others look to social aspects of prison to feel at home, and friendships, as described by this woman:

> I wouldn't call it home away from home. But I feel that my friendships here have helped my people skills and be able to deal with different situations that have come my way. I was showed how to do what's expected of me and the programs have helped me grow.

Prison Friendships

Finding support and developing a few friendships among other trusted women lifers is often a key to adjustment. This woman put it this way:

> Your [*sic*] in a different world with thousands of people but your [*sic*] still alone. Sometimes you need someone that can deal with all the hurt, anger, happiness and laughter. You find that person with someone that has a life sentence as your self—they feel the same way.

As a part of their prison adjustment, woman emphasized support from other women "like them." Between 60 and 70 percent of the women responded affirmative that they could: "depend on fellow inmates," "confide in fellow inmates," and "call on friends in here when I need them." They had other women they could "talk to about my day-to-day problems" and that their "relationships with fellow inmates provide a sense of well-being." The vast majority were satisfied with their friendships (76 percent) and indicated that their friendships in prison were very important to them (86 percent).

A Few Good Friends . . . More Like Associates

In written survey responses and face-to-face discussions, women lifers were often careful about describing their relationships with other women in prison as "associates" instead of "friendships."[14] They made clear distinctions between these terms to the point where some marked through the word "friendships" on the paper surveys and wrote "associates." In addition, some marked through the word "some" describing their friendships and indicated they have "a few" or "one" good friend in prison. A few elaborated on these responses—*"I have met a lot of people over the past 27 years, I have one friend that I have been friend with for over 20 years and she's very positive."*

As the women talked about their friendships, they repeatedly referred to the "good" people in prison. Of their adjustment and prison supports, these women said:

> I had never been in trouble before and this environment was scary. I have discovered that there really are good people in prison and you can make the decisions [of] what type of people to hang with.

> I was happy to be around people sentenced to time like me. . . the ones doing good are an example to me that I can make it.

Use of the term "good" by these women implied that friendships in prison can also be dangerous, devastating, and you must be selective in carefully choosing whom to trust with your friendship *"because trust is hard in here."*

Again, using the term "good" to refer to prison friendships this woman said: *"There are good and bad people everywhere. It's important to use discernment in friendships. My circle is very small. I know who my friends are."* Women lifers learn through experience and by observing other women what it takes to make "good" friends among the other women in prison. Negative relationships in their early adjustment periods helped some develop alternative strategies for successful, positive prison friendships and supports. Speaking of their early experiences, these women shared the following:

> I was involved with people I shouldn't have been. I pick my friends very closely. It try to have positive Christian friends.

> I was very nice and kind, people liked me and preyed on me because I was young and financially settled. I learned a lot quick. Over time I learned from my mistakes and that it's best to have few friends and not fit in with everyone. I've done a lot with my education and religious services. I do my best to stay out of trouble and remain positive and encourage others to do the same.

> Well during my incarceration being around people that believe in me and didn't use my past against me. Overall I have had positive people around including staff.

Friendships often develop in assigned dorms, education programs, and religious groups. Defined by so much time behind bars, women serving a life sentence are constantly reminded of the fact that they are always there while others leave to go home or are transferred to the other women's facility in the state. This makes developing and maintaining friendships with other women in prison difficult and disappointing, but it is also the rationale for why women lifers seek and offer support among one another.

Prison friendships are not only invaluable, but inevitable for some—*"Well I have friends* [in prison] *that I've known 18 years and consider family."* However, early on in their sentence, finding each other and being such a small proportion of the prison population presents obstacles for developing these supports, especially if the prison does not offer a support group specifically for lifers, or women are not housed together. Dorm and cell assignments are not based on a woman's sentence. While many of the women lifers thought it would be helpful for them to have a "lifer's dorm," women lifers are housed throughout the institution. This changes over time for some as they age and move to a unit for "special needs" or earn a space in the "honor" unit. Making friends is also difficult for women who spent years in abuse and isolation.

> I have met some incredible women here—I'm talking inmates—women that I will forever be proud to call friend. If I had allowed myself to have the support

network out there that I have in here, I would not be in here. I have friends—this is such a small sentence, but for someone like me it should be in Bold, Big letters.

Other women lifers do not develop friendships for support because they do not want to—*"I don't have close friendships in here but I get along well with the others. I am somewhat a loner."* Or because they have work details that are isolated from other inmates/women lifers, or solitary, such as cleaning, landscaping, or office work. They may be surrounded by staff or other inmates with whom they have no connections. Some women request these types of work details which fit their personality and approach to doing time. For example, one woman who performs all of the prison landscaping said:

Some lifers keep girlfriends or work/use other women, I don't. I have never been in a relationship. I do positive time, keep my mind busy, and I work 7 days a week. Some look at it like they don't have anything to lose, I look at it like I have everything to gain . . . Parole.

Closer Than Family.

Of her prison friendships, one woman said: *"I've met great people in here."* She added: "but they aren't family." Early studies of women's adjustment to prison pointed to the way women developed "pseudo-families" or "make-believe families" to address the pains of family separation as well as for support within the prison environment.[15] Although there is evidence that these patterns are changing in contemporary women's prisons, for most of the women lifers we surveyed, the supports they developed over time with women in prison were more like family to them, or as several women agreed: *"serve as family."* When women are disconnected physically and emotionally from family, or have no family for support, prison friendships are invaluable for adjustment and survival behind bars. In one woman's words: *"Sometimes friends are closer than family."* Others remarked: *"I have good friends in here who care for me more than any family"* and *"My friends in here is considered family. We motivate, encourage, and support each other."* Elaborating on the types of supports prison friendships provide, these women said:

I have found some real good friends in here who I really enjoy hanging around and being real close to. Since my family isn't here with me it makes me feel like people here are my family especially when I'm crying and depressed they comfort me and I feel better.

My friends are those here who check in on me. We've invested in each other's lives here. Keep up with families, their friends, how things are going. They share in successes and let downs here.

Some women lifers described specific family roles such as mother, grand-mother, and sisters they perform for/with other women. An older woman said: *"Now, I can cook for these women and I feel like they are my children. I can't cook for my children so these women are my next choice."* Others discussed "creating families" for survival and to help each other:

> You create a family to survive within these walls. To help each other, some become sisters, we help raise each other and help each other grow. I came in as a child and I'm middle aged now (45).

> I've created a "family" environment in here being a mother figure to the younger inmates coming into the system.

> I was young when I came into the system. I was scared and . . . met a few young ladies that helped me along my way. There was an older lady that became like a grandma to me as well.

Interactions with Prison Staff

With or without support from family and friends, women lifers must rely on others in prison as they "do their time." This includes interactions with prison staff. Just as women designate some other inmates as "good," there are "good" and "bad" officers. An us-versus-them attitude pervades when women lifer's experiences are shaped by the "bad" officers.[16] Despite this dichotomy, which is a very real and traumatic experience for some women, prison staff, and officers specifically, play a vital role in the prison experience. Over 60 percent of the women responded that they were satisfied with their relationships with prison staff. Women lifers who are satisfied with their relationships with prison staff seem to be better adjusted to life in prison. As evident in this woman's response: *"Prison staff here are firm, but fair and not prejudice because of a life sentence. The prison is not home but it's livable and tolerable and the staff has acceptable conduct that I can respect."* Of the prison officers and staff, the woman who said, *"prison changed me for the best,"* also said that she had *"been treated with compassion."* Others noted that staff *"treat us like humans"* and *"with respect."* In another account, a woman spoke of how she maintained good relationships with staff:

> I have a lot of favor from staff—mainly because I am a low maintenance inmate and do what I'm told. I also have had good, long-term details that I take pride in and work hard.

These views of prison staff and officers stand in stark contrast to women who are still adjusting or who have never/will never adjust to life in prison.

For these women, experiences with "bad" officers were shared in detail, with emotion, and directly correlated with their ability to adjust. For example, an older lifer described her experience with officers each day in the dining hall:

> We are SCREAMED AT in the dining hall and forced to eat our supper meals within 8 MINUTES by cruel staff who have been REPEATED instructed to give us our 15 minutes. We choke down our food while being screamed at.

In addition to overt displays of cruelty, women lifers felt ignored by officers, looked down upon, disrespected, and at other times treated with suspicion. They made comparisons between themselves and animals, specifically dogs, in the ways officers treat them. They also described how officers treat them *"like* [they] *don't matter," "like nobodies," "like* [they] *are the worst people in the world,"* and *"like* [they] *never going home"* because of their sentence.

> Like we are here for life. Some try you up mentally, emotionally, physically attempting to gain some power over you. They are unprofessional (staff) throwing your time, crime in your face; the major issue is the negativity from counselors.

The initial emotions which accompanied the receipt of their life sentence are revisited time and again as officers (and some inmates) work to convince them that they will die in prison. This is especially dangerous for women who have no hope for getting out, lack the opportunity to participate in betterment programs, and lack the support of other women and family. The combination of these missing ingredients and negative experiences with prison staff ensure that women lifers will not "adjust." Further, these interactions demonstrate the important role prison staff play in creating the prison climate in which women lifers must live behind bars.

SUMMARY

Whether women ever truly adjust to a life in prison is a question that depends on one's definition of adjustment. As one of the women lifers asked us in response: *"Do we ever really adjust?"* Some women just do their time. They avoid trouble with other inmates and staff and follow the rules as best they can, but may never, or never want to, "get used" to the prison environment. Women also become part of the institutional culture, or "the mix," and learn the prison game. More than one approach can be used to adjust, and this can vary by and within a person. A woman lifer may "do her own time" but also understand the importance of "the mix" for surviving prison, for women live out their lives in an environment of penal harm where policies and people intentionally make living in prison "hard" and increasing punitive. This main idea of penal harm is that prison should not be easy or comfortable, or a place where people would want to or be able to adjust—it is rather a place of constant fear and anxiety.

Physical, psychological, and emotional forms of survival also point to "adjustment." These vary over time and by situation. For example, the death of a loved one, denial of parole, changing rules or policies within the prison or state, and even "special occasions" such as holidays away from family (e.g., Mother's Day or Thanksgiving) may bring on bouts of depression which women must pull themselves and each other out of. Given time, women lifers grow, mature, and gain perspective, respect, and new goals and purposes for their lives. For these women, adjustment, not just to prison, but to life in general, means changing themselves for the better. In doing this, some women make a home in prison following daily routines and staying busy. They take advantage of every program and limited opportunity afforded to them. But "home" for most women lifers means getting out of prison and going to live with their families. Confined together, though, the world outside does not exist, it moves on, it can be blocked out as "not real," and they must draw on each other including staff for support and friendships, who at the moment may be closer than family. Some call this process institutionalization while others think of it as rehabilitation. Which of these represents what is meant by "adjustment" to life in prison? Is prison an opportunity where women are "better because of prison," or does prison bring on more trauma for the already vulnerable, yet strong survivors, who are kept behind its walls? What we hear from women lifers are experiences with all of these forms of adjustment, from the major life-changing forms of adjustment to the everyday steps they take to simply live a life behind bars until they can "go home."

NOTES

1. Wright, "A Study of Individual, Environmental, and Interactive Effects in Explaining Adjustment to Prison"; Zamble and Porporino, *Coping, Behavior, and Adaptation in Prison Inmates.*

2. Loper and Gildea, "Social Support and Anger Expression among Incarcerated Women."

3. Jiang and Fisher-Giorlando, "Inmate Misconduct: A Test of the Deprivation, Importation, and Situational Models."

4. Liu and Chui, "Social Support and Chinese Female Offenders' Prison Adjustment"; Van Tongeren and Klebe, "Reconceptualizing Prison Adjustment: A Multidimensional Approach Exploring Female Offenders' Adjustment to Prison Life."

5. Irwin and Cressey, "Thieves, Convicts and The Inmate Culture"; Kruttschnitt, Gartner, and Miller, "Doing Her Own Time? Women's Responses to Prison in the Context of the Old and the New Penology"; Sykes, *Society of Captives*.

6. Johnson and Dobrzanska, "Mature Coping among Life-Sentenced Inmates: An Exploratory Study of Adjustment Dynamics"; Mackenzie and Goodstein, "Long-Term Incarceration Impacts and Characteristics of Long-Term Offenders: An Empirical Analysis."

7. Owen, *In the Mix*.

8. Lempert, *Women Doing Life*.

9. George, *A Woman Doing Life*.

10. Dye, Aday, Farney, and Raley, "The Rock I Cling To."

11. Goffman, *Asylums*; Sykes, *Society of Captives*.

12. Owens, *In the Mix*.

13. According to Erin George in *A Woman Doing Life*, a bulldagger is "an inmate who constantly bends or breaks the rules to see her girlfriend," 237.

14. Greer, "The Changing Nature of Interpersonal Relationships in a Women's Prison."

15. Owen, *In the Mix*.

16. Lempert, *Women Doing Life*. See also Girschick, *No Safe Haven*.

Chapter 5

Family Matters

"I often write my family letters, send cards, etc. to let them know my accomplishments."

"I have been forgotten and I'm not loved by my family anymore."

"My family is so busy and sometimes they just get caught up in their own lives."

"I send letters and get no response. I send love in letters but don't know if they are read."

Family ties have important consequences on the lives of women serving time walled off from the rest of society. Viewed as the cornerstone of their world, the family is the social context where identity is affirmed and whereby women in prison practice important traditions and rituals that give special meaning to their lives.[1] Each woman in prison has a unique family history where members have toiled together, making memories both good and bad along the way. The painful process of incarceration disrupts the ability to function as a family, often leading to a full-blown crisis.[2] Typical prison families today often have lived lives marred by bouts with alcohol and drugs, violence, crime, mental illness, and exposure to other traumatic events such as divorce and poverty. Lacking important economic resources, prison families struggle in maintaining ties with those who are locked away for decades. However, remaining connected enables individuals an opportunity to participate in family functions as well as staying involved in routine decision-making.[3] When families make special efforts to remain connected, this helps reassure those convicted that they are not forgotten and are still valued as people.

Women serving life sentences, like other incarcerated women, cite family as one of their biggest worries. Being separated from and worrying about family make up one part of women's adjustment to prison—a part to which they never fully adjust. While most women lifers do eventually adjust to factors inside of prison, they have the most difficulty adjusting to living apart from their families, both physically and emotionally. As one woman told us: *"I usually focus on life in here. Worrying of keeping up with the outside would only depress me and makes life in here more difficult."* However, some women rely on family for support and continue to assist their families in any way they can from inside prison. This sixty-year-old woman summed up the importance of family with this statement: *"Some people don't have no one. At least, I can truly count on my family, had it not been for them, I could not have made it this far—11 ½ years."* Having family support gives women hope for day-to-day life inside of prison, allows them to maintain a role in their family's lives, and hope for one day getting out and being reunited with family.

For women who do want to maintain contact with family, many felt that *"prison discourages family support by giving family a hard time through any type of correspondence."* While visits, phone calls, and letters are a way for women to participant as a family member, the quality of family relationships, their worries about their family members, and their role in their family also affect how women maintain their bonds with their families.[4] This chapter focuses on the ways women serving life in prison maintain contact with family, the barriers they face in maintaining contact, the way they are able to participate as a family member, and their worries about their family and relationships with their families.

CASE HISTORY 5.1: THE HARDEST THING IS WATCHING MY CHILDREN GROW UP IN PICTURES

Catherine is serving twenty years to life for being a party to murder. She is fifty years of age and has been incarcerated since 2001. Married for ten years, Catherine was a stay-at-home mom until just recently before her incarceration. Even though prison has taken Catherine away from her children, she still occupies her role as a mother to her children and as a daughter to her mother. As she states, *"Those roles have never changed as I was very close to my children and mother."* Incarceration has also taken her away from family rituals such as the usual Sunday night dinners at her mom's house referred to as *"family night at Nanna's."* She misses the family vacations to Chattanooga, Tennessee, or Cherokee, North Carolina, or just going camping on the lake with her family. Most of all, she misses not getting the chance to watch her children play football or basketball or to dress up and going to church with her kids. The hard part is having to watch her children grow up in pictures. Catherine is allowed to have a total of twenty pictures and any over that amount is confiscated. As the years go by, she misses the opportunity to be an even better mom to her kids—*"There were so many places I wanted to take my kids."*

SOURCES OF FAMILY SUPPORT:
"SOME PEOPLE DON'T HAVE NO ONE."

Only 3 of the 214 women serving life sentences listed no immediate family members. Either parents had already passed or they never had a relationship with their parents. Slightly less than 30 percent of the women do not have children. One of these women explained her situation:

> I have an aunt but mostly friends are my family and they keep in contact. I encourage them to share their problems with me and I give advice when asked. I'm pretty well informed about their lives, jobs, and concerns.

Thus, the vast majority of women serving life sentences have a variety of immediate family members (parents, siblings, children, and grandchildren) who, at least, provide a pool from which support may be possible (see table 5.1). Most women report having living parents (70 percent), siblings (87 percent), and children (70 percent). A little over one-third of the sample (35 percent) report having grandchildren. About 8 percent of the women do not have living parents or children, and nearly one-quarter (22 percent) have out-lived parents, but have children and/or grandchildren. Also, about 22 percent of the women have children, but have never been married.

The most common sources of support women lifers receive from family members come from parents and children.[5] For those women with living parents, they receive visits, phone calls, and emotional and financial support to a point. Once parents reach a certain age and/or when their health problems worsen, they can provide less support. After serving eight years, a thirty-three-year-old woman explained: *"My mom who is 70 years old cannot visit as much as she would like because of health problems, mobility problems, financial constraints and transportation. I see her maybe once a year even though she lives not even 15 minutes away by car."*

A similar pattern is evident for support from children. Women attempt to provide support to their young children, and many receive support from grown children, but this is also to a point. Adult children lead their own busy lives, and as is the case for mothers outside prison, their children do not visit or talk as often as they once did.[6] Support lessens with time. A forty-four-year-old divorced mother stated: *"I don't see them much. I have been in now 20 years. My children were babies ([ages] 10 and 2) when I left. They are grown with children."* Similarly, a mother who had served fifteen years said, *"Now that my children are older I talk with them whenever I am able to catch them on the phone."* Another woman, thirty-one years old and never married, added a similar experience: *"Well, my family is so busy and sometimes they*

Table 5.1 Family Support Profile for Women Lifers (n=214)

Marital Status (%)	
Married	9.4
Widowed	18.4
Divorced	24.5
Separated	9.4
Never Married	43.9
Cohabitating	1.9
Living Family Members (%)	
Parents	69.3
Brothers/Sisters	86.9
Children	70.6
Grandchildren	34.9
Receive Family Visits (%)	
Never	23.6
Occasionally (1–2 times a year)	42.8
Fairly often (monthly)	26.4
Very often (weekly)	7.2
Receive letters from family (%)	
Never	7.6
Occasionally (1–2 times a year)	31.4
Fairly often (monthly)	38.6
Very often (weekly)	22.4
How often do you talk to family on the phone? (%)	
Never	23.0
Occasionally (1–2 times a year)	14.8
Fairly often (monthly)	28.7
Very often (weekly)	33.5
Encourage visits? (% yes)	86.4
Receive regular financial support from family? (% yes)	65.1
How satisfied are you with your family relationships? (%)	
Very satisfied	32.5
Fairly satisfied	36.3
Not very satisfied	31.1

just get caught up in their own lives. But when I first got locked up they used to write all the time and come to see me."

Although women are more likely to have siblings than either living parents or children, only a few described having relationships with siblings, and these were not sources of support for many of them. Sibling relationships were often the most fragile and inconsistent. A woman incarcerated at age seventeen said: *"I am an aunt and I have 2 sisters, one I haven't spoken to since I got locked up. I don't know how to show them love in here."* She explained:

> My sister is still mad so everything is my fault . . . I cry a lot 'cause I know nothing can be the same again. I just try to make things right but she is still mad. I beg her to come see me."

In a similar case, a woman explained how her sisters *"distance themselves from me as much as possible so they can deal with their own lives."* Another added *"[my] Brothers and sisters act like I don't exist."*

Several women also mentioned siblings' "busy lives." Referring to her brothers and sisters, a woman stated: "[They are] *constantly working, not enough time I guess and they have families of their own to see about."* Other women have older siblings with serious health issues which hinder their ability to offer support. For fourteen women, their siblings are their only living family members, and they never or only occasionally receive support from them. One woman, fifty-five years old, who had been incarcerated for over twenty years at the time, told us she had not had a visit from her siblings, or an aunt she still talks to, in over ten years.

When looking beyond immediate family, only about 10 percent of the women lifers indicated that they are currently in either a married or cohabiting relationship. Less than half (43 percent) have never been married. Over 25 percent of the women are divorced or separated, and an additional 18 percent are widowed. Only a few of the women mentioned support from a spouse/husband. Specifically, they worried about how they would never see or touch him again. For some wives, their husbands were also incarcerated or deceased:

> I and my husband didn't have no money for proper representation in court. Our family is so poor, so this cause us to be found guilty of crime we didn't even commit. . . . So this whole situation is taking a toll on our family members who are for us.

Her explanation also indicates that she receives support from some of her family but not others. As women shared their experiences with family and their life sentence, many found support from a few family members, but felt

ignored or forgotten by others. An overwhelming majority of the women encourage family to visit them in prison (86 percent), and despite the fact that
most women have living family members, visits and other forms of contact
are not a reality for a sizable portion of the women serving life sentences.

CONTACT: VISITS, LETTERS, AND TELEPHONE EXCHANGES

External support from visits, letters, emails, and phone calls has been shown
to reduce prisoner's worry, but can also be a source of worry.[7] One-fourth of
the women lifers received visits on a monthly basis, with another 7 percent
on a weekly basis. However, a significant number (43 percent) reported that
visits are infrequent (1–2 times a year), and for about one-fourth, visits were
nonexistent. More commonly, women maintained contact with family through
phone calls and letters. Some 60 percent of the women reported phone conversations very often (weekly) or fairly often (monthly) compared to 23 percent
who never talk to their family by phone. Letter writing is by far the most common form of contact with family. In fact, when asked how they participate in
their families lives, many indicated *"I write."* As one woman shared: *"The
only way I am able to participate in my family's lives is by mail, phone, never
any visits."* Nearly 60 percent of the women received letters from family
monthly or weekly, and another 30 percent received letters occasionally (1–2
times per year). Only 7 percent never received letters from family members.
Even though they may write to their families, they may not receive a letter in
return. This was a common experience for women serving life. Serving seventeen years, this thirty-three-year-old mother and daughter stated:

> I often write my family letters, send cards, etc. to let them know the accomplish-
> ments I have made in here and to keep the lines of communication open. It's
> often frustrating because I don't always get a response (unless I call if I'm able
> to.) That leads to feelings of abandonment that I try to deal with.

In recent years, families have stayed connected through electronic means
including email and Skype. Each dorm has a kiosk for video communications
with approved family members, and all incarcerated females in the state now
have small tablets they can use to send and receive email. About 42 percent
of the women lifers communicate with family via email very often. Currently,
it is more economical for women and their families to use email instead of
phone calls (thirty-four cents per email). In addition, email communication
provides quicker responses, and is less likely to be lost in prison mail or un-
delivered. Family can share pictures which further connect women to family
members' everyday experiences and their milestones. However, 28 percent

of the women never email with family. Some have lost all family members or relationships with family members, while others have aging family members or are aging themselves and unfamiliar with the technology.

BARRIERS TO MAINTAINING FAMILY CONNECTIONS: FACE-TO-FACE VISITS

Overall, maintaining ties with family members has been one of the most positive behaviors leading to improved prison adjustment as indicated by fewer disciplinary reports; however, the ability to remain in close communication with families on the outside can be a constant struggle.[8] While communication between women and their families provides the most concrete and visible strategy that families use to manage separation and maintain connections, numerous institutional and family obstacles frequently prevent optimum exchanges.[9] Some women cannot afford stamps, paper, or envelopes to send letters to family. Thus, they can only write to their families when they can afford stamps. Barriers to visits and phone calls are even more substantial for women and their families. For example, the women in our sample list, on average, around three specific barriers that they feel hinder family visitation. The primary barriers to visits are distance from prison and financial issues associated with taking off from work, and gas and lodging expenses. Another significant barrier related to travel involves family members' health. Aging parents with deteriorating health, and siblings and children with cancer or physical disabilities make transportation especially difficult.[10] When family has health problems, they may not be able to drive and must depend on others (including non-family members) to provide transportation for them. This sometimes adds additional financial hardships when they pay others to drive them—*"I live 7 hours from my home town. My mom is sickly and it ways* [sic] *on her to ride so far. My mom cannot drive so* [she] *pays other family members to bring her."*—and when family members must take off work to do so. When asked about her family's barriers to visits, this almost sixty-year-old widow listed the following:

> All of my sisters are older than me—oldest 70 years old with colon cancer, heart condition. Widows on fixed income. Oldest daughter mostly has to drive and she has had two heart attacks. Baby girl has cancer.

Given the rural locations of two of the women's prisons, even when family manages to travel to visit their loved ones in prison, they must stay overnight in the area. When her family does visit, they *"have to have a place to stay all night to come see me the next day."* Simply finding hotels is added barrier and cost. As this woman added:

My parents don't have the money. Both are sick. One lives in Orlando, FL, the other in Cumberland, KY. Don't have any transportation. Brothers and sisters act like I don't exist. No place to stay, don't have money for hotels.

As this woman indicates, many of the women do not have family members close enough to visit. In fact, the typical prison family lives, on average, 150 miles from the prison.[11] At least 10 percent of the women lifers in Georgia report their immediate families reside out of state, causing significant travel and financial hardships. For example, a recently incarcerated thirty-year-old described her family situation:

My family lives out of state so not only do they have to travel far, the hotels aren't reasonable and there aren't any forms of public transportation in the area. This means that they have to spend to rent a car but there aren't any rental agency's in the area. Luckily, my mom met a church lady here who provides her with transportation to see me.

A nineteen-year-old Hispanic woman who was incarcerated as a juvenile also explained: *"When my sister comes from California to visit me . . ., she tell[s] me how hard it is for her and it is a lot of money. She also talks about her health issues and why she can't come to see me like she would like to."*

For women whose families live in the state, the geographic location of prison and policies regarding prison assignment are another added barrier. This woman described the barriers her family faces with visiting as well as the policies that further reduce women's ability to stay connected with their families.

Living so far away in the same state. The rule is you can't live within a certain mile radius of your crime to be housed at either (3) women's prisons in the state of Georgia. If you live too close to the prison then you will not be housed there.

Whether deliberate or unintentional, these policies extend the punitive nature of the prison experience, and further disrupt family connections and supports—in both directions.

Other prison policies regarding the scheduling and timing of visits create additional institutional barriers for maintaining family connections. Work conflicts or scheduling visits within a specific time frame are noted as important barriers for families by about a fourth of the sample. These women explain how the scheduling of visits works (or doesn't) for them:

We have select days for visit. A-J on Sun[day], rest (K-Z) on Sat[day] with a 3 month rotation. If families were allowed to come every weekend when their time frames permitted it would be easier.

Each inmate is assigned one visiting day according to the 1st [letter of the] alphabet of last name. When my visiting day falls on Sundays, I rarely get visits because my family attends church faithfully. When visiting days rotate every 3 months and my day is on Saturdays—I have visits every weekend.

While weekends are possible for most of the women whose families do visit, it does not fit with schedules of those whose families have to work on weekends. In addition to the days, the hours which are set for visits can conflict with or produce constraints on the amount of time a woman has available to visit with her family.

The time we are allowed is not enough. The only problem my family and I have in maintaining our connection is that all of my family lives out of state, Texas, California, and Arizona. So the period of time we are allowed is not enough considering there are only two visitation days per week! I think if you have out of state visitors they should be allowed more days considering your [sic] only getting a few visits a year.

Travel distance, work schedule conflicts, and prison policies in combination were noted by this forty-five-year-old mother:

Coming to visit during limited hours conflicts with my son's work schedule. For my birth family members who must drive 8+ hours to visit it is a financial hardship and the actual visiting hours are so few with them processing in taking so much time often visitation does not actually begin until 10 am. Special visit arrangement is difficult to arrange since family can't call us for us to initiate visitation approval.

From these women's accounts, it is also clear how families experience the visitation process: they must arrive to the prison early in the morning, wait/ stand in line, be searched, and meet all prison policies before being granted access to the prison and a visit with their family member. This procedure is taxing on family members with health issues as well as small children.

My child lives with his grandparents which have health problems. They also live two and a half hours away. It's a long ride for older people. If your [sic] not here by ten-thirty then you can't get in until almost twelve-thirty. That's a waste of time that you could be spending with love ones.

Additional time is required for the women lifer to be called to the visiting area to see her family, and sometimes a miscommunication with prison staff results in women not being able to visit with their families. Women may be sent to the wrong area of the prison, or delayed in being called for her visit.

Although these women did not elaborate to any extent on how prisons may deny family visits due to disciplinary reports, this does occur.

The woman quoted above concludes her description by adding that, "*Vending machines are* [pricewise] *outrageous. There's nothing for kids to do.*" These passing comments also point to the visitation experience itself as a barrier families and women face when attempting to maintain connections. Mothers and grandmothers may not want their children to visit them if the experience will be negative for all involved, especially their children. Negative experiences lead to fewer visits and less support, and diminish women's ability to participate as a family member. This mother/grandmother shared her experience with a visit from her daughter and grandson:

> My daughter and grandson came for a visit. They drove 4 hours to get here. They were told to wait from 10 am to 12:30 pm before they could see me. My grandson, 4 years old, was rambunctious and my daughter and he were constantly harassed by a prison guard about his inability to sit still. They were told they would get in trouble. The guard was extremely rude to my daughter. My daughter has written me only one time since then.

As she described, the fear and shame associated with their interaction with staff led her daughter to not only never visit her again, but also to write her infrequently. As such, positive programs and interactions for mothers and grandmothers are at the top of these women lifer's "wish lists."

Staff also implement prison visitation policies in ways that the women and their families view as inconsistent, rude, and negative, which impact the visitation experience. One woman described the inconsistencies in this way. She said: "*Each weekend different staff work. The rules are always changing. Family members don't know what to expect from one weekend to next.*" Others added how rules regarding clothing and what family members can and cannot wear are applied inconsistently. For this woman her "*surviving son in military [was] turned away in uniform before deploying the same day . . . Did not know his uniform was banned.*" This woman felt that:

> When my family has come to see me the officers are very prejudice. When it comes to what they wear, but often times the officer will let other people come in with something they are wearing and send my family to change.

She added: "*Also the way the officers and staff treat my family like they are incarcerated as well.*" Several women felt this same way. As this woman described the financial barriers her family faced when trying to maintain connections through visits, she continued by saying:

With some of the security regulations it really don't make any sense. All that our family has to go through just to come in and see us, it is like their [*sic*] being processed in on visitation day and it makes them feel like they are locked up as well.

When family members or the women feel their family members are treated like inmates being locked up, this humiliation and negative experience can result in fewer visits, less support, and a further fracturing of families.

All women, regardless of the frequency of contact with their families, reported barriers to visits. The number of problems reported by those who never receive visits was about two, and those who receive weekly visits also reported about two barriers. Likely, those who never receive visits face barriers such as financial and distance issues that prevent visits, while those who receive weekly visits face institutional barriers. Women who faced the greatest number of barriers received visits only one to two times per year. These families face barriers that prevent visits more often as well as other institutional barriers when visits are made. This twenty-year-old woman, whose siblings visit occasionally, is a good example of these combined barriers: *"My family works on weekends and it's a good distance away. When they do come they are treated rudely and made to wait a long time in the sun (or cold) to visit."*

BARRIERS TO PHONE CONTACT:
"THE CALLS ARE HIGH AND THE MINUTES ARE FEW."

For women whose families cannot visit face-to-face, phone conversations may serve as the next best form of contact, and a way to maintain connections and stay involved in their family's lives. However, women confront just as many barriers to contact via phone as they do with in-person visits. Two of the most common problems with phone calls to family involve costs and privacy. Making a phone call from prison can cost family members between $20 and $40 for a single, fifteen-minute call, which could be higher during holidays. These are *"collect calls, not calling cards,"* which women argued would be more affordable for them and their families. For families who already have substantial financial problems, these added costs mean that either a family will have to forego a necessity (e.g., food or medicine) or not hear their loved one's voice.

I'm unable to make calls because the phone system, GTL, is too expensive for my family to maintain. The calls are $25 for 15 minutes and my family is already having a hard time trying to maintain their households and send me money. I'm left without visits or phone calls because nothing [here] is convenient or cheap. Everything is about money: the store, medical now charges packages, visits and phones are just too expensive for any family members to have to try to maintain for a life sentence.

The telephone system referred to as Global Tel Link, or GTL, which was contracted by the state, presented problems for women and their families. Another woman explained that to just make the call carries a relatively high charge and then each minute (up to fifteen minutes) is then charged. For an in-state call it is *"$2.35 for just to say hello and the call go through . . . 35 cents for each additional minute"* [about $8 for a fifteen-minute call, in-state]. While in-state calls range from $5 to $8 for fifteen minutes, which some women say is *"not too bad,"* costs become exorbitant when women's families live out of state. In this woman's experience:

> The cost for out of state calls is $25 for 15 minutes. Sometimes the phone disconnects in the middle of a conversation. It's very difficult to call cell phones and that's what everyone on the outside has. The phone company makes things difficult. We can only change our phone lists every six months.

Phones are often broken or cut off during conversations, work only sometimes, or have static in the line—all problems with the phone system mentioned by many of the women. Given the costs and the dropped calls, this woman explained: *"I could call right back, but then that would cause my parents to have to pay the initial fee for accepting the call, which costs more than the minutes. I feel it is set up this way on purpose."* She added: *"Some people I can't call because they don't want to switch phone companies."* In order to even make calls, family must be on an approved list of numbers, which is itself a lengthy process and often excludes cell phone numbers. In addition, families must change their phone service to GTL. This woman explained: *"You have to have your phone connected to a certain service. Being that I'm from Mississippi, my family has had numerous of problems obtaining the correct phone service for the prison. The prison system in Mississippi uses a different phone service than Georgia."*

After initial setup and a few calls, cost becomes too much for families to cover. Siblings and children may refuse to accept calls. Or women decide they cannot make calls to parents and other relatives when they know they really cannot afford it. In other cases, women lose connections with their family because their families cannot pay their phone bills and their phones are disconnected by the phone company. Many women shared a similar story: *"Most of my family is in NYC. My sister's phone got cut off because of my long-distance calls to her. She tried but could not afford to pay the bill."* Others added that, without notice, *"if $ reaches a certain amount the phone company will put a block on their phone."* To resume receiving calls, a family member would have to pay the costs of the calls, plus fees, or get a new phone/number. Either way, they must go through the setup and approval process again—all of which takes time. Family members may complain about the costs of the calls and the bills they receive, placing more worry and burden on both the women and their families, and ultimately straining their relationships even more. For some women, during the process, they lose touch with family members and do not know how to reach them by phone (and sometimes by mail).

Ironically, when women are able to make phone calls, they find that there is not enough time—*"The calls are high and the mins are few."* Phone calls are restricted to certain times of the day (e.g., evening) when women may not be able to reach their family members by phone. The fifteen-minute time limit on calls also prevents women from meaningful conversations with family members and their children, or sharing their true feelings. This woman described this feeling as *"a monumental struggle of trying to sound ok."* She went on to say how *"even if I wanted to the total inability to explain why this is so hard and I really want to not 'be' anymore. There's no way to tell someone who loves you that little nugget of truth."* If possible, women *"try to address family issues when in visitation because the phone calls are just not long enough."*

Regardless of the amount of time (or costs), women do not feel they can talk about their problems (with family or prison) out loud with other inmates and staff listening. Issues of privacy and a related problem of noise are additional barriers to making phone calls, and making meaningful connections through phone calls. Phone location and availability contribute to these problems. As these women explained:

There are numerous problems with the phone situations. First and foremost no privacy. All our calls are subject to recording. The cost per call is ludicrous. Furthermore, there's only one phone per range. This can become a problem when there's 30 inmates on one range.

Privacy—the phone is in an open area and so you are subject to have others listening to your side of the conversation. There is only one phone for 42 women and sometimes there is a long line to be able to use it.

As the first quote above indicates, phone conversations are recorded, but a more immediate concern for women is that staff and other inmates are close by and listening in on their conversations. Referring to the lack of privacy, this woman said: *"We have 4 phones beside each other with 7 tables close by. We (on the phone) make a move, switch from one foot to the other or even turn around, everybody looks at you."* The lack of privacy also inhibits women's meaningful conversations with family. Surrounded by the noise of the dorms and dayrooms where phones are located makes hearing difficult, and for some is not worth trying to have a phone conversation with their family members. When asked about the problems with phone calls, one woman said she does not like to talk to her family on the phone because she cannot hear them, and another shared this experience saying, *"You are lucky to hear your family."* According to the women lifers, when other inmates and staff are not listening to your conversations, they are constantly talking loud, nearby, or yelling orders, calling over the intercom, or calling people to appointments. Describing the noise, they explained how *"inmate and officers are right there in your face sometimes, you can be on the phone and the officer tells you to hang up for a phone call that the family has to pay for."*

SATISFACTION WITH FAMILY RELATIONSHIPS

While maintaining connections with family through contact was a source of comfort and worry for women, the degree to which women were satisfied with their family relationships was also an important component. When asked to report their level of family satisfaction, 32 percent said they were very satisfied compared to 36 percent who are fairly satisfied and 31 percent who are not at all satisfied. Satisfaction with family relationships varied significantly by the types and frequency of contact as well as the number of barriers with family visitation such that more contact and fewer barriers is associated with greater satisfaction. For example, 56 percent of those who never received visits from family were "not at all satisfied" with family relationships compared to 19 percent who were "very satisfied." Likewise, none of the women who received weekly visits indicated that they were "not at all satisfied," but 67 percent who received weekly visits were "very satisfied" with family relationships. Similar trends were evident for letters and phone calls. While all of the associations are very strong in magnitude (> thirty percentage point difference) and statistically significant, letter writing seems to have a pronounced impact on family satisfaction. Of those women who never received letters, 80 percent report they are "not at all satisfied" with family relationships. Not surprisingly, then, barriers to visits were significantly related to satisfaction with family relationships. Those who were "not at all satisfied" with their family relationships were those who faced a significantly greater number of barriers to family visits while those who were "very satisfied" with family relationships faced fewer barriers. Although connected, satisfaction with family relationships seemed more important for women's lives behind bars than the amount of actual contact with family. Contact with family was not correlated with depression or overall prison adjustment. Increased contact with family improved satisfactions with family relationships and decreases worries about being forgotten by family but had no effect on overall prison adjustment. Instead, contact with family seemed to work indirectly on adjustment through worries about family and satisfaction with family relationships. Women who were very satisfied with their family relationships compared to those fairly or not at all satisfied report less depression and better adjustment.

Women with no living parents or children had the least amount of contact with family, were the least likely to encourage family visits (67 percent), and were the least satisfied with their family relationships. In comparison, women with living parents and no children were significantly younger (thirty-three years) and less likely to have ever been married (16 percent), but were significantly and substantially more likely to encourage family visits (91 percent), remain in contact with family, and were more satisfied with their family relationships than other women, especially women who have outlived their parents and have children. Given the age differences (fifty-four years, on average), women in this later group likely have older children whom they encourage to visit (85 percent), but do not receive many visits or contact with their children and were therefore not as satisfied with their family relationships and frequently worry about being forgotten by them. Women with no living parents or children were the most depressed and worst adjusted than those with living parents and/or children. Interestingly, women with living children only (no living parents) were the least depressed and better adjusted than the other groups of women, despite their worries about being forgotten by family.

WORRIES ABOUT FAMILY

The women's worry about being forgotten by their families is prevalent and distinct. This is a real concern and a reality for some women. As time goes by, they are, or at least feel they have been, forgotten. After fifteen years, this thirty-seven-year-old woman felt this way about her family:

> The problem is too big for them, they do not know how to get help nor do they seek help. I believe that because it is overwhelming to them, it is easier to ignore me and as time goes by, months into years pass without visit or letter or phone call.

A younger woman, after serving eight years, already felt that her family *"just don't care enough; better things to do."* She observed how *"1 to 5 years the*

*memory of you is fresh, people think of you in present tense. 6 to 10 years
memory fades, you fade. 10 + you disappear as a person and are at best a
fading memory."* This forty-four-year-old wife and mother expressed her
feelings about this experience with these words:

> Prison has totally cut my life out of my family's lives. I don't have a significant
> relationship with my mom, dad, brother, sister and especially my only child, my
> son, at all. It's like I've died. I don't have any type of a relationship with any of
> my family any more. My worries I have about my family are that I never wanted
> to be forgotten or not loved and that's what happened. I have been forgotten and
> I'm not loved by my family anymore.

Women's accounts about their family are consistent with the fact that 79
percent of the women reported that they are always worried about separation
from family. Over 34 percent of the women are "always" worried, while 22
percent and 26 percent "often" or "sometimes" worry about being forgotten
by family. Worries about family vary significantly by types of contact frequency, barriers to visits, and satisfaction with family. Maintaining contact
with family through letters or phone calls (but not visits) is associated with
greater degrees of worry over separation from family. In contrast, for all types
of contact, the more contact with family, the less women worry that family
has forgotten them. The more satisfied they are with family relationships,
the less often women feel they are forgotten by family. Women who face
the greatest number of barriers to visitation are often bothered by feelings of
being forgotten also.

When we asked women what they worry about most when it comes to their
families, we found that they live with constant worries about specific family
members and maintaining their fragile relationships with their families. Three
primary themes are evident in their responses with regard to worry about
family, including being forgotten by family, losing loved ones (e.g., aging
parents), and a variety of worries about their children.

In the first theme, what we might think of as a focus on "self," some for
the women's worries about family are directed inward—what will happen
to me or how will this affect me? As already discussed, the most common
worry was being forgotten by family. However, they also worry specifically
that they would be a burden to their families who would get tired of them,
give up on them, and forget them. Fourteen years of incarceration for this
twenty-nine-year-old woman resulted in her biggest worry being: *"Becoming a burden more than anything. After being here so long I start to feel and
worry that they are tired of taking care of me and all the other burdens that
come with my being away from home."* Another woman spoke specifically
about the way she felt she was a burden to her family: *"I worry that I am no*

longer a viable part of the family. Because I cannot earn money in the prison I am also a burden on them for basic hygiene supplies and lunches for Fri, Sat, and Sun" [forty-four years old, divorced, served thirteen years].

Women also reflected on how much they were missing out on by not being there with/for their families. They wanted to offer their support, but could not. For a few of the women, they tried to support and encourage family members who worried about them because they were serving a life sentence in prison—for the first time or unjustly. They worried that their families were sad and heartbroken over their crime and sentence, and how they had disappointed them. This woman explained: *"My family worries about me. My emotions and how I am holding up. That makes me worry about them. Plus, just not being there takes its toll on me missing out on family functions."*

Others worried that their families would not accept them or would not be there for them when they do make parole and get out of prison. This concern was related closely to a second important theme—losing loved ones (a) while incarcerated/ "in here" or (b) before they get out. As this woman said, *"I'm not a mother but my mother is all I have. And I worry that something might happen to her."* Another talked of losing her father: *"My biggest worry right now is losing my father (dying) while I'm still locked up. Prisons do not allow lifers to attend funerals. My father is my sole support mentally, financially. Basically my whole world and last parent alive."* Siblings, children, and especially parents were reportedly in poor health or otherwise aging while others lost family members to accidents or violence. For example,

My biggest worries and fears about my family are about losing someone I love from death or someone getting sick and me not being there. I know no one lives forever and that scares me. I've already lost my 17 year old little sister to a car wreck.

As a result, women worried about physically losing family and any emotional support they provide. A distinct concern was not being able to attend a family member's funeral due to their sentence. However, they were also concerned about who would take care of their kids if something happened to their kids' caregivers. With tears, this mother told us: *"That if something happens to my aunt or grandma my kids will be left to defend for themselves and there* [sic] *only babies."* Another mother worried about her parents and only son. She was sixteen years old at the time of her sentence. She said:

I worry that I am going to miss everything in my son's life. I was pregnant when I got incarcerated and he's now 15 years old so I've missed a huge chunk already. I worry about more family dying or getting sick—especially my parents. If that happens who would take care of my son?

These and similar concerns about their children make up the third prominent theme among women lifers' worries about their families. Foremost
were worries about children's well-being, safety, and health. But they also
outlined worries about education, making "good" decisions, and making sure
their kids did not end up *"like me."* These women, all relatively young when
sentenced, shared these thoughts about their kids:

> I sometimes find myself concerned about whether or not my folks have all that
> they need, whether my child is safe at school, coming from school and them
> being safe on the highways, etc.

> My daughter is 18—she was a baby when I got locked up so I'm always writing
> letting her know how easy it is to come to prison and how it is in here. I give
> her advice on life and education on how important it is.

> I'm scared my 15-year-old is following in my footsteps. He is very rebellious
> toward my mom and he is always fighting with his little brother. They hit each
> other a lot and I think my 15-year-old has an anger problem.

Although they blamed themselves and felt guilt about their separation from
their kids, they also worried that their kids would blame themselves for their
sentence and feel abandoned, unloved. In this same thought, they worried
their kids would hate them and no longer respect them as their mother. As
these mothers described:

> I worry that my children will think I abandoned them and don't love them. I
> worry about how my mother will pay her bills when I could be helping, work-
> ing too. I worry if my children are being raised right, their father is racist and
> I don't want my children having the same views. I really hate that I'm missing
> everything, all their school years, birthdays, holidays, marriages, first kiss, teeth
> falling out, every little scraped knee. I'm missing it all and I can't get that back
> and that's what hurts the most.

> I worry that my kids will grow to hate me for not being there. But I try to write
> as much as I can to let them know that I care and love them. I let them know that
> they are never far from my mind and to write me and let me know how they feel.

Then, there are about sixty-three women who are not mothers. They worry
that they will never have the opportunity to be a mother. This is a realistic
concern given their ages and amount of time served/left to serve. About 44
percent were incarcerated when they were eighteen years old or younger,
and the average age at their sentence was twenty-three. They have served
an average of twelve years (range one to twenty-seven years). Current ages

range from nineteen to fifty-nine years old, with an average age of thirty-five. Nearly three-fourths have never been married.

PARENTING AND GRAND-PARENTING FROM PRISON

Over 150 of the women lifers in this group (70 percent) were mothers, with children ranging in ages from *"just babies"* to adults with families of their own. These women's age at incarceration ranged from sixteen to seventy years, with an average of thirty-two years old—significantly older than women lifers who are not mothers. However, about 5 percent (eight mothers) were under the age of eighteen when they went to prison for life. Another sixteen mothers were between the ages of nineteen and twenty-one at their sentence. As such, all of these women either had very young children or were pregnant when they received their life sentence. Overall, mothers have served an average of twelve years (range < one to thirty-five years); therefore, some of them had been incarcerated for most of their children's formative years while others still have hope for "mothering" their children when they get out. Current ages for mothers range from twenty-two to seventy-eight years old, with an average age of forty-four years—again much older than women without children. About half of the mothers are now grandmothers.

Being a mother or grandmother does not necessarily mean they have more support from and contact with family. In fact, mothers seem to have less contact with their family/children in face-to-face visits and phone calls—70 percent never or only occasionally have visits. Compared to the 40 percent of women who are not mothers, only 30 percent talk on the phone weekly. Rather, they are much more likely to send letters as their primary form of contact and as a way they can participate in their family's lives as mothers and grandmothers. As a result, mothers (and grandmothers) are more likely to be on opposite ends when it comes to satisfaction with their family relationships. A much larger percentage of about 47 percent of women without children are "fairly satisfied," while mothers are either "not at all satisfied" or "very satisfied" with their relationships with their family. This pattern is understandable given that a portion of mothers are cut off from the family and are not able/ allowed to participate in their children's lives. One of the women, who, at age twenty-eight, had served four years, had not seen or talked to her children in three years. Two other mothers also shared their unsatisfactory experiences in mothering from prison:

> Basically, I don't participate as a mother. 2 of my 3 children no longer talk or write for 11 years. I send letters and get no response. I send love in letters but

don't know if they are read. . . . I am missing being there for them and that a chasm has been created that I won't be able to be overcome.

I don't make any family decisions. They won't allow me to make any kind of decision. The only love I can give my kids is sending them letters and expect not to get a return letter back. I can't give emotional support when the other parties won't let you.

A woman in a similar situation continues to "mother" even when she is not able to see or talk to her children. So that they will not forget her and will always know how much she loves them, she said, *"I write them every week and send the letters to my grandmother. She keeps all the letters in a notebook that my boys will one day receive."* But, for women who lose, or lose touch with family, they would participate if they knew how to reach their loved ones: *"Right now I don't have a current address on two of my children. One of them is in the military."*

Whether mothers or not, a portion of the women lifers simply responded *"I don't"* or *"I can't"* when asked how they participate as a family member. A thirty-six-year-old woman (no children) told us that after eighteen years in prison: *"I no longer feel a part of a family or have a right to anything due to my circumstances. . . . It's hard trying to fit into a life that is no longer yours."* Although her parents are still living, for women whose parents are deceased, they may have no one remaining to participate with as a family. This thirty-year-old woman with only one brother said: *"I have no responsibilities/obligations at home."*

Despite these struggles to remain involved as family members and mothers, most of the women serving life were able to participate in decision-making and "mothering" from prison. As this woman concluded: *"I have to continue to be a mother no matter where I am. I write letters and call my family at least once a week. I am involved in all decision making when it comes to my daughter."* As she explains, most women who can afford to do so continue to "mother" through letters and by phone. This includes decision-making, offering opinions on family matters when asked, staying up-to-date on their children's lives, sending encouragement, gifts, and love, and marking special events and milestones in whatever way they can. They also share their own accomplishments and achievements, reassuring their family members that they are okay and doing well, and still living life. Along with their families, they maintain a hope for one day getting out of prison and returning to their family and children. The following are some of their accounts of how "mothering" takes place while they are incarcerated:

I talk to a family member daily, most often my daughter. We discuss everything and I am asked for my input in decisions. I make sure that my family members know that I care for them because I tell them and I offer my support especially during visits.

My family keeps me up to date on things that go on at home and within our family. I'm not really able to make major decisions but I do give input. I write my parents, sisters and son on a weekly basis and help them with things that may be going on in their lives.

I write my children and keep up with their school grades/activities. I try to encourage them and show them love by sending cards I've made or how proud I am of them.

I'm notified by mail of anything that my kids participated in. When I call home the kids still look [to] me if I approve of a certain activity that they want to participate in. I ask their opinions on certain things and we have open discussions during visitation with each other to find out what is going on in their lives.

I try to participate in my son's life as a mother as much as possible. We talk about everything before a decision is made.

Through phone calls, visits and letters I can provide emotional support/advice and definitely love. Some decisions I'm asked about but after 16 years I can't be there in person to assist in care for a sickness, help with an issue, life goes on and I can't linger in worry for something I have no control over.

Evident in these voices is the way participation with family and as mothers changes over time. While this is the case for all mothers, in prison or not, these mothers' greatest fears is that they will be forgotten. With time, change also brings changes in the composition of a family. Another fear is that family members will die. At the same time, new family members are added—grandchildren and great-grandchildren. "Grandmothering" from prison brings its own struggles and emotional challenges. Most grandmothers serving life sentences have never met their grandkids. For those who have, they have had few opportunities to interact with their grandkids as parenting programs in prison are reserved for mothers, not grandmothers. This sixty-year-old grandmother who has served eleven years of her sentence said the following:

I have missed so much bonding with my grandchildren, my youngest grand[child] was 1 month old when I was sentenced so I've never had the chance to actually play a game with her. They should have a children's center for grandmothers as well as mothers!

Instead, they send letters, handmade gifts/crafts, and write them stories—all things a woman expects to be able to do with her grandchildren. This grandmother explained the way she participates: *"Writing stories to my granddaughter so she will know when she gets older. She'll know the things we would have done together: making mud pies, movies, dress up, etc."*

SUMMARY

From their accounts, women lifers never adjust to being separated from their families including parents, children/grandchildren, and siblings. Most have some level of support and contact with family, but this is limited by distance, resources, and prison policies. Barriers to maintaining family connections are common whether negative visitation experiences or costly phone calls. In addition, women worry about being a burden to their family, their family's health, and especially their children's safety and future. When women worry less about family on the outside they are often more satisfied with their family relationships, regardless of the amount of contact with family members.

Family matters for women's adjustment to prison and mental health. The way women maintain connections with family during their time in prison also has direct effects on the successful transition outside of prison. Outside emotional support especially provides women serving life sentences the necessary social capital they need in order to maintain the hope of reunification with family decades later. By continually participating in positive communication, women can draw on the support of family and friends to better normalize their life. Being able to actively participate in either a daughter, sibling, or parenting role can serve as an important motivator improving self-esteem and encourage a more positive outlook on life. With the ebb and flow of life, those serving long sentences have the necessary time to carefully weigh the value of their outside supports. For many of the women, questions remain regarding what the future might hold for women serving lengthy sentences and their families. Will those left behind in the free world continue to convey empathy and a willingness to reciprocate when women lifers seek help or understanding? Will family and friends remain steadfast in their support as life goes on or will they move on while those behind bars are stuck in time? Will family members or lifers themselves remain alive long enough to have an opportunity to reconnect? For many women, these are some of the issues that bring constant worry as they sit and wait.

NOTES

1. Aday and Krabill, *Women Aging in Prison.*
2. Poehlmann, "Representations of Attachment Relationships."
3. Casey-Acevedo and Bakken, "Visiting Women in Prison."
4. Mignon and Ransford, "Mothers in Prison: Maintaining Connections."
5. Celinska and Siegel, "Mothers in Trouble."
6. Travis, McBride, and Solomon, *Families Left Behind.*
7. Mancini, Baker, Sainju, Golden, Bedard, and Gertz, "Examining External Support."
8. Cochran, "The Ties That Bind or the Ties That Break."
9. Aday and Krabill, *Women Aging in Prison.*
10. Aday and Krabill, *Women Aging in Prison.*
11. Hoffman, Dickinson, and Dunn, "Communication Policy Changes."

Chapter 6

Health Concerns and Practices

"[My] Health [is] deteriorating due to prison conditions."

"They cut back on our portions and we do not get equal required food servings."

"Medical is entirely too quick to disregard symptoms and tell you it's a figment of your imagination."

"I wanted to kill myself and still do every day."

Over the past three decades, virtually every aspect of the punishment system ranging from mandatory minimum sentencing to penal policies has shifted to a more punitive stance.[1] An intentionally harsher form of "deprivation of liberty" has emerged such as rationed or unappetizing food, delaying adequate medical care, overcrowded dorms or cells, hard bunks, lack of access to lower bunks, insufficient protection against extreme weather conditions, sleep deprivation, and strip searches.[2] The penal harm movement, apart from introducing harsher prison conditions, has been extended beyond the custody and control of inmates and into policies impacting healthcare treatment.[3] With prison food and health services contracted out to independent providers, private officials are with more reluctance providing the minimum services necessary under the health mandates. Some have suggested that penal harm medicine has become so commonplace that such practices now pass for standard operating health care procedures.[4] These issues are particularly troubling for incarcerated women who have significantly more health concerns than their male counterparts.[5]

One of the most striking aspects of meeting women lifers face-to-face is their aged appearance and readily apparent physical health problems. For most, it is surprising how woman lifers look more like your mother or grandmother, and how many have trouble walking, use canes or walkers, or are in wheelchairs, compared to the image of the "monsters" that most people possess when it comes to women serving life sentences. However, physical health and other medical issues are a major concern for women lifers because of their later ages at incarceration as well as their long sentences. Short-term inmates have more choice in when and where they receive medical care for health issues. They can more readily wait for outside services and care when they are released. With as many as twenty to thirty years to serve, lifers do not have this option or many options when it comes to preventing and treating physical health problems or healthcare. For instance, a thirty-seven-year-old woman, who had served fifteen years of her life sentence, told us this:

> The changes that happen in prison only affect those with a long sentence the most, loss of contact with loved ones, lack of medical care (good care), . . . if it is a death sentence tell us and let us decide how we die; [I want] honest information given to me about the situation, better food, building (all of the prison!), being treated like a human and not a mindless junkie or dumb animal.

Paradoxically, lifers are viewed as "waiters"; because they do have so much time, they can wait for programs and services including medical care. In addition, their life sentence is sometimes referred to as another death sentence. Carrying this stigma can result in a lack of care, concern, and treatment, and worsening health conditions. This relatively young woman is a good example of these health issues as experienced by women spending their lives behind bars:

> When I got locked up I was 25, married, and had just suffered devastating pre-term births. My children did not live and I'm fiercely afraid that I will never have my own children b/c of me being too old to have kids when I get out!! . . . There's nothing worse than the feeling that you are sitting in here literally rotting in prison. I feel like my life is over. I'm doing nothing with my life. It is empty. No kind of sense of purpose. I'm only 33 and feel 63! These people do not care nothing about us.

As her description implies, she came to prison with some health issues (both physical and mental), but being in prison also affected the way she felt physically. Women lifers are often physically older than their actual age, and they age faster in prison. This has been attributed to either poor or a lack of access to proper healthcare prior to prison, pre-prison structures (e.g., poverty and inequality), and behaviors (e.g., drug addiction, mental illness, and abuse history) that negatively impacted their health, and the experience of living in prison.[6] As to the latter, research has concluded that "thwarted by rules, custodial priority, poor healthcare management, incompetence, and indifference" become major impediments to prison-experienced healthcare, which negatively impacts women's physical and mental health.[7] Whether imported physical health problems or problems that come with or are exacerbated by being in prison (i.e., healthcare, diet, sanitary conditions, etc.), this chapter portrays the physical and mental health problems reported by women serving life sentences, and the attempts they make to receive proper care despite the many barriers to access, delivery, and proper treatment.

PHYSICAL HEALTH STATUS AND CHRONIC ILLNESSES

Two-thirds of the women lifers self-reported their physical health as either "good" (43 percent) or "excellent" (24 percent) while the remaining third rated as either "fair" (26 percent) or "poor" (7 percent) (see table 6.1). Not surprisingly, older women (ages fifty and over) are overrepresented among those in the fair/poor category. Only 19 percent of women in the good/ excellent category are age fifty or older compared to about half of the fair/ poor category. While the overwhelming majority of women in the good/ excellent category are "younger" lifers, one-quarter of the younger women self-reported their physical health as fair/poor.

CASE HISTORY 6.1: I'M IN POOR HEALTH AND I JUST WANT TO GO HOME NOW

Helen is seventy-seven years old and has been incarcerated for thirty-six years. She describes her mental and physical heath as poor with her health getting worse each year. Although atypical of most women serving life, Helen is currently receiving twelve medications due to her wide array of health problems. She suffers from arthritis, asthma, circulatory disorders and severe leg cramps, digestive issues, hypertension, heart condition, a respiratory disorder, and frequent urinary tract problems. Comorbidity issues such as Helen's are associated with worse health outcomes, more complex clinical management, and increased healthcare costs. She also frequently experiences chest pains and weakness in parts of her body. Now with limited mobility, she required an "inmate aide" to help her navigate the prison grounds. She requires ground-level housing and a lower bunk. She has difficulty standing for periods up to fifteen minutes at a time or walking long distances. Due to her declining health and dissatisfaction with the medical care received, Helen is constantly worrying about getting sick in prison. Showing symptoms of depression, she very often feels hopeless about her future as well as feeling lonely and blue. Similar to other lifers, she was physically and sexually abused prior to incarceration. Despite her health challenges, Helen only visits the health clinic once every few months, although would go more frequently if not for the co-pay expense.

Table 6.1 Health Profile for Women Lifers (n = 214)

Self-Reported Health (%)	
Excellent	23.5
Good	43.2
Fair	26.3
Poor	7.0
Self-Reported Mental Health (%)	
Excellent	19.9
Good	45.5
Fair	29.4
Poor	4.2
Visits to Health Clinic or Sick Call (%)	
Weekly	1.0
Once or twice a month	10.5
Once every few months	42.4
Hardly ever	46.3
Does a co-pay prohibit your visits to the health clinic? (% yes)	57.8
Daily Number of Medications (mean)	3.1
Number of Chronic Illnesses (mean)	4.4
Have you ever had a drug/alcohol problem? (% yes)	43.0
Have you ever been treated for a mental health problem? (% yes)	64.8
Do you ever have suicidal thoughts before prison? (% yes)	45.5
Have you ever attempted suicide? (% yes)	43.9
Health Compared to Two Years Ago (%)	
Better	7.5
About the same	60.3
Worse	32.2
Satisfaction with Medical Care You Receive (%)	
Highly satisfied	6.6
Somewhat satisfied	28.6
Somewhat dissatisfied	29.6
Highly dissatisfied	35.2

On average, women lifers reported between two and three chronic health problems (range zero–eleven). While 28 percent reported only one condition, roughly 20 percent reported four or more conditions, the most common being hypertension (24 percent), arthritis (33 percent), heart conditions (12 percent), respiratory problems such as asthma (24 percent), digestive disorders (18 percent), skin problems/eczema (11 percent), and menstrual or menopause issues (28 percent). Roughly 10 percent of women serving life sentences were diagnosed with diabetes, 6 percent with obesity, 7 percent with osteoporosis, and a little over 3 percent with various cancers. Women also reported problems with high cholesterol, acid reflux, heartburn, constipation, and anemia—all related to their in-prison diet and nutrition—and stress-related health problems. Experience with more general problems such as leg cramps, swelling limbs, back, neck, and shoulder pain, migraines, and allergies/sinus issues were also common. In addition to these more common problems, a few women suffered from rare genetic conditions including connective tissue disorders (e.g., Marfan Syndrome) and skin disorders (e.g., Pityriasis lichenoides et varioliformis acuta [PLEVA]). Others reported specific cases of degenerative disks, bone issues, nerve damage, and Lupus; severe thyroid conditions (hypo- and hyper-); and HIV/AIDS, Hepatitis B, and Human Papillomavirus (HPV).

With lack of adequate healthcare prior to imprisonment, it is common for women entering prison to have either untreated or undertreated health conditions. Women may have first learned of their diagnosis when they entered prison even if these conditions were present prior to incarceration. Although not considered life threatening, chronic health conditions can affect the quality of life of women in prison. These types of conditions are often exacerbated by the prison environment including their living conditions, diet, physical demands of prison life, and insufficient medical care. Complications from surgeries or injuries suffered from years of battering can linger causing persistent mobility problems. Also suffering from constant pain due to severe arthritis, menstrual problems, and disabilities can interfere with sleep habits, exercise, or work assignments. Older lifers in wheelchairs or those requiring walkers are greatly hindered in their ability to participate in the regular functions of the prison.[8] Others with advancing age may lack the sufficient stamina or strength to feel comfortable getting to an upper bunk or using stairs or any uneven terrain.

Whether based on existing health problems or ones they developed after their incarceration, about one-third of the women serving life sentences reported that their health had deteriorated over time. That is, their health was worse than what it was compared to two years earlier. About 7 percent indicated their health was "better" than it was two years ago, and for the rest, their health was "about the same." Older women lifers are overrepresented among those with "worse" health (by about 20 percent). For example, this fifty-three-year-old woman told us: *"[My] Health [is] deteriorating due to prison conditions and they say no money to address needs."* These women are aging, aging faster than they would outside of prison, and their health is worsening as a result. Without proper treatment, many of the chronic conditions experienced by women lifers will become worse, threatening their quality of life or life itself. Women lifers worry about these health problems and their health deterioration in prison. Health habits and accessibility to unique healthcare needs of women lifers and their perceptions of service delivery deserve more attention.[9]

NUTRITION, DIET, AND HEALTH PROBLEMS

In the prison dorms with just a microwave and packaged foods are many examples of great and creative cooks, however, this pattern of limited food availability has direct consequences on physical health conditions, including obesity, diabetes, and digestive issues. In fact, by all indications, women are at risk for developing diabetes after entering prison and changing diet habits for the worse.

> I hate the weight I've gained from the constant carb diet and being an age where it's NOT easy to take it off, at least not in here. I try to stay physically active as much as possible but as a result of poor diet and exercise, as well as from the added weight, I lack flexibility and mobility.

For these reasons, women lifers seek better, healthier food, food with no additives, and more vitamins. Like other prison services, food service is contracted out to lower costs. Women report small portions, starchy, bland foods, and a lack of food service on the weekends. To improve their lives and health, women point to the need for *"better servings."* One explained "[portions are] *too skimpy unless we're having visitors."* Another added: *"The food here they serve you are portions you would give your 3 year old child. They cut back on our portions and we do not get equal required food servings."* In addition, they criticize food services for cutting back the meals, as this woman requested, *"get us three meals on weekends."* Hungry, unsatisfied, and providing their own meals on weekends, they rely on approved foods on the commissary lists including high-sodium and high trans-fat processed foods, potato chips, candy bars, and sodas. Addressing the costs and quality of foods, one woman added: *"It would be cheaper to buy seed than buy canned food."* Others also recommended planting gardens and flower beds for dietary and health-related benefits (e.g., exercise). Several vegetarian and vegan women made these comments about their diets and healthcare:

I only ate organic vegan food away from prison, so I wish they offered healthier options at the commissary store. I wish they understood that not everyone prefers to each junk food. I also wish they offered holistic alternative medical care to sickness or issues because I don't believe synthetic treatments are the safest options. [thirty years old, served three years, excellent/good but worsening health]

[We need] better quality food, . . . quality of vegan food is poor, not enough vitamins and minerals, doesn't get soy milk with breakfast as the other regular diet does every morning. [fifty years old, served eight years, poor/fair and worsening health]

[We need] food that is better quality—fresh vegetables and fruit—less processed junk and a larger variety (not peanut butter 5 days/week) Note: I'm a vegetarian. [sixty-seven years old, served twenty-seven years, poor/fair and worsening health]

Women were concerned specifically with the chemical additives in the foods. For example, this fifty-five-year-old woman, who had served eight years and was in poor/fair and worsening health, offered the following comment about the quality of food and its effects on their health: she argued they should be served *"real meat, without the chemical additives that make us gain dangerous fat."*

Women also mentioned that it is not just the food quality, but staff expectations in the dining hall for "rapidly" eating their meals, which affects their health. Regarding this concern, one woman added: *"We choke down our food while being screamed at."* Another woman agreed, saying: *"Stop the horrible yelling at chow at us for minor 'talking'; do not rush us at chow—should be 10 minute to eat, but is usually (not always) around 5-7 minute. (The capt. is great. If he's around, the officers and staff do right)."* Eating too fast and under stress leads to stomach cramps, acid reflux, and issues with constipation for these women.

The policies reported here reflect the general approach states have taken in feeding "our prisoners." An analysis of menus from various states found that incarcerated people were served a diet too high in cholesterol, saturated fat, and sodium, and insufficient fiber.[10] A lack of fruits, vegetables, and milk as well as watering down recipes and serving small portions have made it impossible for prisoners to get the nutrients needed for a healthy lifestyle. While the purpose to serve unhealthy and unappetizing food is to save additional costs, the cost-cutting measures have been shortsighted. The consumption of processed unhealthy foods has led to three quarters of people incarcerated now being overweight or obese.[11] With dramatic increases in hypertension and other chronic health problems, the cost of providing healthcare especially for those serving long sentences will only rise. While some women have turned to commissary foods as an alternative, they too have been found to be of poor nutritional value as well high in sugar, sodium, and trans fats.

FUNCTIONAL HEALTH

The activities that people can comfortably engage in are important indicators of both how healthy they are and what services and environmental changes they need in order to cope with their limitation. While the majority of women in our sample were able to function, age, injuries, and worsening health conditions often result in or exacerbate numerous functional health problems reported by women lifers. For aging women, the most common functional challenges are loss of vision and hearing, which "can cause older prisoners to unwittingly break prison rules and risk punitive consequences"[12] and make it difficult to negotiate the prison environment. In addition, walking and standing can be a challenge for older women and those with physical health conditions which affect mobility. Over half of the women lifers indicate that they require a lower bunk (55 percent), and 21 percent require ground-level housing because they also have difficulty walking up or down stairs (13 percent). About 11 percent cannot walk independently, 16 percent require flat terrain when walking, and 25 percent have difficulty walking long distances (e.g., from their dorm to medical unit or to dining hall). More than 36 percent of the women lifers have difficulty standing in line for more than fifteen minutes at a time.

Despite pain or physical difficulty/inability, without a medical approval, woman are expected to follow prison custodial and security rules when it comes to walking, standing in line, cell assignments, and clothing. In particular, the types of shoes women are required to wear as a part of their uniform are problematic for women with foot injuries and pain, especially older women. In more than one account, women described the need for soft sole shoes and arch supports. A sixty-seven-year-old lifer had served twenty-seven years of her sentence, and her number one concern and recommendation for what could improve her life in prison was *"remove the mandatory men's boots required during business hours and allow soft soles (especially for over 65)."*[13] Also related to their functional health and physical pain, women complained about the effects of sleeping on thin, uncomfortable mattresses. This forty-eight-year-old woman pointed to the need for *"better living conditions as not to create future health problems, . . . better mattress, a lifer's dorm with added comforts/benefits, different rules."* These types of problems are clear examples of how little power and choice women have when it comes to addressing their physical health. Where a woman outside of prison can more easily change her type of shoes or mattress, or make accommodations for walking or standing, women in prison do not have this option. They must abide by prison rules, or receive a disciplinary report. When they do pursue some form of relief, it comes through a lengthy approval process. In the meantime, their health problems, and sometimes painful conditions, continue to worsen.

PRISON CONDITIONS, PAIN, AND SOMATIZATION

In addition to diet and nutritional deficits, the stressful conditions surrounding food consumption, and lack of healthy foods, women also cite how prison conditions are harsh on their bodies. We found one common pattern where women are often low in energy (27 percent), sore in muscles (23 percent), and weak (20 percent) or numb (25 percent) in parts of their body. About half report poor appetites. In other cases, women are often faint/dizzy (5 percent), have trouble breathing (13 percent), and have pains in their chests (5 percent). These symptoms are partly due to diet but also are attributed to living conditions such as thin mattresses, standing for long periods of time, heavy lifting in work details, lack of exercise, and overall adjustment to life in prison. While these conditions may be related to mental health or psychosomatic issues, there is a correlation between the extent of somatization, self-reported health, and health deterioration. Those with poor/fair health and those with worsening health report somatization more often than those with stable or improving health which is good/excellent.

In addition to the assortment of somatization symptoms, the high rates of other chronic health conditions reported by the women also contribute to significant pain issues often needing attention. With high rates of arthritis, osteoarthritis, back pain, diabetes, and chronic issues, many of the women have difficulty participating in a healthy lifestyle. Constant pain and discomfort tend to influence mental outlook, sapping energy and mobility while contributing to depressive symptoms, difficulty sleeping, and an overall decline in mental health. The physical structure of the prison can create significant undue stress especially for older, frail lifers who may find the prison environment oppressive due to their physical limitations.[14] It is not uncommon for women to report falling trying to get up into an upper bunk or when completing a work assignment. Stale air, top bunking, and being housed too far of a distance from dining services or bathrooms have been viewed as serious environmental and health issues.[15] These structural concerns become more problematic when women are suffering from symptoms of chronic pain. While pain medications have been found as the more prevalent means of treatment in the free world, most women are generally dissatisfied with the lack of access to pain management in prison. Living with both emotional and physical pain has become a common practice for women serving life.

MEDICATIONS

For these and other health problems, women take an average of three medications daily (range zero to twenty-eight), with the vast majority taking between one and five medications. Women in the fair/poor health category take more medications than those in the good/excellent category. However, even among women in the good/excellent category, especially those age fifty and over, about 75 percent of them take at least one medication every day. These medications include both prescription and over the counter, but for most women, typically consist of vitamins and minerals such as iron, calcium, and vitamin D to supplement diet and nutrition as well as age-related health issues. In general, there is a lack of medications for health problems. About 25 percent of the women take no medications. While some women may take specific prescriptions such as Zocor for high cholesterol, most complaints, even when extreme (e.g., broken foot, torn ligaments, or back injuries), are treated with ibuprofen, acetaminophen, and antacids indefinitely or while awaiting their appointment with medical. Antihistamines are often used for anxiety. Prescription pain medications and muscle relaxers are not dispensed at "pill call" due to concerns about misuse and mishandling among inmate drug users or women wanting to "get high," and are restricted to those admitted to the infirmary. Similarly, women are not allowed medications on an as-needed basis. They must be part of their medication list and schedule. Each medication and refill must be requested by form, along with their $5 co-pay, and then approved by the licensed doctor on staff. This process is slow, takes time, and may go unfilled even for chronic conditions such as heart problems.

Once a woman receives her correct medications during "pill call," there is a lack of follow-up on dosage and side effects. Thus, the prescribed medications can make their health worse overall. This possibility is complicated by the fact that the wrong medications may be dispensed at "pill call" in a "mix up of meds." Women must be knowledgeable about the types of medications and appearance of pills to know when/if this happens to them (or others) or else risk further health complications.

ACCESS TO AND SATISFACTION WITH HEALTH SERVICES

Given barriers to access and quality of health services in prison, health-related worries and deterioration are understandable, but not acceptable. Almost half of the women hardly ever go to "sick call." About 10 percent go once or twice a year, and roughly 40 percent go monthly. Only two women indicated that they go to "sick call" weekly. For one, a fifty-four-year-old woman in poor health, she has multiple chronic health conditions including cancer, a heart condition, high blood pressure, and digestive issues, for which she takes numerous medications (twenty-eight pills daily). The other woman, a forty-two-year-old in fair health, has only two, fairly serious, conditions—a back injury and asthma. She has support from her family, talks with them on the phone weekly, and thus can afford, more so than others, the weekly visits to the medical clinic. She would go more often if she did not have a co-pay. However, for both women, they indicated their health was about the same as it was two years ago, and they were somewhat satisfied with the health care they receive. Despite this, a clear pattern is evident among women with worsening health: they are more likely to go to "sick call" at least once or twice a month than those in relatively better health. Only 16 percent of the women lifers in "worse" health (compared to two years ago) hardly ever go to "sick call."

Regardless of their health status, about 58 percent of the women would be more likely to go to "sick call" if they did not have a co-pay—typically $5 for each visit to the prison medical unit and $5 for each medication. When asked about "sick call" and medications, many women said they *"can't afford it."* According to their explanations, the state cannot afford their care (or better care), so they must pay. However, Georgia is one of only two states that do not pay inmates for their labor. Given their financial situations both inside and outside prison, seeking medical care is simply not affordable for most, especially when they reserve their limited funds for hygiene and food supplies. As a result, women forgo medical care, especially preventative care if/when it is available due to costs and other demands on resources.

In addition to costs, women lifers may not seek medical care because of the process itself or because of the "uncaring" or "overworked" medical staff. For any medical-related service, inmates must fill out a medical request form describing their illness or grievance. Reviewed by a limited staff, several hundred requests are received daily, triaged, and scheduled accordingly. Depending on the condition, it is almost impossible to obtain immediate medical treatment unless it is without question a life-threatening situation, and even then, may depend on the time of day/shift, holiday, location, and staff on schedule. Doctors and nurses relegated to the "uncaring" category remind the women that they are inmates and that in contrast they were hired to save the state money (and in turn make more profits for corporately contracted health providers).[16] Acting as gatekeepers, this interplay results in women with multiple visits to the medical unit, and requisite co-pays, being told there is nothing wrong with them—treated as the stereotypical hypochondriac or attention-seeker. Stretched over time, women's conditions worsen—infections may take hold, they lose mobility, or reach a point beyond viable treatment—and women also lose any hope they ever held for being well or improved health.

Consequently, over 35 percent of the women lifers are "highly dissatisfied" with the healthcare they receive in prison. One woman with worsening health said: *"Medical is entirely too quick to disregard symptoms and tell you it's a figment of your imagination. You must be on your death bed to receive partial assistance"* [age thirty-six, served eighteen years]. Similarly, a forty-two-year-old woman with good but worsening health was highly dissatisfied with the medical care she had received over the three years she had served of her sentence. She self-reported nine health concerns ranging from arthritis to seizures, but indicated *"they tell me my illness is not real, except for asthma."* Others described their dissatisfaction with *"mainly health issues . . . because medical does not want to take care of you the way they should."* Like others, they felt strongly that staff did not listen to their grievances, and requested *"more caring staff"* and *"more professional staff."* Another fifty-five-year-old woman had problems with staff when she transferred prisons but her medical profile did not. She explained: *"Give us our profiles or honor them coming from different prison. Medical took my soft shoe profile and no chemicals profile. Wouldn't honor it. The deputy warden and treatment goes along with whatever doctor says."* She described her experience and interactions between inmates and medical staff as *"just a losing battle."* In another example, a fifty-year-old woman said: "[We need] *proper healthcare, myself for example, can only be treated for any that is life threatening. I have 3 issues with my right foot but cannot get treatment."* A forty-six-year-old woman who had served eleven years suspected she had a serious condition such as cancer or a heart condition. She was highly dissatisfied with her medical care because she had not received *"proper testing"* to determine the cause of her symptoms. In her case, she explained: *"I would like to see a new medical doctor replace Dr. 'N' . . . We need an internist I believe. We also need tests provided and proper healthcare done. They have said they are not sending anyone out except for life threatening conditions."*

What is unfortunate and cruel is that by the time life-threatening conditions, including cancer, are discovered, it is too late for women to receive appropriate treatment. These concerns are compounded by the fact that most cannot afford care for even life-threatening conditions. When they do receive care, they have almost no follow-up or monitoring after surgical procedures or treatments. They live with pain and the knowledge that they will likely die in prison. Many of them fear and refuse to go to the medical unit to live out their days behind bars because at this point they realize that a lonely and often further humiliating death is near. As this thirty-six-year-old woman with HIV/AIDS and emphysema spoke about these fears and the high costs of healthcare, she said: *"I want to go home one day and live the rest of my life with my cronic* [sic] *disease in peace, loved by my family."* If this outcome is not an option, they would prefer to die in their prison cells (i.e., their "homes") surrounded by their closest inmate supports.

Another 30 percent of the women lifers are "somewhat dissatisfied" with the medical care they receive in prison. Most point to general concerns with a need for "better medical," while others provide specific examples of insufficient services and care. After serving ten years, this forty-five-year-old summed up these health/healthcare-related experiences when she said: *"We/I need better dental care; we/I need a healthier diet, fresh fruit/veg, vitamins; we/I need preventative dental care; we/I need cleaner/more sanitary environment."*

A consistent theme among the women lifers involved the need for better dental care and more preventative dental care. For most, dental services are nonexistent or minimum. Cavities are not treated even when significant. Teeth may fall out or be painfully extracted. For older women, dentures are not available or are too costly. This fifty-two-year-old woman has served time in *"some prisons* [that] *have no hygienist."* She continued by saying: *"I've lost too many teeth due to no proper care and we can't get dentures anymore! Keeping up our appearance is important."* Although aesthetics is an important consideration, the loss of teeth can create many problems from vanishing bone structure, loss of facial support giving an amplified appearance of age and wrinkles, and possible damage to the remaining teeth that must still bear the full stresses of chewing. Once enough teeth are missing, then food choices and nutritional changes can cause medical problems such as malnutrition and loss of self-sufficiency. Older people with missing teeth are especially at risk if certain foods are difficult to chew or time restraints are placed on meal consumption as suggested earlier in this chapter. Certainly, more attention should be given to those who have become more vulnerable healthwise due to missing teeth.

Infectious diseases are also a concern in correctional populations who are more susceptible through exposure to blood, bodily fluids, poor healthcare, prison overcrowding, security issues, and high-risk behaviors. Older women lifers are particularly vulnerable to a variety of diseases that are spread within institutions. Of particular concern is the spread of infections due to unsanitary living conditions. After seven years, this forty-year-old woman described how she felt infections spread and what they could do to prevent illnesses. She said: "[There are] *too many housed in one room, sharing same toilets, the spread of infectious diseases. . . . I would like the budget to allow more bleach and disinfectant products, and toilet paper and pads for the inmate population and to help the spread of germs and infections."* Various other viruses and infections contribute to the health threat among women in prison. Airborne viruses such as influenza and respiratory viruses are common. Gastrointestinal infections have been frequently identified in prison settings. Foodborne gastroenteritis outbreaks may also occur when people are housed in close quarters. Hepatitis and pneumonia are other infections that can quickly strike older inmates. Elderly inmates with chronic diseases such as congestive heart failure, chronic lung disease, and diabetes are quite vulnerable to infection and need appropriate vaccines.[17]

Only about 7 percent of the women lifers indicated that they are "highly satisfied" with the healthcare they receive in prison. Those who are at least "somewhat satisfied" are reportedly in "better" health and among those in "good/excellent" health categories than those who are dissatisfied with their healthcare. However, because those who are mostly satisfied are in better physical health, they hardly ever go to "sick call." In contrast, though, as women are more dissatisfied with the healthcare they receive, they go to "sick call" less often. Thus, those who go to "sick call" most often are more likely to be somewhat satisfied with the healthcare they receive.

Among those who are dissatisfied with the healthcare in prison, between 60 percent and 68 percent would go to "sick call" more often if they did not have a co-pay. In fact, women lifers were particularly concerned with preventing health problems and improving their health. If given the opportunity and resources, they would. However, they often lack the ability/freedom to engage in basic self-care. For example, central to this thirty-five-year-old woman's concerns are *"not being able to take care of one's health appropriately from a preventative perspective."* In addition to better diets and nutrition, women wanted to see *"more activities"* and *"exercise programs"* to help them maintain healthy lifestyles, prevent future health problems, or manage symptoms of existing conditions. This fifty-seven-year-old woman offered her ideas for *"more physical activities (not for social meetings)"* including *"aerobic classes, weights for 50+ inmates to help with bone problems."*

OLDER WOMEN LIFERS

Older women (fifty+) in our sample indicated that they had four chronic illnesses and consumed, on average, five daily medications, which suggests declining health in later life. The installation of ramps, shower handles, other modifications, and care assistants are now required for those who become too frail to walk independently. Accommodating older women with special needs in prison environments built for younger people will continue to challenge prison staff. This point and the healthcare demand of older prisoners is best illustrated by the following lifer now in her seventies who possesses a wide range of chronic health problems:

> I was assigned a top bunk at age 64, fell and broke my hip. As a result, I now have a titanium hip, which was replaced after two years of suffering. A laparoscopic surgery following that surgery was needed two years later to correct internal injuries sustained in the fall. This procedure was followed one month later with emergency surgery to clear a blockage in my intestines.

With corrections departments across the country reporting that healthcare for older prisoners cost between four to eight times that for younger prisoners, new practices have emerged to control cost which has affected the quality of healthcare for those women making prison their permanent home.

Keeping older female lifers confined to a maximum-security bed when they pose no risk to society serves as an expensive cost to taxpayers. Prisoners serving a life sentence in the thirty-year range can easily consume $1 million or more of taxpayer's money excluding medical expenses. While the average prisoner costs in the neighborhood of $24,000 annually to retain, the cost to care for older prisoners is in excess of $50,000.[18] For those individuals who have extraordinary health problems that require hospitalization, the cost is dramatically higher. As we have pointed out, women in prison are generally less healthy than the general population, typically attributed to pre-prison risky behaviors, poor healthcare, and abusive histories.[19]

HEALTH MANDATES VERSUS PENAL HARM

As these women explain, preventive care and healthy lifestyles other than smoke-free policies are not a priority for most prisons. Instead, correctional administrators place more weight on keeping financial costs low more so than individual health. Policies based on penal harm, or the idea that women lifers do not deserve better healthcare, food, or opportunities for life improvement activities, also influence these decisions about healthcare programs. From a policy perspective, there is a formal recognition that inmates are entitled to health services consistent with prevailing community norms. Early in the 1900s the Supreme Court of North Carolina ruled, "It is but just that the public be required to care for the prisoners, who cannot, by reason of the deprivation of his liberty, care for himself."[20] A number of years later, the U.S. Supreme Court's decision in *Estelle v. Gamble* in 1976 mandated that having custody of a prisoner's body and controlling his or her access to treatment imposes a requirement to provide needed care.[21] Federal courts have indicated that a serious medical need is one that has been diagnosed by a physician as mandating treatment. Correctional facilities also have the responsibility of providing competent medical employees and to ensure they are capable of providing proper healthcare services.[22] Correctional healthcare staff should continually monitor access, quality, and healthcare expenditures as part of a comprehensive plan to ensure quality care.[23] This recommendation is important for the more vulnerable prison populations such as women with an extraordinary number of mental and physical health issues. In spite of previous court mandates, cases have frequently been brought forth complete with accounts of inadequate and inhumane healthcare systems. The obligations of healthcare standards set forth by *Estelle* remain one of the largest unfunded federal mandates in state and local budgets.[24]

MENTAL HEALTH CONDITIONS

Given their vulnerable backgrounds, lifestyles, environment, and abuse histories, women lifers present officials with a variety of mental health conditions requiring care. Research comparing inmate mental health needs to the population at large suggests that inmates are two to four times more likely than community dwelling individuals to experience mental health problems.[25] Estimates indicate that 20–50 percent of women serving time in the criminal justice system have severe mental health symptoms.[26] While depression has been described as the most prevalent and lingering form of mental disorder among incarcerated women, bipolar issues, PTSD, drug and alcohol abuse, anxiety, personality disorder, schizophrenia, and various other mental and emotional problems are common.[27] Entering prison with a low sense of self-esteem and fractured external support group, the prison environment can also serve as a source of stress leading to a further decline in mental well-being. If left untreated, additional problems may arise prohibiting the ability to adapt to prison life. In fact, levels of depression, specifically, are one of the best predictors how well women "cope" with living in prison.

Although 65 percent of those in our sample indicated they had been treated for at least one mental health problem, a majority of women lifers rated their current mental health as either "excellent" (20 percent) or "good" (45 percent). Five percent of the women lifers reported their mental health as "poor" while 30 percent indicated their mental health was "fair." However, when asked about specific experiences over the past few weeks, the majority of women reported psychological distress at least sometimes. We used the

Hopkins Symptom Checklist (anxiety, depression, and interpersonal sensitivity) to measure psychological distress.[28] Of these mental health measures, depressive symptoms were the most common among women lifers, including feeling lonely and blue (81 percent), feeling anxious about the future (76 percent), feeling others do not understand them (74 percent), and blaming themselves for things (72 percent). One-quarter felt hopeless about the future pretty/very often. Women lifers experienced thoughts of suicide and lack of interest in things less often. A little over 5 percent of the women reported experiencing all eight depressive symptoms pretty often or very often, which represents severe or clinical levels of depression. Close to 76 percent of the women lifers represented moderate to high levels of depression, experiencing a combination of symptoms at least sometimes.

Women also reported high levels of general anxiety, the most common being feeling tense or nervous. Levels of anxiety were highly correlated with indicators of somatization including pains in heart or chest, trouble getting breath, and numbness or tingling in part of the body. Indicators of "panic" disorders were not as common—only about 7 percent of the women reported often feeling scared or frightened at unexpected times or certain places.

Given their levels of depression, anxiety, and abuse histories/trauma, women lifers reported a variety of interpersonal sensitivity indicators. Of these items, women lifers felt others did not understand them, others were unfriendly or disliked them, and were easily annoyed and irritated by others. Relatively few of the women felt critical of or inferior to others or had uncontrolled temper outbursts, but two-thirds reported their feelings are easily hurt at least sometimes.

As we concluded in the abuse chapter, levels of depression, anxiety, and interpersonal sensitivity are higher among women lifers with histories of abuse. Sexual abuse was also related to higher levels of somatization. Physical abuse history was associated with significantly greater levels of depression and interpersonal sensitivity, but less anxiety or somatization.

People who come to prison for the first time experience a wide range of negative emotions (e.g., fear, anger, frustration, sadness, regret) that can influence their mental health outlook. Those with high levels of anxiety or personality disorders may find adapting to their new way of life difficult. Encounters with others may be filled with emotional reactions built on a lack of trust not only of others but also the system in which they now reside. One of the common negative emotions is that of fear. One thirty-six-year-old shared her view of fear: *"I do my time and stay in my own world because it is a safe place and follow the rules to the utmost as they come; the fear of not knowing, the fear of survival, the fear of never leaving, the fear of our files collecting dust because repeaters get off so easy."* Another forty-year-old with high levels of anxiety shared: *"My initial adjustment was fear of the unknown, being around strang-*

ers and how I would be treated by the other inmates and staff. Now I have no fear." Being able to manage negative emotions appears key in making a successful transition into a prison community of strangers. For those affected by interpersonal sensitivity, living in close, forced proximity with other women inmates is stressful and they have increased difficulty adjusting to prison.[29]

Overall, measures of depression, anxiety, and interpersonal sensitivity were all strongly correlated and tend to co-occur with one another. Each also was associated with women lifers' self-reported mental health ratings. Those who rated their mental health as "poor" had the highest (worst) scores for depression, anxiety, and interpersonal sensitivity while those with "excellent" mental health ratings reported lower (better) scores. Symptoms of anxiety seemed to better discriminate between women lifers' ratings of mental health than depression. For example, women with "excellent" mental health, on average, never/rarely experienced anxiety. However, even those in "excellent" mental health category, on average, reported experiencing depressive symptoms at least sometimes. Further, women's reports indicated that overall depressive symptoms do improve with time served, but compared to anxiety and interpersonal sensitivity, remain a mental health factor despite the passage of time.

Mental health, in general, improves with the amount of time in prison, as women lifers adjust to the prison setting and life in prison. Although the statistical correlation is weak, those with less time served reported experiencing mental health symptoms more often than those with more time served. As time passes, some psychological distress experiences become more common, but then subside. For example, after serving five up to fifteen years in prison, women lifers tended to blame themselves, felt tense or keyed up, and were easily annoyed and irritated more often than other women lifers. During this time frame, these women lifers also were more likely to report thoughts of ending their life. However, these feelings wane with more years behind them. In contrast, some psychological distress experiences do not change with time. In particular, women with less than five years, five to fifteen years, and more than fifteen years served were equally likely to report feeling anxious about the future, feel that others do not understand them, and feel trapped. In fact, these are the most common mental health symptoms experienced by women in the sample precisely because they continue to be experienced by women at all stages of prison life.

Despite the ebb and flow or constancy in these feelings, women lifers cling to hope for the future. As this woman stated: *"This is my life for now, but I never gave up hope. Hope has seen me thru."* According to the women serving life, their hope (or hopelessness) is principally based on the belief they will get out of prison (or not). The feelings of hope about the future, ironically, increase with their time behind bars. As one woman shared: *"Initially I was on a one way road to self-destruction. 17 years later I am hopeful and very positive about one day receiving my second chance."* Others mentioned the value of hope in their lives: *"When I first came I felt as though I would die in prison but now I feel hope of going home one day.* Yet another stated: *"I have done 21 years. At first it was all anger. Now, it is hopeful for a future."* In addition to their length of time served, each of these women indicated relatively low levels of current depression and anxiety, and overall good mental health.

Hope for the future and for getting out of prison is not a lifesaver for all women. Hopelessness is an indicator of psychological distress and depression for some of the women lifers. At fifty-two years old and having only served four years at the time, this woman felt that *"people just don't go home and that there is no hope."* She describes *"living with that but also being diligent that no little trickle of hope sneaks in."* Evident in her statement is the idea that letting even a "trickle of hope" "sneak in" negatively affects her mental health and psychological distress. In order to protect her mental health or as an indicator of her mental health struggles she does not or cannot experience hope for the future. Consistent with these statements, she reported relatively high levels of current depression and anxiety.

Depressive and anxiety symptoms vary by situation and in response to day-to-day outcomes. Women lifers must deal with a mix and fluctuation of emotions as they confront a life outside prison that moves on without them, a monotonous life inside prison that can also be unpredictable and change in an instant, and an incomprehensible system of parole and uncertainties of when and if they will get out of prison. In the extreme, women lifers may commit or attempt suicide. Although completing suicide is very rare in prison and among women lifers, of this group, more than 45 percent indicated they had attempted suicide at some point in their lives. Of the 8 percent who currently think about ending their own lives pretty or very often, suicidal ideation is a very real indication of the mental health state of these women serving life. As this woman simply but powerfully stated of her life sentence: *"I wanted to kill myself and still do every day."*[30]

While prison conditions may prompt suicide thoughts, especially early on in their life sentence, suicide ideation/attempts may be imported with women into prison. We identified four groups of suicide risk among women lifers.[31] The most at-risk groups included fifty-three women with pre-prison ideation which continued to manifest after incarceration, and another twenty-six women who indicated no pre-prison suicide thoughts but some degree of current suicide ideation. Both of these groups had relatively high levels of current depressive symptoms and feelings of hopelessness. The primary difference in these groups was more extensive abuse histories and prior mental health treatment for those with pre-prison and current ideation. Two additional groups of women lifers reported no current suicide ideation, including those who never thought about suicide whether prior to prison or after, and those who experienced thoughts of suicide before prison, but none currently while in prison. Interestingly, and indicative of experience with intimate partner violence, the most common predictors for this final group was abuse history but currently low levels of depression and hopelessness about the future.

Mental and physical health problems are aggravated by the prison living environment, including both structure and culture. With a deeply rooted history of trauma characteristic for most women serving life sentences, the punitive nature of prison can trigger stressors requiring mental health intervention. We have already mentioned that women with abuse histories are often retraumatized by strip searchers and pat downs that can produce flashbacks to previous traumatic events. Also, when living in overcrowded quarters with excessive noise, unfriendly exchanges, and lack of privacy are the general rule, constant tension leading to emotional distress can further aggravate those already suffering from anxiety and other mental health disorders. One woman indicated that living in prison was *"horrifying,"* and numerous others remain scared and withdrawn after years of imprisonment. Relationships when severed by imprisonment may lead some women to experience emotional trauma, resulting in symptoms of depression, sadness, and uncertainty.[32] The physical structure of the prison can create significant undue stress for older, frail lifers who may find the prison environment oppressive due to their physical and mental limitations.[33]

(Dis)satisfaction with health, healthcare, food, housing, programs, interactions/relationships with other inmates and staff as well as family including loss of loved ones in and outside of prison impact mental health and frequency of symptoms. While women lifers may adjust overall to living in prison, the daily stressors and dissatisfaction with specific situations or outcomes result in changes in mood, outlook, and mental health experiences. Women may alternate between depression and anxiety depending on the circumstance or event.[34] Few receive needed, appropriate, or adequate counseling and mental health therapy to deal with these mental health struggles.

It became apparent that the women attempted to manage their feelings on their own and with each other by modifying their thought processes. Maintaining a sense of purpose and hope was frequently mentioned as an important mood elevator. In visiting with these women on multiple occasions and with additional letter exchanges, it became obvious that the ability to draw upon their sense of humor when describing characteristics that they thought made them unique was an important coping tool. They perceived humor as an important medium for finding relief from the sadness and regret they frequently experienced. One woman captured this sentiment saying: *"Laughter is the best medicine being in a place like this. You have to be able to laugh and let*

God's word shine through. I just try to stay upbeat." As we watched these women interacting with each other, we could see that humorous relationships with other women are an important factor in helping women normalize their daily activities while coping with a life in prison.

CONNECTIONS BETWEEN PHYSICAL AND MENTAL HEALTH CONDITIONS

We found substantial and significant overlaps between physical health and mental health ratings and reported symptoms. That is, generally, the better their physical health, the better their mental health. For example, only 8 percent of those in the "excellent" mental health category reported their physical health as "poor" or "fair," whereas nearly 54 percent of those with "poor" and "fair" mental health rated their physical health as also "poor" or "fair." In addition, women who rated their mental health as "poor" take more medications (six versus two medications) and report more chronic health conditions (three versus two) than women in the "excellent" mental health category.

Examining women's mental health symptoms in combination and for individual items also revealed a general pattern where perceptions of worse and worsening health over time as well as dissatisfaction with healthcare resulted in worse mental health. Compared to the average woman lifer in the sample as well as those with better health than two years ago, those who reported worse health showed significantly elevated levels of depression, anxiety, and somatization. Specifically, women were more likely to experience feeling lonely or blue, worrying about things, feeling hopeless about the future, feeling low in energy, and a variety of other elevated somatization symptoms including faintness/dizziness, sore muscles, numbness and weakness in parts of their body, and heaviness in arms and legs when they perceived their physical health as worsening. Somatization and anxiety symptoms were also greater for women lifers who rated their physical health as "poor/fair" compared to "good" or "excellent."

Levels of satisfaction with healthcare also revealed this general pattern—greater dissatisfaction, worse mental health—especially for somatization and anxiety. Women who were highly dissatisfied with their healthcare in prison evidenced scores on somatization and anxiety that were two times greater than those who were highly satisfied. This equates to those who are highly satisfied with their healthcare never or rarely experiencing these symptoms. Among the individual indicators, temper outbursts, having bad thoughts, feeling inferior to others, feeling trapped, and feeling hopeless about the future were two to three times greater for those who were highly dissatisfied compared to highly satisfied with healthcare in prison. Many of these symptoms represent depression and anxiety, but also point to problems with interpersonal sensitivity. Thus, clear sets of symptoms are indicative of women's perceptions of their physical health and healthcare. Women who rated their physical health as "poor" or "fair" also report more symptoms of somatization and anxiety. However, when women viewed their health as worsening over time, they were more likely than average to report depressive symptoms along with somatization. In addition, when women were dissatisfied with their healthcare, they experienced more problems on average with interpersonal sensitivity. The connections between physical and mental health are complex and reciprocal—mental health symptoms lead to more physical health problems/poorer health and physical health problems lead to more mental health symptoms.

SUMMARY

Health concerns, both physical and mental, are prevalent among women lifers. In addition to the number of chronic problems, women's aging, worsening health, and lack of preventive practices stand out in their stories, and impact all facets of life in prison including the basics of food, clothing, and housing. Unhealthy diet and poor nutrition, lack of exercise and mobility issues, and dental problems are detailed. Despite existing mental health problems attributed to histories of abuse, trauma, and poverty, and continued bouts of depression and anxiety, most women lifers report good and excellent mental health. Their feelings and thoughts depend on family support and the care and comfort they provide each other. They draw on religious meanings, hopes for the future, and humor to cope with life behind bars and maintain positive mental outlooks.

The ability to care for themselves and the way the system provides for (or hinders) inmate health are limited by both policy and practice. Without compensation for their labor, many women simply may not have the necessary money for co-payments, and the state does not pay for these services, at least not to the extent that makes services available or effective. In keeping with the mandates of the Eighth Amendment which prohibits against inflicting "cruel and unusual punishment," correctional healthcare policy must continually monitor access, quality, and cost together as a part of a comprehensive plan to ensure quality care.[35]

NOTES

1. Clear and Frost, *The Punishment Imperative*.
2. Haney, *Reforming Punishment*.

3. Vaughn and Collins, "Medical Malpractice in Correctional Facilities."

4. Maeve and Vaughn, "Nursing with Prisoners."

5. Aday and Krabill, *Women Aging in Prison.*

6. Braithwaite, Arriola, and Newkirk, *Health Issues among Incarcerated Women.*

7. Stroller, "Space, Place, And Movement as Aspects of Health Care in Women's Prisons," 2263.

8. Aday, *Aging Prisoners.*

9. Fearn and Parker, "Health Care for Women Inmates."

10. Sawyer, "Food for Thought: Prison Food Is a Public Health Problem."

11. Sawyer, "Food for Thought."

12. Aday and Krabill, *Women Aging in Prison*, 55.

13. Today, women wear orange "crocs" instead of boots unless they have a medical profile or work detail which requires another type of shoe.

14. Aday and Farney, "Malign Neglect: Assessing Older Women's Health Care Experiences in Prison."

15. Aday, *Aging Prisoners.*

16. Webb and Hubbard, "Voices of Incarcerated and Formerly Incarcerated Women," 34.

17. Webb, "Voices."

18. Fellner, "Old behind Bars: The Aging Prison Population in the United States."

19. Aday and Krabill, *Women Aging in Prison.*

20. Rold, "Thirty Years after *Estelle v. Gamble*: A Legal Retrospective," 11.

21. Rold, "Thirty Years."

22. Granse, "Why Should We Care? Hospice Social Work Practice in a Prison Setting."

23. Fellner, "Old behind Bars: The Aging Prison Population in the United States."

24. Rold, "Thirty Years after *Estelle v. Gamble*: A Legal Retrospective."

25. Lurigio, "People with Serious Mental Illness in the Criminal Justice System."

26. Lynch, Dehart, Belknap, Green, Dass-Brailsford, Johnson, and Whaley, "Prevalence of Serious Mental Illness."

27. Aday, Dye, and Kaiser, "Traumatic Effects of Sexual Victimization."

28. Derogatis, *"Brief Symptom Inventory."*

29. Greer, "The Changing Nature of Interpersonal Relationships in a Women's Prison."

30. This woman is currently thirty-seven years old and has served eighteen years of her sentence. She reported alcohol/drug use prior to prison to cope with life's problems, as well as pre-prison suicide thoughts. She had the highest score on the HSCL/BSI of any woman in the sample, and although "adjusted" to the prison environment, continues to experience PTSD and suicide thoughts very often.

31. Dye and Aday, "I Just Wanted to Die."

32. DeHart, Lynch, Belknap, Dass-Brailsford, and Green, "Life History Models of Female Offending."

33. Aday, *Aging Prisoners.*

34. Krabill and Aday, "Exploring the Social World of Aging Female Prisoners."

35. Fellner, "Old behind Bars: The Aging Prison Population in the United States."

Chapter 7

Enduring Grief and Loss

"I've lost all future generations of my family."

"I've lost my individuality. I'm one of the bricks."

"The loss of a good friend in prison is deeply felt."

"I won't be able to properly grieve my losses until I am released."

With exclusion from the outside world, prisoners find they will be required to cope with a number of losses which bring considerable emotional pain. Many of the psychological and social issues surrounding grief and loss in a prison setting are considered to be quite different from those who live on the outside.[1] Compared to death on the outside, women in prison are required to grieve alone and often without counseling resources needed to complete the grieving process.[2] Already suffering from emotional grief due to separation from family, women prisoners will often experience an intense level of guilt for their incarceration during a time of family need. Although the literature on prior negative life events of inmate populations has focused predominantly on the experiences of younger offenders, researchers are now recognizing significant differences between age groups in the types of losses previously encountered, the subjective levels of distress caused by losses, and trajectories of mental health complications from having endured such losses.[3] The scope and depth of loss for prisoners is enormous and can be especially difficult for older offenders who have spent the majority of their adult life behind bars.

Long-term offenders frequently encounter the greatest problems of acknowledging, accepting, and adjusting to a wide range of losses. Over the past several decades, considerable literature has documented the pains of indeterminate imprisonment in both men's and women's institutions.[4] Research conducted with women lifers specifically suggests that losses may be even more detrimental to the offenders' well-being as they tend to have lower levels of self-esteem and less developed coping mechanisms.[5] Since most women serving life sentences have no prior prison experience, the initial "shock" from the realization that their lives have been drastically changed for future decades can be a devastating blow. Many recall memories of the initial "prison shock" throughout the duration of their sentences. Although long-termers frequently overcome initial feelings of depression, anxiety, anger, and hostility as they establish niches within the larger prison regime, many still view their lives as having been wasted.[6]

Women lifers have often experienced a multitude of losses over the life-course that, taken together, significantly impact their ability to successfully adjust to imprisonment. For example, in response to our question on losses, one woman mentioned her *"losses had started with the loss of childhood in-nocence resulting from years of sexual abuse at the hands of her father."* The earlier chapter on abuse confirms this was a typical occurrence. Other trau-matic events often experienced at a young age included the loss of the daily presence of a parent due to divorce, drug addiction, or other tragic events. Upon becoming an adult, losses experienced include the loss of a job or place of residence, or the death of a parent or other family and friends. Women with histories of domestic violence talked about having already grieved losses such as a warm intimate relationship, a sense of security, support of family and friends, or the happy ending they so desperately wanted. While these losses are all different, they do have in common the experience of being dis-connected from and divested of the lost object, status, person, or relationship. These cumulative loss experiences and subjective levels of duress are often imported into prison making a successful transition most difficult.[7]

NON-DEATH LOSSES

Loss of Identity

The very first devastating non-death loss experienced by those serving life is the loss of identity or the person they were prior to incarceration.[8] The nega-tive label of "inmate" often associated with being immoral, menacing, dan-gerous, and untrustworthy becomes the new identity marker. A person's name or title on the outside is no longer relevant—only an inmate's number. Even more compelling is the newly assigned status of "lifer" which often becomes detrimental to one's sense of self. Often viewed as a flawed person, social retorts such as the abrupt loss of a job or profession, loss of ability to practice important roles (such as parent, child or as a spouse), and loss of one's reputation accompany this new "master status." For example, comments like *"I miss being a wife," "I miss being a part of the family,"* or *"I miss my job and the people I used to see at work"* were frequently noted. Another shared the loss of autonomy as she noted: *"The one thing I struggle with behind these walls is not being able to take care of myself financially. Working a job and earning my own paycheck is the hardest part for me doing time."* Already diminished by an unfriendly criminal justice system or an abusive childhood filled with neglect and rejection, this explicit portrayal of prison can be an overwhelming experience.

With the multiple losses associated with their pre-prison community identity, lifers in particular are often singled out as a negative force in the prison culture. For example, lifers in our sample frequently mentioned that they are viewed as people with special character flaws as a result of the stigma attached to the sentence. The emphasis on sentence length was frequently used as a weapon to inflict pain on those labeled as "lifers." Comments such as *"you'll never go home"* or *"oh, she has life, she'll never get out"* were regularly mentioned with others testifying that the remarks were so hurtful they should be considered verbal abuse. In the words of one lifer, *"We get cursed out by officers and inmates. They terrorized us. I heard a staff member say they should put a gun to our head and pull the trigger and then the budget won't be so bad."* To combat such negative criticism, several of the lifers mentioned that good people can come to prison, too, and we found that many women were just in the wrong place at the wrong time.

Rather than receiving some measure of support from cohorts serving time, some women acknowledged experiencing feelings of hopelessness, feelings of uselessness, loneliness, and being ostracized in an environment already filled with painful everyday deprivations. Feeling institutionalized and an added burden to family, this subgroup of incarcerated women often masked their stigmatized identity. This rejection of social support for the newfound identity of a lifer ignores the fact that some of the women serving life are probably innocent of their charges. Many of the women indicated they were simply in the company of men who actually committed the crime. Others claim that *"many people are here because of ineffective court appointed attorneys who didn't effectively try to get them acquitted or bullied them into pleas."* Of course, others are here because they were forced into taking a life to save their own.

> I don't know why other inmates are serving a life sentence, but I know a man was trying to kill me and told me he was going to. I fought for my life. I wanted to live, not die. I was beat and a gun was held to me head. I think any other person would have done the same thing. Nobody wants to die.

Prison has been described as a place where the mortification of self is fully enforced leading to a series of humiliations and degradations.[9] Not only do lifers lose their identity and sense of freedom, they also lose control over their self-presentation as a ward of the state.

Loss of Luxury Items

The act of imprisonment also has an immediate and dramatic effect on an individual's daily social life. As the chapter on pathways to prison suggested, hearing the judge pronounce a "life sentence" can be a tremendous shock to the system like none other, especially if this is a first-time experience. Women lifers learn very quickly that with entry into the criminal justice system every aspect of a person's life will be controlled by others. The comforts of home (food, shelter, and clothing) are abruptly taken away along with the opportunity to engage in spontaneous social activities. As mentioned by one woman: *"One of the main things I miss most about being free is REAL food. I miss having my own apartment especially when depression kicks in."* Others mentioned little things taken for granted such as having access to a washer and dryer, clothes hangers, sunsets and soft beds, the feel of carpet on feet, the smell of food baking in the oven, the laughter of small children, going for a walk, going to a movie, having a mixed drink, ordering a pizza, or being able to pick a fresh tomato. Personal effects such as clothes, jewelry, pictures, shoes, nail polish, lotions, hair care products, and other items often so

---

CASE HISTORY 7.1: THE GRIEF IN MY HEART HAS HURT TO THE DEEPEST CORNERS OF MY VERY SOUL

Joyce is a sixty-four-year-old divorced Caucasian woman who has been incarcerated for twenty-three years. Not only has she lost the opportunity to actively serve in the role of mother and grandmother as well as other important roles, Joyce has suffered countless personal losses due to death. Her personal losses began many years before her incarceration when she experienced the sudden death of her three-month-old child. A short time later her father, who was an officer of the law, was murdered in his driveway with a shotgun blast in the back. Since her incarceration, Joyce has been notified of the deaths of her half-sister, a grandmother, two uncles, one aunt, a cousin, one brother-in-law, one sister-in-law, her father-in-law and mother-in-law, and a nephew as well as three close friends on the outside. More recently, Joyce found herself grieving the loss of yet another child, who died at the age of forty-one. Over the years, dear friends she has made while incarcerated have died while others have been released or transferred to other units. As she states: *"The losses I have experienced are still very much a grief in my heart, mind, and spirit. I do not have freedom to move forward yet as I have not had the opportunity to fully heal confined in this space."*

important to a woman's identity are stripped away. As one woman expressed: *"We used to get packages sent from home where our families shopped for approved items such as makeups, lotions, clear nail polish. Now our packages are all ordered from one company where our options are very limited as to what they sell."*

Loss of Freedom and Autonomy

Freedom in the United States is often associated with the opportunity for the pursuit of happiness. Realizing that the opportunity to pursue this dream in the free world may have been lost forever can have a devastating impact on those serving life sentences. Prisoners are deprived of their liberty, which consists of not only the confinement to but also restrictive movement within the institution.[10] Life in a total institution is highly controlled and unpredictable and, following incarceration, those retained lose the basic freedoms to define and manage their personal schedules, move about at will, the loss of time, freedom of speech and expression, and the ability to make basic decisions such as who and when they can receive visits from or communicate with loved ones on the outside. Those imprisoned are managed through continual surveillance, monitoring of spatial activity and classification. For those with life sentences, the question is constantly asked: *"How long will I be deprived of my freedom?"* Lifers in our sample shared grief-related stories of how demoralized they were by the parole board after time and time again being denied their request for parole. With each denial came setbacks ranging from one to eight years before consideration for another parole opportunity. After repeated denials, several women in our sample offered little hope for release and acknowledged that such a loss could very well be permanent.

> I have thought a lot about lifers and there are those here who in their own hearts think we can go home if we are good. I was in a preferred class for 20 years and did I get freedom? A girl who is in the Christian Halleluiah Choir has done over 30 years and she still can't go home.

> I am a damaged vessel. Truth is the longer I remain locked up the less I feel. After numerous denials for parole and other disappointments you begin to withdraw from your own feelings. Sometimes this numbness can be overwhelming. Perhaps one day I will just fade out like the morning mist.

Once incarcerated, prison rules that are constantly changing become the ordinary way of life. Prisoners are told where to live, what to wear, what material things they can possess, which prison programs they can participate in, and how many phone calls they can make. As one person countered, *"I have learned not*

**CASE HISTORY 7.2: AN OFFICER CAN SHAKE YOU DOWN
AND TAKE YOUR THINGS AT WILL**

At age five Casey suffered the traumatic loss of her father, causing a constant struggle with her childhood identity. Coping with the loss of her father lead to her rebellious teen years, eventually leading to a life sentence as a young teenager. The loss of those important childhood years leading to adulthood can never be recovered. She has literally grown up behind bars. *"Privacy is something almost unheard of in here and over time I have numbed myself to certain aspects of having my privacy invaded because the reality is that your life is no longer your own."* However, this realization has been most difficult to accept especially since *"at any time an officer can shake you down and take your things without provocation or even strip search you."* On a practical level, this is the only "life" Casey has ever known as an adult. For that, her meager material belongings are a very important symbol to her. When even small material things are taken, this results in a tremendous sense of loss. More importantly, the unpredictability of the prison environment creates a sense of fear as well because Casey, like others, never know when their world will be disrupted. As she states: *"It is truly a form of structural violence that is lived in many ways within the prison environment."*

---

to collect too many things because whenever they felt like taking things such as a shake down they do. Even if it's something we are allowed to have." Other women also shared the repercussions of having personal items taken away that were important to their identity be it pictures, clothing, or artifacts.

At a time when many of the older women in our sample entered prison, the structure of women's prisons tended to be less strict. In comparison to twenty years ago, several of the older lifers spoke about how the prison environment today has become harsher and with a strictness more in keeping with men's prisons. For example, there was a time when more informal prison regulations permitted women to wear their own personal clothing or clothing that had been donated from outside groups. Prior to technological advancements, there were no security cameras constantly viewing each prisoner's every movement and with a smaller female prison population, prison management provided a supportive environment.[11] This is no longer the case as contemporary women's prisons have significantly changed over time. As one older lifer having served over two decades and now witnessing the invasive role of technology as a controlling mechanism illustrates:

We have no privacy, even in the shower. A curtain doesn't hide us. We feel violated still. My grief is not having clothes to hide my body. It's awful and I'm an emotional wreck. I hide behind the dark of night to mourn because I have no place to mourn my loss of freedom. That's my best opportunity for privacy and still someone is looking at me. The lights are out but the staff is up looking at the camera to see what is happening so my freedom or privacy is impossible. I try not to care anymore. After more than 25 years, this is home to me. I have accepted it.

Other research found using a model assessing institutional structure, some association between the degree of depersonalization of the environment and the effects of self-imagery.[12] As one woman acknowledged, *"I'm institutionalized. I'm now part of a system. I've lost my individuality. I'm one of the bricks."* The more total the institution (based on such items as orientation of activities, scheduling of activities, provisions for dissemination of rules and standards of conduct, and observation of the behavior in inmates, type of sanction system, how personal property is dealt with, decision-making about the use of private property), the greater its depersonalizing effects. One woman describes the results of this highly structured prison setting:

My life has been reduced to a small space. My house here in prison is a metal box about 10 inches deep, 30 inches long and 28 inches wide. It holds all my property and personal items and state issue, except for what I'm wearing and my bed covering. What little space I have is not private and unless you have ever lived in a glass house you'll not know the experience.

Loss of Roles and Relationships

The losses associated with external relationships is a key element for women who realize the tremendous challenge to maintain a physical presence in their lives of their outside family and friends. Being unable to fulfill the role of child, spouse, sibling, parent, grandparent, or friend is extraordinarily difficult for women offenders. The loss of contact with family and friends on the outside is a major concern, especially for those who are serving long sentences. As summed up by a couple of the women:

We all feel a sense of loss. We ache and cry a lot for our families. We are scared within. The ones under the 7-year [sentencing guidelines] does 20 to 23 years and the 14-year lifer are probably doing more and it's all a concern to us. We reach out to one another. We all have lost a lot in life.

Distance and life often create a lack of contact even though today's modern times provides electronic technologies at one's fingertips and even face-to-face chats when separated miles apart from our families. Still it's the personal visits that can be important making our relationships full. When I no longer receive letters or the phone never rings, the loss is felt deep and I wonder do I matter anymore?

The fear that these relationships will be irrevocably lost creates a unique set of concerns since over time families can change dramatically. For example, several women discussed the fact that they simply did not know where their children were living or how many grandchildren they had. A feeling of loss and abandonment was often shared by those with disrupted family ties.

> Knowing when you can expect to reconcile and reconnect with family and loved ones and will it even matter when you finally do. While our families on the outside grieve the loss of our presence and they heal, we continue to experience anger and a loss abandonment.

> I don't have any family who cares about me. None of my 8 children ever make contact. All I have are those who I've been with here for the past 30 plus years. You know I think of them as family and it helps. I miss my family but it is like a dream now and hard to believe it was real at times.

As a result, some women serving long sentences without family contact have a frozen picture of life on the outside—the way life was when they left the free world. Although most do maintain contact and perceive relationships to be relatively close, barriers such as distance, travel expenses, scheduling concerns, and lack of privacy restrict the frequency with which visits, phone calls, and letters can be exchanged.[13] However, some may be shunned by relatives who are shamed by their crimes, and in some cases may have their parental rights terminated. Others mentioned that family members remain estranged and unforgiving due to the crime of taking another person's life. The following narrative extends this thought and captures the essence of this type of loss associated with incarceration.

> I keep my head down. My daughter was kidnapped, beaten, sold into slavery, and sexually assaulted. Not only have I lost my life, my daughter has lost hers. I will not be allowed to have my interaction with my grandbaby because her father doesn't agree with having me involved because I'm a lifer. When I lost contact with my daughter, I lost my grandchild. I've lost all future generations of my family.

Also, some reported losing all contact with siblings with whom they once shared a close relationship while others may have no knowledge of family or their whereabouts.

No longer viewed as a pillar in the community or someone the family could count on is a loss that is difficult to accept. In the words of one individual: *"I can't be with my daughter. I can't be a mother."* The notion of a "disrupted life-course" results in these ongoing grief reactions as those serving long sentences begin to realize they will miss important developmental milestones in children or grandchildren's lives such as birthdays, special holidays, gradu-ation, weddings, and newborn grandchildren.[14]

> I've missed out on all my grand babies being born. Time has continued on with my family but time has stopped for me in here. It's like I'm living in a box with no ties to those on the outside.

> I'm not feeling that well because I am missing my children and husband. My oldest son has a birthday tomorrow. He will be 16 years old. My wedding anni-versary will be a few days later. I am kind of broken because those are supposed to be special occasions in our lives physically.

Awareness that loved ones have responsibilities of their own and reluctance to request relatives (many of whom are also growing older) to make sacrifices result in the offenders missing out on many of the developmental milestones. Long-term prisoners, in return, may report being so out of touch with life outside the institution they have relatives that are now considered total strang-ers. As one offender remarked: "*I have lost hope for the reunification of my family. It is lost forever.*"

Being separated from family members for long periods of time encourages lifers to turn almost exclusively to their peers in prison for support and com-fort. For numerous women, the people they have shared a major portion of their lives with now function as typical family members. The interruption of these special ties are significant losses when such close friends are transferred to another prison, preventing personal contact, or paroled back to the com-munity. One lifer provides thoughts on how the loss of a good friend presents a void that is difficult to overcome. As she conveys:

> Most of these separations holds a loss of contact. We can't correspond, we can't telephone, we can't be approved for visits. It's a void in my life just like another death. For we can't encounter one another or share with one another—be it as to a family matter of joy or sorrow or a health issue we may be experiencing or a study of God's word together.

The narratives provided here support previous findings that the friendship ties women lifers developed with each other were a critical component of the way they did their time, and the significance of those losses should not be underestimated as women cope with the pains of incarceration.[15]

Loss of Health

For many aging prisoners, the most important "role loss" influencing in-stitutional adjustment is that of health. Loss of appetite, sensory processes,

memory, and ability to complete activities of daily living such as walking independently, climbing stairs, or working a regular job become more prevalent
with age. Research has noted that older female offenders suffer from at least
four chronic illnesses, creating a significant concern regarding deterioration
and accelerated aging.[16] For example: *"I am old and done 22 years already
in here. Now I am just getting older and sicker every year."* Others have
reported that many long-term inmates are obsessively concerned and highly
self-conscious about outward signs of deterioration.[17] As one lifer described:
*"I have a fear of growing old in prison and being unable to get around or
do for myself, having to solely to depend on someone else due to my declining health."* The loss of choice over one's own medical or dental care can be
particularly difficult, especially for those coming to prison much later in life.
Many of the women indicated that every time they go to medical they see a
different provider, which was troublesome in receiving consistent care.

With an abundance of time to fill and limited opportunities to fill it, older
women often become preoccupied with physical aging and their increasing
health problems. For example:

> Sometimes it's hard to be old and in prison away from family and loved ones.
> Sometimes I feel like I will never be able to be with them in the free world be-
> cause of my age and my time remaining. I have been here for over 20 years and
> since I'm now in my 70s it scares me to think about my future.

As older lifers experience a restricted life, chronically ill persons become
more cognizant of the fact that they cannot engage in many of the activities
they valued and enjoyed in the past. An older lifer coping with declining
health acknowledged: *"You are expected to keep up a certain pace like
the others who are much younger. Some of the jobs are physically demand-
ing and it is just not possible."* The restrictions the disease imposes on
normal daily activities make the individual feel controlled by the disease.
For some, this change in lifestyle is overwhelming. For example, chronic
incurable conditions require major adjustment in personal identity as individuals must assimilate the fact that impairment and constraint will become
a permanent loss.

DEATH-RELATED LOSSES

Coping with the death of a loved one is an event that nearly half of all women
in prison encounter while incarcerated.[18] Death-related losses are considered
to be the ultimate injustice that threatens self-esteem for female prisoners cut
off from the outside world. The loss of loved ones while incarcerated is a

common occurrence, especially for those doing a significant amount of time. As one lifer indicated: *"I am pretty used to loss by now. I fully understand that term: God giveth and God taketh away."* Another shared: *"I have lost everyone except for my father and these losses have had a very damaging effect on me causing extreme emotional pain and distress, and desperation."* Mothers confronted with the loss of a child while confined in prison is especially difficult. This fact is illustrated with this mother's grief-stricken comment: *"I lost everything when my son died."* This sentiment is shared by another woman who had experienced any number of overwhelming losses including her mother, friends, and other family members. However, she states: *"the most difficult personal loss was my child being murdered."* Yet another expressed a similar view: *"The most hurtful loss that I have had to endure was the death of my baby daughter who died at age 35."*

While sudden losses bring their own coping challenges, anticipatory grief often helpful in the mental preparation of a loved one in a prolonged state of decline is often unacknowledged for those in prison. In some cases, women will not have the opportunity to share with other family members during the last weeks of a loved one's life. Often guilt, shame, anger, and a sense of helplessness are common emotions expressed by those walled away from family. For example, while guilt is a natural reaction for those working through the grief process, incarceration generally will heighten those emotions. The women frequently felt they had let their family down by not being present to function as a part of the family during this time of loss. This was particularly difficult for those lifers who were already feeling guilt over having to abandon their children. This added stress can often lead to feelings of anger that may be displaced in the form of hostility aimed at other prisoners, staff, and in some cases, themselves. A woman grieving the loss of her son stated: *"You agonize and tell yourself if only I wasn't locked up, this never would have happened."* Others in expressing their anger voiced their displeasure about the nonchalant nature in which they had received word about the death of a loved one. Women mentioned they were able to share this hurt with others, although most preferred to remain silent about their underlying feelings. As deaths continue to occur over the years of incarceration, prisoners often see their social circle disintegrate and with these changes, emotions and memories from the past often surface recounting the good and bad experiences. The following narrative puts such losses into perspective:

> When one loses a loved one, no matter how (death, divorce, desertion, dementia, disability or disagreement and sometimes due to distance) no matter where we are in our daily life our emotions and feelings trigger old memories and those thoughts get tangled up with all of them. We often ask ourselves, "how come?, I wish, I could of [*sic*], should of [*sic*] and then did not do.

The loss of significant family members and friends through death may also result in losing the frequent interactions that have served to normalize one's existence behind bars. Inmates consider their family as the social context whereby their identity is confirmed. The regular phone calls, the letters and cards sent on special occasions, the simple fact of just knowing someone is on the outside doing your time with you are all significant losses that shrink the inmate's social world. The loss of a loved one is particularly difficult if it also includes elements of financial support as suggested by the following comment:

> The death of a loved one won't impact our lives in here unless it also incurs a financial loss. Say, the relative was sending us money and/or packages. We then feel it on a whole other level. We're not only grieving them but also the security we had by their support.

Facing the fact that death has eaten away at their social support network is especially true for aging prisoners who may have outlived any number of family and friends on the outside and now must either turn to others inside prison for social support or simply go it alone. Of course, the loss may not be felt as painfully in the case where there was a lack interaction or attachment with the deceased.

Losing close friends in prison may be a dreadful experience as inmates frequently establish close personal relations with prison peers, which in many cases is considered more significant than family on the outside.[19] Research indicates that survivors experience many of the same challenges adjusting to life without the close friend as they would the death of a spouse, siblings, children, and other family members.[20] As one lifer shared: *"I have lost an aunt that I knew well but it feels it has happened to someone else. I am more affected by my fellow inmates who have died in here."* Another shared: *"Our friends in here who pass we mourn differently and harder because we spend time with them in here every day."* This reaction may be particularly true for long-term inmates having served the majority of their adult lives together. They have been moved from facility to facility and over the years have shared many of the same experiences. For example: *"The loss of a good friend in prison is deeply felt because the loss separates two people of similar experiences—women of like time periods. I am missing such a dear friend now."* Some women lifers become very close through their prayer groups and other church-related activities and are often a vital social support. As one woman shared: *"I miss the times we have spent chatting and sharing."* The death of friends may also heighten older women's awareness about the meaning of life, the aging process, and one's own mortality behind bars. As one woman declared: *"At one time it looked like all my friends would die in prison and it made me feel sad and all alone. I really just try not to think about it."*

GRIEF AND BEREAVEMENT

The concepts grief and mourning are often used interchangeably.[21] Experiencing the pain of grief, both physical and emotional, is a positive and necessary task of bereavement. The process of mourning involves the actions and manner of expressing grief. However, how this process evolves is contingent upon the types of practices common in a particular culture or in this case a closed prison environment. Regardless of place, following the death of a family member or close friend, it is important to be in a position to acknowledge the reality of death and to share the experience of loss with significant others. All bereaved persons have a need for knowing the facts about what happened during the process of death. This is an essential step in making the event real in one's inner world. However, people in prison rarely have this opportunity to formally acknowledge the loss of a loved one or may never fully learn the details surrounding the loss of a loved one:

> When we receive news of the loss of a loved one here in prison, we cannot do the normal things that free world citizens can to honor the deceased. We cannot process our grief by gathering with others to share tears, laughter, memories, or comfort foods. Typically, we receive no condolences even from the administration. Our only choice is go through the grieving process alone.

> You don't experience the death with them and there is no way to explain to others what it is really like. I've lost family members out there three weeks or a month before I found out. They worry about how to tell me because they don't want to upset me in a place like this. Everyone is watching you to see how you will react to the loss—whether they will have to box you up and send you to the mental health wing. There is no place you can go just for 10 minutes to be alone.

When applied to the prison setting, the concept of disenfranchised grief suggests that a prisoner does not have the right or opportunity to function as a bereaved person. In this instance, disenfranchisement may remove the very factors that would otherwise facilitate mourning such as a role in planning and participating in funeral rituals or to obtain social support such as speaking about the loss, receiving expressions of sympathy, or finding solace within some religious tradition.[22] Rarely does the opportunity arise in most prison environments. Grievers are especially disenfranchised when they are not recognized by prison staff as persons who are entitled to experience grief or continue to mourn. As one lifer mentioned: *"The people here feel like I should not grieve those I've lost since it's been so many years."* This lack of responsiveness is further illustrated by two women who have suffered extensive losses over the past two decades:

> It is very difficult to process my grief inside these prison walls. When one of my sons died the first week I came to prison, the nurses did try to comfort me, but the guards gave me little sympathy. One commented to me you shouldn't have been locked up when he died. This was very hurtful since I was already overwhelmed with guilt and grief.

> When you are locked behind bars you don't have the adequate time and support to grieve. We have a very uncaring and uncompassionate chaplain who can care less. And most staff have a very negative and indifferent attitudes towards us inmates.

In addition to feeling they didn't have permission to grieve, women in our sample also spoke of the difficulties of attending funerals or visiting the gravesite. Funerals are considered an important rite of passage enabling loved ones to express what is known about the deceased. Attending the funeral or perhaps obtaining a furlough to visit a next of kin in the hospital serves to help resolve any unfinished business (i.e., past regrets, relationship conflicts) or physically viewing the body at services. In regard to the death of her father, one woman talked about the opportunity she had of getting to see him in the hospital before he died. Although this short visit was bittersweet, she recalled how meaningful this opportunity was to her:

> I got to spend 15 minutes with him, just me. He wasn't awake, but he knew I was coming. And they say that as soon as I left he changed his breathing. He knew that I was coming and he waited for me to get there. I got to talk to him and to hold his hand and tell him that it was okay. My sister paid for my visit which was two hundred dollars, but well worth it. I would rather do that than not see him at all.

In some cases, women expressed that the furlough experiences were constrained, where viewing was only permitted in isolation of other family members. In fact, eligibility criteria for temporary furloughs may systematically exclude many inmates due to their security classification level, relationship to the deceased, prison conduct or activities, physical and mental health statuses, geographic proximity to the critically ill, and personal finances.

Although grief is a normal reaction to death, women lifers may experience complicated grief, a condition recognized by symptoms, intensity, and duration deviating from socially recognized norms. The most common found in correctional settings is delayed grief, a defense mechanism characterized by intentional decisions survivors make to postpone grief until they have the time, space, and resources to fully process the loss. Incarcerated women, in particular, delay grief to maintain a sense of agency in an environment where surveillance is constant and empathy from administration, staff, or peers is inadequate.[23] Under these circumstances, suspending grief until release and community reintegration appears to be the most rational decision. As one woman recalled: *"I recently lost my sister and was able to go to the funeral. However, I have yet to be able to grieve her passing. This environment does not allow one the time to mend their wounds."* For other prisoners, the grief process may not be fully completed until they are released from prison, can place flowers on the grave, and generally have an opportunity to say good-bye in a more personal way. As one woman expressed:

> I have lost a daughter, a brother, and a mother in here and I have never mourned yet. I think I will once I am out of here. If you have never had a visit from your family, it just doesn't seem real. I keep a lot in me and I don't share because people talk and they turn things around to make you look bad.

Another who had lost both sets of grandparents stated: *"The grieving process in here is very limited and I believe that I will only be able to properly grieve these losses when I am released."* One person, having served well over fifteen years behind bars, shared her realistic vision of the main barriers preventing them from grieving in a way that might be accustomed in the free world:

> Most of the time your humanity is taken away in being able to process things grieving the loss of a loved one a normal way and makes it difficult because of the lack of compassion and kindness from staff. They are overworked and underpaid so they have more important things to worry about than a person grieving the loss of a loved one. Being in for so long I have seen the steady rise of the system being understaffed, which makes it difficult to do a proper job concerning each person's personal needs. You just have to swallow your losses and figure out a way to make it through.

This view is supported by others who shared: *"It's pretty much touch and go. They tell you someone has passed away and then send you back and you have to find a way to deal with it the best you can."* While some may be trapped at the point of not being able to let go of losses in lives, other women appear to take a different approach. This departure is illustrated by this comment: *"I fully understand the process of death. By our very nature we are selfish people. We want our loved ones with us forever. And unfortunately, that is not the law of God; he alone is forever. This is how I've carried and will carry every loss."*

Sometimes death-related losses can also trigger other painful emotions associated with previous experiences prior to incarceration. Two women shared with us such experiences, which frequently make the grieving process even more complicated because of the retraumatization from past victimization:

The abuse histories I had was and is still in my mind. I have regrets of course but yet it still remains a part of my grief. I can say that no amount of time will make the hurt go away. Living with loss, grief, and death is an everyday occurrence. It is like everyone and everywhere there is someone or something you see or remember what that person said or did. You will laugh or cry at the memory.

I, of course, have never mourned my husband. My nights used to be filled with dreams of him—never about the things he did, rather always about the times when I could have been a better wife—learned to cook better, cleaned better, been more adventurous with sex, been more fun for goodness sake. My life and joys and failures before prison are in a box and now this is my prison life.

From our findings, it is apparent that people in prison rely on differing patterns to express their grief experiences. The nature of the relationship (e.g., parent, child, grandparent, friend, etc.) as well as how instrumental that person was to their identity tended to make a difference. While some women expressed anger against the system, others more or less took the losses in stride or in some cases remained in a state of denial. It should be mentioned that memorial services are held when a prisoner passes, permitting the opportunity to honor their life, and these have been proven to be successful for some of the women. As one woman commented: *"The memorial services held for my roommate who died helped the acceptance of my loss. Several had an opportunity to speak about her life, often sharing her humor."* In addition, Grief and Loss groups are routinely offered and are considered helpful by those who attend. Regardless, due to the perceived barriers associated with coping with loss in prison, being able to let go through a structured grief process appears to be a far more challenging task than adjusting to losses suffered in the free world.

AGING, DEATH WORRIES, AND WISHES

Living in a harsh prison environment designed primarily for younger people presents significant challenges for older offenders who must cope with declines in functional health. With long sentences heaped upon their bodies, these women will eventually face the reality of being entrapped in the prison time machine. It has been stated that "women's bodies become the object of the prison gaze as they spend their time compelled to watch the clock as their bodies age."[24] With advancing age and fraught with mental and physical frailties, older females construct their identities within the constraints of a stigmatized setting where they are all but invisible. This negative view of aging has been reinforced by a society that has consistently viewed women's aging bodies as lacking sex appeal and ridiculous looking. Since our society generally has devalued older women by perpetuating stereotypes and portraying older women in negative, often degrading ways, growing old with respect in prison becomes an even greater challenge.

As women enter middle and later adulthood, they experience a wide range of new challenges, as they must begin to notice, acknowledge, and accept distinct reminders of their own mortalities. Without exception, older incarcerated women report a continued struggle to negotiate some of the same challenges their free world counterparts experience on a regular basis. When asked about what aging in prison meant to them, several women placed considerable emphasis on recent changes they had observed in their health statuses, personal appearances, or the roles they now will occupy while participating in familial affairs. The top fear voiced about growing old among this group was being separated from family. Comments like *"It just is scary thinking about not being with your family"* or *"I do not want to grow old here; I want to be with my family"* were common. Others mentioned numerous losses related to aging behind bars, such as: *"I've missed out on all my grandbabies being born. Time has gone on for my family, but time has stopped for me in prison."* Of course, women serving life sentences are constantly confronted with these losses in various stations of life.

Others spoke of fears related to their own health deterioration. As people age, they experience frequent reminders of decline in every body system. For example, a seventy-one-year-old woman who began serving her current sentence twenty years ago described the events older women who are residing in any environment can anticipate experiencing as they reach later life:

> The aging process, regardless of where you are living, hurts because we must all go through certain changes. . . . Our hair changes color, our faces wrinkle, and we no longer look the same as we did when we were young. It's horrible to be getting old here. I worry about medical needs being met.

In fact, almost one-half (47 percent) of women reported that their health had progressively worsened over the past two years, and it is no surprise that the majority of participants (79 percent) were more likely to worry about getting sick and dying in prison with little confidence in the healthcare system. As health declines and greater physical problems emerge, higher levels of death anxiety are reported in elderly people. As one lifer disclosed, *"Death anxiety is pretty high in here. We have lots of time to think about our health problems and the lack of medical attention we receive. It is constantly on our minds."* Vulnerable older adults when confronting their own mortality may experience greater uncertainty and profound fear. Women housed in correctional facilities in remote areas spoke of the fear of having a heart attack or some other sudden life-threatening symptom and the response time of getting to a medical facility for proper treatment. This is particularly the case for some of the older women who are battling a variety of acute diseases.

The existence of ongoing chronic illnesses can create a sense of vulnerability among aging inmates who frequently have to rely on an unfamiliar or untrusting medical system for critical care. For instance: *"I'm 70 years old and growing older, possibly getting real sick and dying in prison. This bothers me all the time."* Another woman indicated that she feared not being able to make her next birthday due to declining health. In this sense, older inmates are not only grieving their own deterioration, but often are mourning the loss of others as well. For the older women in this sample, there appears to be a significant link between the preoccupation with death thoughts and death anxiety. For example: *"It's hard to be old and in prison away from family and loved ones. Sometimes I feel like I will never be able to be with them in the free world because of my age and my time remaining."* These anxious thoughts creating an immediate emotional response tend to be more prevalent when another prisoner dies.

Reactions about dying in prison fluctuated from feelings of hopelessness, sadness, disgust, and fear to *"I don't allow the thought of dying in prison to bother me."* Three-fourths (76 percent) of the women in our sample indicated that the thought of death frequently entered their mind, and about one-half (43 percent) said that such thoughts were quite bothersome. A large number (82 percent) said that they often dwell on how short life really is. One of the most common thoughts held by women sentenced to life in prison is that they might possibly die in prison. Others described a life sentence as just another form of death penalty because of the indeterminate amount of time they face behind bars, especially for those in their later years. Numerous women expressed that their main fear was the fear of *"not knowing about possible parole"* or whether dying in prison will become their fate. One woman voiced her concerns: *"I deal with loneliness, pain in my mind, heart, and soul wondering if this is where I'm gonna die, not knowing if this is where I'm gonna be in 5 years."* The not knowing if/when they will get out of prison (dead or alive) slowly eats away at the women's peace of mind, producing real anxieties about their own death. Of course, some women who were younger or anticipated a more immediate release gave less thought to dying in prison. For example: *"Thoughts of dying in prison aren't a concern to me. I'm getting to the end of my sentence and I'm not coming back."*

Given the stigma associated with incarceration, many prisoners hold a negative view of dying in prison, considering this final act as the ultimate failure. Prisoners frequently associate dying in prison with an experience lacking a dignified death. As one woman commented about leaving prison in a body bag: *"It's very emotional for a lot of us in here. It bothers me a lot because it's one of the things I pray not to happen to me. It's a terrible feeling. I don't want to die in prison."* Additional concerns about leaving prison in a *"pine box"* or with a *"toe tag"* illustrate the women's concerns about the impersonal nature of death behind bars and thoughts of being forgotten. The stigma of dying in prison is often associated with consequences of dying alone. One of the most important privileges is the right to die with dignity and peace in a place of our choosing surrounded by family and friends. A remote uncaring prison is not that ideal place, and women serving life sentences are reminded of this fact on a daily basis. One woman who prays daily asks the Lord: *"Please let me go home so I won't die in prison. I want to spend the last days with my family."* Similar sentiments were expressed by other women in response to other inmates who had died in prison. They were generally saddened by the fact these women didn't get the opportunity to go home.

Many of the women also indicated that they fear dying as a "convicted felon" will have a direct negative bearing on their children, grandchildren, and other family members. Numerous women wondered how their families would cope should they die in prison. Some suggested it would be an *"embarrassment to their family,"* while others felt it would be *"such a waste to die behind bars"* and place a tremendous burden on the family. There is a general view that dying prisoners are considered a highly marginal group and devalued by society and prison staff alike.[25] Women lifers may feel the added shame from dying in prison and may regret the lack of opportunity to return back to their family and redress their criminal past. For example, for one woman dying in prison would mean: *"I would not have the opportunity to rejoin my family. I want to repair my relationship with my family and live as a law-abiding, productive citizen."* In general, one of the biggest concerns for women lifers was the fear that their family would, over the course of time, forget all about them. This fear continues for some women who, should they die in prison, wonder whether surviving family members will be willing to claim their body. Some older lifers may have outlived immediate family members, or the expense of a funeral may be too much for some families to bear. As one older woman with numerous health problems mentioned:

> I have wondered what would happen if I died in prison. I wonder if my family (what is remaining) will have the notification and resources to claim my body. If not—then donate it to science. This way I can make a final contribution to mankind.

If formal arrangements have not been made to dispose of the body, those who die in prison are buried alongside other inmates with their grave identified only by their inmate number. This is the reality many women serving life fear.

For some, the process of dying is actually more troubling than death behind bars itself. As one woman expressed: *"My main concern is not with what happens after death, but with the process of dying in here. I fear dying in pain and without dignity."* Others voiced concern about the security measures taken when someone dies in prison (e.g., the handcuffing person). Experiences with other prisoners' deaths and the lack of access to end-of-life health services often influence views on death and dying in prison. Although most of the women had not personally witnessed a death in prison, they are made aware of the fact when a death occurs. The news passes rapidly in a prison setting, and there is a general interest about the nature of the death and how the prison system handled the situation. As one woman mentioned: *"They die here all the time. I have been to plenty of memorial services here. It upset me at first but I had to accept some will not make it out of prison* [alive].*"* Losing close friends in prison, in fact, may be a harrowing experience, especially if the person is present at the time of deterioration and ultimate death. When offenders witness their friends die due to a perceived lack of healthcare or neglect on the part of prison staff, words of anger were common reactions to such experiences.

In correctional environments, under conditions such as substandard medical care and stigma associated with the dying process, emotions surrounding death can be intense.[26] When having negative thoughts, we found religious faith to be very comforting in dealing with the topic of loss. One lifer having served over twenty-eight years commented about the prominent role her faith provided in giving her a measure of comfort:

> I've cried over a lot of losses in my life—both family and prison family. They won't be there when I'm free, but I'll see them again heaven, which I am bound. I dreamed once that we were all standing at the graveyard and a short distance away was the entry where I could just walk into heaven.

Another older woman considered to be among the higher-risk, vulnerable populations including those who have chronic or other life-threatening illnesses explained that the general aging process inspires persons to begin thinking more seriously about their own mortalities:

> As I get older and begin to see that death looms ahead, I feel that I need to know more about where I stand with God. There's something about the transition from this physical life to the afterlife that is scary—the unknown. Heaven or Hell—that's all there is. As a Christian, I believe that death is a transition to a new existence and body which is very exciting to think about.

In sharing their thoughts, numerous women tended to rejoice in the realization that their prison "sisters" have moved on to a better existence. For some, death represented a better alternative to isolation, illness, and other pains of imprisonment. Those serving long sentences may welcome the prospect of ending the physical fatigue, pain, and suffering. The recognition that the future is limited, that health declines, and that there is a lack of outside social support may influence a person's view of death as an escape. This thought is reinforced by *"knowing that one day I will not suffer any longer in this house and one day I will have a new one that will be mine forever."* Another shared: *"I have known around 20 inmates who have died in prison. I always just say a prayer for they are now free and the creator will take them on their last journey home."* Thus, to soften the thought of dying in prison, the women often viewed death as a safe passage into a new afterlife. Several women mentioned: *"When the Lord gets ready for me I got to go. It will be a better place,"* *"I really don't think about death very often, nor am I afraid for I know where I'm going when I die,"* *"Dying anyplace in the world means if I'm absent from the body I'll be present with the Lord God Almighty,"* and *"Yes, we all have regrets but honestly I feel as if I die I will finally be at peace."* These comments support our findings that those women who participated in a greater number of religious practices were less anxious about death.

SUMMARY

Life-sentenced women encounter the greatest challenges acknowledging, accepting, and adjusting to a variety of non-death and death-related losses. The constant daily churning of the total institution fails to acknowledge inmate losses and offers very little empathy for those suffering losses due to the death of family and friends.[27] This interruption of grief and mourning prohibits any routine participation in celebrating rituals which highlight the important contributions of the deceased. For many, the pain intensifies from the initial arrest to courtroom hearings, incarceration and appeals processes, to the acceptance of multiple decades behind bars.[28] Unlike other social contexts within which individuals may experience similar losses, long-term incarceration is unique in the fact that the pain associated with losses is cumulative while increasing in intensity over time. We found that the normal grieving process is often interrupted or in some cases delayed permanently due to the restraints found within the prison environment. Such barriers inhibit the opportunity to mourn personal losses, often resulting in complicated grief reactions exhibited by depression, anger, or withdrawal. For these women, prison is not considered a suitable place to grieve.

Sensitivity should be given to the experiences of women who are simultaneously trying to negotiate losses within the contexts of their pre-incarceration experiences, non-death experiences, as well as the loss of loved ones due to both tragic or timely natural deaths. From the narratives shared by this group of lifers, we were able to provide a greater understanding of the obvious negative effects associated with the loss of self, life, and liberty. In particular, we found that these shared losses indicate the need for a greater understanding of how women struggle with loss during such prolonged stays behind bars. The question remains, how can prisons acknowledge and respond more humanely to such a vulnerable group? Even in institutions constrained by limited resources, opportunities can and should be available to disseminate general information regarding bereavement, grief, and mourning. This population should be encouraged to educate themselves about practical strategies they can engage in to restore a sense of equilibrium following trying circumstances. Careful monitoring of women in the aftermath of death is important, with an individualized approach for necessary healing. For those who will eventually be released and will resume key roles in mainstream society, some degree of consideration and preparation must be given to the grief process most likely to be encountered in the transition back to the free world.

NOTES

1. Aday and Krabill, "Grief and Loss: The Silenced Emotion."
2. Harner, Hentz, and Evangelista, "Grief Interrupted: The Experiences of Loss among Incarcerated Women."
3. Maschi, Morgen, Zgoba, Courtney, and Ristow, "Age, Cumulative Trauma and Stressful Life Events, and Post Traumatic Stress Symptoms among Older Adults in Prison: Do Subjective Impressions Matter?"
4. Leigey and Ryder, "The Pains of Permanent Imprisonment: Examining Perceptions of Confinement among Older Life without Parole Inmates."
5. Crewe, Hulley, and Wright, "The Gendered Pains of Life Imprisonment."
6. Leigey and Reed, "A Women's Life before Serving Life: Examining the Negative Pre-Incarceration Life Events of Female Life Sentenced Inmates."
7. Aday and Krabill, *Women Aging in Prison.*
8. Lempert, *Women Doing Life.*
9. Goffman, *Asylums.*
10. Stevenson and McCutchen, "When Meaning Has Lost Its Way: Life and Loss 'Behind Bars.'"
11. Aday and Krabill, *Women Aging in Prison.*
12. Haney, *Reforming Punishment: Psychological Limits to the Pains of Imprisonment.*
13. Aday and Krabill, *Women Aging in Prison.*
14. Jewkes, "Loss, Liminality, and the Life Sentence: Managing Identity through a Disrupted Lifecourse"

15. Severence, "'You Know Who You Can Go To': Cooperation and Exchange between Incarcerated Women."

16. Aday and Farney, "Malign Neglect: Assessing Older Women's Health Care Experiences in Prison."

17. Wahidin, *Older Women in the Criminal Justice System: Running out of Time.*

18. Harner, et al., "Grief Interrupted."

19. Aday and Krabill, *Women Aging in Prison.*

20. Lalive d'Epinay, Cavalli, and Guillet, "Bereavement in Very Old Age."

21. Hansson and Stroebe, *Bereavement in Late Life: Coping, Adaptation, and Developmental Influences.*

22. Doka, *Disenfranchised Grief: Recognizing Hidden Sorrow.*

23. Harner et al., "Grief Interrupted."

24. Wahidin and Tate, "Prison (E)scapes and Body Tropes: Older Women in the Prison Time Machine," 73.

25. Byock, "Dying Well in Corrections: Why Should We Care?"

26. Aday and Krabill, *Women Aging in Prison.*

27. Harner et al., "Grief Interrupted."

28. Jones and Beck, "Disenfranchised Grief and Nonfinite Loss as Experienced by the Families of Death Row Inmates."

Chapter 8

Keeping the Faith

"My faith is more important to me today than ever. . . . It is the rock I cling to!"

"God is my very best friend. . . . I talk to him a lot."

"I know God still loves me and has my future mapped out and everything is going to be okay."

"I find peace in knowing that even now I can still be used, make something of my life."

One of the main constitutional rights of Americans is the free exercise of religion even for those who are serving time behind bars. Prisons in the United States were primarily established centuries ago by religious leaders for the main purpose of rehabilitating those responsible for breaking the law.[1] Today, a cornerstone for redemptive opportunities, almost every prison in the United States has a chaplain responsible for assisting inmates as they practice and express their faith. Religious involvement in its various forms is one of the most common activities for structuring prison life. This is especially the case for female prisoners, who report higher rates of religious participation than for their male counterparts.[2] Regardless of faith, prisoners engage in a variety of church services: informal Bible study, prayer, and meditation, all of which counteract the noxious pains of imprisonment. With everyday life in prison a constant struggle between the godly and worldly influences, the need for positive social support mechanisms is critical in bringing about lasting change.[3]

For women serving life, religious engagement provides a number of important functions contributing to successful prison adaptation.[4] Religion allows those convicted of often serious criminal offenses the opportunity to find a new way of life, to build a new social identity, gain a sense of self-

157

worth, inner peace, and dignity.[5] Incarcerated women have also commonly used religiosity/spirituality as an important means of coping with the daily challenges found in a harsh, unforgiving prison environment.[6] Involvement in these activities buffers stressors for those with a history of victimization, deteriorating health, loss of loved ones, and reduced social networks.[7] Losses, specifically those that are permanent and involve a loss of personal control, can be spiritual turning points during which those serving long sentences begin to communicate with, rely on, and receive strength from God with greater regularity.[8] The intensification and focus on the inner life serve to help prisoners find refuge in a world filled with hopelessness and despair. While prisoners suffer extensively from worldly deprivations such as materials and services, the real pain results from the attacks on the psyche.[9] To alleviate the pain often associated with guilt or betrayals from others, religion serves as a soothing balm that provides a sense of hope when all seems lost.

EARLY RELIGIOUS EXPERIENCES

We start our discussion of the meaning of religion in prison among this group of women serving life by examining some of their religious experiences prior to incarceration. Although various criminal actions had led them to prison, many of the women indicated that religion was always an important force in their lives. Those women who were firmly grounded in their respective

---

CASE HISTORY 8.1: THE BEST DECISION IS TO OPEN THE WORD OF GOD DAILY AND FEED SELF

Samantha is a seventy-one-year-old woman who is serving a life sentence for homicide. Incarcerated for well over twenty-five years, she relies heavily on her religious faith for guidance. Although a person of faith prior to incarceration, her dedication to the word was not as steadfast as it is today. *"I was not always so conscious of my actions. Obedience takes a willingness that must be learned and practiced."* Bible reading and prayer are a daily given, and Samantha often rebukes the ungodly behavior of others when the opportunity arises. Her faith has gotten Samantha through many troubled times as she has coped with one major life event after another such as deaths in her family and numerous rejections from the parole board. As she states: *"I am disappointed for so many, many different reasons yet I know only God holds a redeeming hand for any of us and the mess we make of our lives."* Over the years by using humor, she has been able to discard her anger and has left any remaining vengeance to God. Through her faith, Samantha has found the love necessary to forgive, including the forgiveness for her own actions which brought her to prison. As a regular churchgoer, this lifer claims: *"There is not a waking moment of my life I don't know that his presence is with me."*

religious beliefs from childhood were able to immediately call upon their religious faith in this critical time of need. The following two women were able to share how crucial their faith was in helping them make the transition to a life behind bars:

> Religion has always been important in my life. . . . In fact, it was the way I was brought up. . . . Early acknowledgment and awareness of the Lord has made it easier than if I had not been involved in the church. . . . Because of it, I have been able to study the word of God and better understand situations that I may have otherwise been bitter about.

> Since I was raised in the church, religion has always had an important place in my life. I was determined that God was coming with me to prison. Since arriving over 13 years ago, I can honestly say that my relationship with Him has become solid, personal, and loving.

Numerous other women with religious foundations rooted in the context of the church shared the fact that their faith was nourished and solidified at an early age in a supportive home environment. These lifers acknowledged that, early on, family members had provided them the necessary guidance that, in the end, served to fortify their ability to accept their fate when incarcerated years later. For example:

> I was very spiritual as a young girl and began attending the Baptist church at age 9 . . . where I learned what it meant to be "a good Christian." My parents ensured that I was always at Sunday School and worship service so I could learn values such as being honest, loving others, and working for the Lord.

> My faith goes back as far as I can recall. As a young child, my grandfather introduced me to God from stories told Sunday School Style. At home, my parents also shared with me the light of joy, happiness, love and pride that only God can provide in their eyes. Remembering their positive influences, my faith remains—just as strong today as it was the day I surrendered my sinful self to God at a young age.

In sharing these early experiences, however, several women noted that their faith had been rigorously tested along the way. Overall these women confirmed that major life transitions, including those closely connected with changes to their interpersonal relationships, often contributed to declines in formal religious programming, private beliefs/practices, and general commitment to their religious beliefs. For example: *"Before I was incarcerated, I did not know God personally. As many other people in church, I was completely lost."* Other women reported that the role of religion was an insignificant part of their early adulthood years—periods when issues including non-marital sex, cohabitation, and alcohol or drug consumption become increasingly more prevalent. Some women voiced the lack of a faith-based outlook as well as doubts of the sincerity of religious conviction.

> Prior to incarceration, I had read the Bible, but not on a daily basis. I attended church too, but I'd never studied the Bible to get personal with my creator and savior. I simply was a Christian in name only for I did not live a life putting God first nor talking to Jesus like I'd do as a friend.

> Religion was never a major issue in my life until I got locked up. So many things happened to me when I was growing up. I felt there wasn't a God because how could there be a God when there is so much hurt and pain in this world?

These accounts indicate that prior to incarceration, religion was not an important vehicle for coping with life's problems. However, after being thrust into a prison environment fostering painful deprivations, people often turn to their faith as an important coping mechanism. While being uprooted, disconnected, and removed from the religious or spiritual figures in the free world, those faced with a life sentence discover a need to reinterpret their current life situation and manage the negative emotions of being in prison.

> It's important for people to understand that life "before" prison was so selfish for most of us inmates! And we mostly were spoiled brats. Putting God first was a superficial front—"me, me, me." was most of our priorities. Then prison happens and we all mostly RUN to God.

Other individuals who spoke of transitions experienced along the life-course prior to incarceration, however, spoke of a disengagement altogether from their early beliefs. One offender recognized the value of capturing periods of spiritual loss in constructing narratives by noting the association between declining faith, abuse, and criminal behavior. Given the prevalence of intimate partner violence in women serving life, the connection between the loss of religion and power, control, or domination in her marriage is worthy of noting:

> Although I was saved as a young girl, I fell from my walk with God as an adult. After my husband died from a freak accident, I had much anger at God for taking Him from me . . . so I simply stopped going to church—began to drink a lot and engage in a life of crime. I became involved with a man who did not share my spiritual upbringing and let him introduce me to lots of sin. I let him order me to do things to hurt others. How wrong I was.

Women encountering similar experiences may need religious communities to extend empathy, compassion, and care to initiate healing. Such positive religious experiences have been known to promote a transformative process significantly improving their psychological well-being and life satisfaction.[10] For others, however, such support is considered to be inadequate—leaving them in states of spiritual distress rather than growth.[11]

As we spoke of earlier, the initial entrance into correctional facilities can elicit intense negative emotional reactions, and some may naturally ameliorate their symptoms of distress by directing these frustrations and feelings of anger toward God. For example, women serving life may harbor confusion and discontentment with the possibility of a loving God abandoning them when his guidance, love, and support are most vital as they transition into prison.[12] The arrival into prison accompanied by the fresh emotional anguish of an uncaring justice system may lead to the questioning of their underlying faith. As these women noted:

> My walk or relationship with God declined after I was incarcerated. Because going through trial and losing my children to devastating circumstances, losing my other 3 children to someone else in custody, then getting a life sentence with the possibility of parole—daily you got to live as an inmate including being treated and talked to like trash.

> I was very hurt when I first came into the system and I have slipped in my faith since then. I had to learn it was not God's fault, it was my choice and the lies that was spoken against me only came to pass because God allowed it. He has work for me to do and I had to go through in order to share with others.

The above example illustrates the worthy recognition that religious discontentment without resolution can result in a variety of mental health concerns for those maintaining these views. Long-standing unresolved religious displeasure, for example, can increase feelings of depression, anxiety, or suspiciousness leading to poor prison adjustment.[13]

> I've been trying to walk right with God . . . and it hasn't always been easy. . . . I'm dealing with a lot of mental things right now, but I'm beginning to develop a sense of faith again so all things will eventually come together. God doesn't say that we won't have trials and tribulation. However, he does say that he will see us through them.

In retrospect, most individuals recalled that any initial feelings of discontentment or doubt they may have formerly held concerning their faith had proven extraordinarily beneficial when approached in a constructive manner. Although the pressures of prison sometimes got the best of them, the majority seemed highly committed to retaining their faith-based identities.

RELIGIOUS RITUALS AND PRACTICES

The meaning that religion holds for those serving time in a prison setting is highly subjective with each practicing religion in a highly subjective and personalized manner. For example, religion can serve as a motivational tool providing direction and meaning for their life behind bars. It can bring hope for the future, peace of mind, positive self-esteem, and an overall change toward a new way of life. For others, attending religious services may be for the mere purpose of meeting other inmates, to interact with volunteers, or to gain access to prison resources. While some individuals expressed little or no commitment for maintaining a religious identity behind bars, most of the women reported that their views of religion have become increasingly more positive with time, enriching the quality of their prison experiences. Eighty-four percent of the women described religion as a "very important" aspect in their daily lives. A similar number (82 percent) pray every day, with a sizable number doing so multiple times. Thirty-nine percent of the women indicated they attend at least one service each week and sometimes more, which is comparable to the free world. While one in five never attend formal services, they may be more inclined to profess spiritual activities such as meditation.

The power of prayer is an important focal point of worship for all the major world religions. Prayer behind bars is a popular ritual and coping mechanism for the incarcerated. When it comes to engaging in religious activities behind bars, prisoners have a distinct advantage over those living in the free world in that they have an abundance of time. Prison can be infamously boring and where a person's thought process can get stuck in an endless loop of self-loathing and resentment. By using this gift of time to pray, women lifers often testify that they are rescued from their own selfishness and shame to a fresh vision for their future lives. When asking God to come into their prison cells and assist them in turning away from the thoughts and behaviors that landed them in prison, the potential for change is ever present. Comments such as *"I talk with God and Jesus multiple times throughout my everyday life," "The more that I pray the closer I get to Jesus," "God is my very best friend . . . I talk to him a lot," "I frequently ask God for help. He knows my heart, but he wants to hear it from me,"* and *"When I feel down I pray"* reflect the importance that these women gave to the purpose of prayer. Participants, for example, identified prayer as being extremely effective in relaying stories and feelings they would be unable to share with family, friends, or external supports via letter for fear of disinterest, disbelief, or personal judgment.

While personal prayers were considered to be effective vehicles through which the women found strength, personalized devotionals and daily Bible reading also were frequently mentioned as a preferred way to express their spiritual/religious beliefs behind bars. Typically, private prayer, studying the scripture, and meditating have been mentioned as behaviors where practicing one's faith in private can be successfully accomplished. However, living in close confinement can often prove difficult for those who search for *"privacy time with the Lord."* As one woman shared:

> Every day is a challenge, I have to study in the word and stay prayed up. It's hard when I have 15 other roommates and you can't really have a quiet moment to yourself. I have to get my quiet time at 3 AM when all are asleep. I don't get to do it every day. Sometimes I sleep through it. But I can tell it makes a difference.

Despite such barriers for private worship opportunities, the personal devotionals are a major source of comfort as these women serving life sentences attempt to grow in their faith. Many of the women mentioned the belief that God has a personal plan for each and every person, and by remaining faithful to his cause and with constant study, *"we will be able to think like God does."* It is the introspective look and precious quiet time where these women lifers sought a personal sanctuary to grow spiritually.

> Nothing has been as beneficial as my personal times with God in the quietness and isolation in his word in my cell for it is available to me anytime. I've read many stories that cover spiritual foundations talking about how to simplify life with principles such as faith, love, hope, mercy, forgiveness, honesty, and trust. While the stories told are not as crude as the actual life going on around me, they provide foundations for lessons that can be applied to the context.

Committed to these daily private rituals, the women felt they could foster a spiritual mind-set that would serve to buffer the deleterious effects of prison life. This spiritual shield can be an empowering commodity, as one woman shared: *"I have integrity everywhere I go because of my walk with God,"* rather than those in despair who otherwise may think, *"I am afraid that life actually has no meaning."* Women who shared their experiences with individual Bible study reported this activity to be an important resource upon which they can draw personal comfort rather than rely on the mentorship of spiritual leaders or camaraderie of their fellow cohorts.

> I focus on working on my thoughts and align them with the Word and try to act on them. I try to build up my faith by reading the Word or a devotional daily. I'm a work in progress and God is truly working on me and I believe He is going to do a mighty work in my life, that will erase all doubt for me as well as others in my situation.

Religion, to me is a very personal, intimate thing between a person and their beliefs. I like to fellowship and be around others who share the same religious beliefs that I do, but my beliefs are very sacred and I prefer personal, quiet time practicing what it is I believe.

In addition to watching religious television programs in common areas, attending formal church programs is another major source of exposure to religious teachings. Participation in these activities provides comfort zones within which the women can share their faith with others, learn to trust, engage in self-disclosure, and change maladaptive attitudes about issues such as suffering, guilt, blame, and forgiveness. The importance of sharing with others is expressed by these two born-again Christians:

It has been a comfort for me to share spiritual thoughts in Bible study which is a part of the Chaplain's program. We pray for each other and their families and this has become a valuable source of support.

Being a disciple of the lord enables me to not only share my thoughts, feelings and confessions with my savior but also works as a therapy—for when I share my past it helps others and eases my own pain.

Connections to structured religious programming was also considered a valuable experience in the everyday lives of these women lifers. As one woman stressed: *"We have religious services during the entire weekend as well as different Bible studies and services during the week."* Another stated: *"I've learned a lot from others since I've been in prison. Some of my knowledge has come through chaplain volunteers that bring the word of God to us weekly."* Others noted that there are numerous churches, some as far as two or three hours away, who come to minister in various ways. As one woman mentioned: *"They are very faithful to God and come frequently to lead our Bible study and provide emotional support."* On special occasions, outside religious groups are also able to provide much needed necessities to those who may need them. These groups provide the opportunity to interact with others from the free world, often making friendships leading to avenues of financial support and other gifts. As one woman recalled:

The church people came to my cell and brought me all kinds of candy, several types of chips plus peanut butter crackers, and cheese crackers, lotion, shampoo, and deodorant. We had a special Bible class and they prayed for us. God's people always stand by us.

While the amenities outside churches provide are considered a definite benefit among church attendees, some critics have suggested that inmates choose to participate regularly in prison ministry programs because of the "consolation" prizes such as free food, party favors, paper, pencils, pens, movies, and so on. However, 60 percent of the women indicated they participate in such activities as a way to occupy time constructively, exhibit signs of personal responsibility, and to prepare for the future.

Sometimes those behind bars are ridiculed for their unique beliefs and practices, creating tension between various groups of religious believers. As a result, some have called for more tolerance for the different beliefs represented behind bars. As one lifer suggested:

> While being here, I have learned that all of the religious programs that exist and are available for inmate participation can be simultaneously helpful as well as confusing. Once you become comfortable with one practice and set of beliefs or values, for example, you soon discover that along comes another group that is sure that "theirs" is the true and only way to God. In essence, each church takes time to verbally bash the others and their members. In a prison setting, this can be very problematical as it leaves the inmates feeling bewildered, guilty, and often convinced that they are, indeed, hell bound.

While there is a general feeling that the various "Christian sects" and Muslim communities are well represented, some suggested that more churches should become involved. As one lifer countered:

> I have had no visits from my faith's clergy since the first year of my prison time. I would welcome even quarterly visits. A kind word or a note in the mail are a great blessing. It helps to know we have not been forgotten. A friendly face at church services is wonderful!

Some women expressed that they are less likely to openly display their exuberant feelings about the active role God plays in their life. As one woman who almost never attends prison church services stated: *"I meditate and do yoga. I believe in God but not organized religion. I'm very moral and live my faith quietly and not just a Bible thumper like many Christians in here do."* Another woman indicated that there was perhaps too much emphasis placed on religion and that empowerment should also come in secular ways:

> Actually, I see that we have enough, if not too much "religion" in the prison system which is very good but bad when compared to education! These women need the basics! Learn to multiply, learn spelling and vocabulary! Learn a trade. Learn their gifts and talents and u-s-e them! That's joy!

While the majority of the woman acknowledged the important role prison chaplains and their volunteers play in their religious growth and assistance in coping with imprisonment, a few women were also quick to criticize the emphasis placed on formal services rather than engaging in a more active hands-on ministry:

> If you feel like going to services, go. But I have a problem listening to long monologues about what we are commanded to do from people whose stories pale in comparison to most of the offenders in prisons today. If the pastors (who visit the prisons) would only invest their time, energy, and resources in other charitable means they would do much in God's eyes, I suspect. Finding an inmate who does not receive visits and make a visit to them once or twice per month. God would really love that as well. What one does for "the least of my brothers" is what really counts.

Others may not participate regularly in formal religious activities because they feel some of the women use the religious services as an opportunity to meet up with a girlfriend, exchange contraband, or other illegal actions. Some women voiced their displeasure with the nature of some religious services referring to them as "pagan" because emphasis is placed on *"vulgar dancing, loud clapping, shouting of an obscene nature to encourage the performers."* Instead, women called for more specific group-study opportunities. They recognized the problem of prison conversions, especially for those who have opened up their lives to Jesus for the very first time. Among these women, there is a belief that more emphasis should be placed on nurturing new Christians. As one woman stated: *"A lot of women are not saved until they come to*

CASE HISTORY 8.2: WE SEEK A WAY OF LIFE OF THAT BRINGS ABOUT CHARACTER AND RESPONSIBILITY

Lucy is an older lifer who admittedly entered prison as a selfish and angry person who took the prideful view that her rights had been violated and those around her had no idea who she was or what she had to endure just to survive in the outside world. With this mind-set, she feels that women serving life often do not recognize incarceration as an opportunity where they can learn more about themselves while learning to help others. For Lucy, exposure to religious training was a major turning point in not only her eyes, but those with whom she comes in contact. The spiritual training that brought about her transformation began in 1998 along with six other women who desired a new lifestyle, yet were ignorant as to where to begin. Turning to a security officer and a pastor from the outside seeking guidance and prayer, a renewed mind filled with Christian principles changed their lives and those around them. Contentment from their purpose-driven lives still abounds twenty years later for this small group of women who not only changed their lives for the better, but also influenced many other women's lives of those released who were influenced by their teachings. Lucy feels that their commitment to their faith and resulting good works dispels the negative label often attached to *"jailhouse religion."*

*prison and most don't know what to do after that and most of the Bible study
groups are full and have a waiting list."*

For those who want to be more involved in religious teachings, one of
the women's prisons offers inmates the opportunity to enroll in a four-year
theological study that is taught on site. This course is designed for those who
want to seriously study the Bible. As one woman remarked: *"Nothing wrong
with the praise and worship but for some of us, intellectual stimulation is
what keeps us going."* Another stated: *"There is a lot of reading and studying
involved which takes up many hours. The only problem is not having access
to reference materials."* Another popular program offered to the women
was the Inter-Change Freedom Initiative. Through this program, volunteer
women come into prison to teach about abuse, mothering, and living positively in a negative world. As one woman said: *"This program is awesome."*
Involvement in programs like these can be very cleansing for souls who have
previously been so badly damaged and broken by abuse or some other crisis.
Faith-based programs such as these can be advantageous to prisoners who are
experiencing problems that would otherwise prove to be insurmountable. Involvement in such intellectual, religious and spiritual activities buffers stress
associated with the consequences of long-term incarceration and is effective
in relaying their stories and feelings.

THE COMFORTS OF RELIGION

Whether inmates bring their religious beliefs with them directly to prison or
experience a religious conversion, the spiritual journey behind bars will involve a pathway reflecting change. For those who have a history of religious
participation, prison becomes a time for renewal, a time to overcome the
lapse in judgment causing harm to self and others. New converts usually are
encouraged by chaplains and local volunteers to become engaged, often for
the first time, in religious activities found inside the walls. Recent religious
converts are taught that no matter what they have been through, the harm they
have endured prior to imprisonment, they now have the opportunity to create
a spiritual beginning. Religious converts typically report a drastic change in
their approach to life characterized by shifts in attitudes, thoughts, and self-
understanding.[14] As one woman said: *"My belief that one God has a plan for
each of us inspires me to use my talents to help others. I am not bitter about a
wrongful conviction because I know that in God's time I will receive justice."*

People who are sentenced to life or life without parole still have a propen-
sity to maintain a sense of hope.[15] They feel that God has a plan and at any
time can sweep down with a miracle providing a pathway to freedom. Many

of the women serving life took pride in living a life with purpose and one of hope. For them, hope appeared to be an elevated emotion felt when they vision a path to a better future. Hope offers those serving life the ability to confront their personal situation even in the most difficult of times, and to try and deal with that adversity going forward. For these same women, their faith in God is more likely than not at the centerpiece for maintaining high hopes for the opportunity to eventually return to a life resembling the one that was left behind decades ago. The following serve as illustrations of the important role of hope:

> My faith is very important part of my daily survival. Without faith there is no hope and no purpose in life. I have lost everything: my family, my home, and all that I had acquired in 55 years of hard work. The hope that I may one day regain my freedom and again be with those I love is all that sustains me. My faith that with God all things are possible makes my hope live.

> My beliefs are my hope. Hope that while I may be paying for past/present karma, I will one day pay my debt and be free. I believe that the meaning to my life is the same no matter the location, however unfortunate the location may be. Faith and the hope of a freer tomorrow are what keep each and every one of us going.

There were a few in our sample who indicated that, for them, religion served to provide a false sense of hope. While these individuals had always anticipated they would be able to return to their previous lives, they were now more realistic regarding their expectations surrounding hope. Even with such doubts, some were still holding on to eternal hope:

> Right now, I do not have much hope and I am afraid that life actually has no meaning. However, if it is anywhere, it's in the Bible. So, I do study, study, study . . . and perhaps just the looking for hope and searching for meaning has given me both: hope and meaning.

Although those who appeared to remain steadfast in their faith were more likely to continue to hold on to hope, other women when exchanging casual conversations often mentioned that they were resigned to the fact that the state would never let them go home or that they would most likely never hear from family members on the outside. One woman described how her religious faith helped her to reinterpret her current situation and more effectively manage the negative emotions that are so frequent in prison life:

> We talk about freedom a lot. I look at this as I am free in here. I just can't do some of the things I did in the free world, but I am just thankful I have freedom

with my Lord. My faith plays an important role in my freedom and how I cope with it. I am free from worldly things in here.

The harshness of prison environments coupled with a lack of access to adequate healthcare often triggers anxieties, especially for those older lifers who are experiencing declines in health. Religion is frequently used as a coping resource for those who are imprisoned with illness and other losses related to incarceration.[16] Overall, women lifers experience multiple losses, with the effects of each being cumulative and often causing psychological deterioration. As one lifer stressed: *"My faith in God has helped me deal with the diagnosis of muscular dystrophy. This serious health issue helped me reevaluate my priorities and learn to trust in God's enduring love and care."* Other women who shared their experiences in this area recalled:

I lean heavily on my religious beliefs simply because the health care in the system today is bad and is getting progressively worse. Prayer and believing in something other than this system is what keeps most of us long term lifers going and mentally stable.

My relationship with my higher power has helped me cope with health issues as well as end of life issues by just trusting God, knowing that He's too wise to make a mistake. I made it through back surgery, I'm healthy.

I have a dislocated right hip. It's not dislocated so much where I cannot walk. It's just enough to be aggravating. In the Bible, Jacob's hip was dislocated after wrestling with an angel of God. So, I figure if Jacob can deal with his I can deal with mine.

In addition, religion can be very comforting to older women in ameliorating death-related fears—specifically when present among high-risk, vulnerable populations including those who have chronic or other life-threatening illnesses. As one woman interjected: *"I consider my religious beliefs as the basis of who I am, how I view and respond to life in general. This has helped me to accept an aging body and mind, even eventual death."* Another explained how her religious faith provided a source of comfort and hope as she considered her own mortality:

Brokenness brought me to God and through his help I was able to better my health, my mind and my spirit. My faith in God has given me spiritual discipline, courage and hope to face possible death in prison. Sure fear, doubt and hopelessness comes at me, but I have learned to apply my faith and God's word to discipline my thoughts and keep hope. He has my life in his hands.

Women serving life often enter prison reeling from a chaotic disorga-
nized lifestyle often complete with poverty and other traumatic experiences.
In the midst of this turmoil, female lifers find themselves striving to achieve
ego integrity, a sense of peace, and acceptance with self. In prison the un-
rest persists as they seek a way to structure their life in a more ordered and
less chaotic manner. Although public shaming rituals erode self-esteem,
religion can counteract destructive influences by providing a place within
which they can construct meaningful lives.[17] Religion provides the opportunity to reframe past negative events and give permission to forgive self
and others.

When responding to the question of how religious beliefs and activities
helped the women cope with their imprisonment, a frequently mentioned
result was a *"sense of peace or a calming effect."* Inner peace for these
women includes a sense of harmony, emotional well-being, and fulfillment
in life despite their daily struggles with incarceration. Numerous women
talked about how they now experience peace through their faith. Comments
such as *"Jesus brings me peace"* and *"I have learned to take it one day at
a time"* indicate how these women have developed patience as they cope
with the uncertainty of their life sentence. Others experience a sense of
peace because they now have confidence in the fact that *"through their relationship with God they now have salvation through Christ."* This internal
quality of calmness and security puts the mind at ease and fills these true
believers with a sense of tranquility. As one born-again believer stated: *"I
now have total peace, it has changed my life."* Overall, the women convey
a sense that they now are in a secure place and they trust that their future is
in good hands. For example:

> God has become my foundation and source of peace. He is now playing a dif-
> ferent role in my everyday existence. This has been revealed to me by the Holy
> Spirit voice I hear. God's voice told me that I have been commanded to forgive
> others as I had been forgiven.

For both Islam and Christianity, inner peace is obtained through a close
relationship with God. This involves accepting the gift of love from God
and accepting that grace is given and not earned. In this regard, forgiveness
is available to the repentant sinner, allowing them to have peace with God,
which is the very foundation of "inner peace." The Protestant tradition places
the emphasis on each person having the responsibility of speaking directly
with God, who will grant salvation. It is the acceptance of the gift from God
of forgiveness for wrongdoing which is the process whereby inner peace is
experienced. Meditation and prayer is a practice that can bring peace, and this
assumption is borne out:

I meditate, pray, seek answers about God, me and the world. I seek the oneness of my mind with the universal mind (God) having compassion for others and myself, seeking inner peace.

I am Catholic, and I also practice yoga and meditation. Believing in God's goodness keeps my perspective positive and gives me hope. Yoga and meditation give my peace of mind and have taught me how to control and cope with thoughts and emotions as well as tap into my inner strength.

A REALIZED TRANSFORMATION

Over time the women's lives behind bars takes on a transformational process, whereby with their newfound faith they appear deeply committed to adhering to strict codes of living a life predicated upon their faith. By engaging in daily prayer and devotionals, frequent study groups, and official church services, it appeared that these women were constantly searching for ways to grow in their faith. This immense attraction to their "born again" lifestyle enabled women lifers, who were filled with the Holy Spirit, to foresee a fresh start in life where sinful ways of the past are discarded and totally replaced by a new and more conscious way of living. Empowered by religious principles, a more positive attitude emerges, often having a profound impact on behavior enabling the women to maintain a future built on trust.

My belief that all things happen for a reason, and that God knows what we will face even before we do, helps me know that all things good or bad are stepping stones to strengthen us and draw us closer to Him. He is there through it all providing all our needs to help us through all things. . . . I know that as long as I believe and have faith God can do all things.

I'm taking captive my thoughts to make them obedient to Christ Jesus. My calling I believe is to turn what the devil meant for bad to good. Even in knowing the truth of the injustice to me, I'm to let go and let God handle and direct my life. I've surrendered all.

Another way that women lifers tended to draw meaning from their religious convictions is the manner in which they perceived God to play a very active role in their daily lives. They reported experiencing a sense of personal empowerment which enabled them to cope with the daily pressures and disappointments of prison life. One woman expressed: *"God is with me through it all and I know and have him to lean on."* By deferring to a higher being, women experiencing this change in their life stance appeared more likely to listen for God's voice in making day-to-day decisions. For example:

I belong to God, He is absolutely faithful to show me every detail of my day to serve Him. Through prayer, meditation and reading my Bible, the Holy Spirit whispers to my thoughts. My day unfolds beautifully with appreciation of what I am able to do to serve others. I have integrity everywhere I go because of my walk with God.

When the women were asked whether their religion was more important today than it was when they first came to prison, most felt religion had become increasingly important to as they served their time. For example:

I believe that my faith is more important to me today than it has ever been. It is the rock I cling to! It helped me get through the fear and anxiety of those first months but now it sustains me. I grow stronger in my faith and purpose as the days go by. I will survive this trial and live to rejoice with my family again.

My faith is so important because I am an active breathing member of Christ's Church and it fills up my days with hopes and dreams of one day being let out of prison. My faith is just as strong today as it was the day I surrendered my sinful self to God's call as a young teenager.

Lifers also regarded religion to be a critical vehicle through which they could expunge deeply entrenched feelings of guilt and instill in themselves a sense of hope for their future.[18] As one lifer observed: *"Because God is just as much here as he is anywhere. Even in a place like this, it is possible to walk with him."* Over time, several individuals recalled having learned to use their faith to support them by looking beyond their statuses as serious offenders:

I was 23 years old when I discovered the reality of God. That was the defining moment of my life. It changed me forever, for the good. I wasn't a bad person, but my decision to follow Christ put me on a rugged journey of emotional healing, personal accomplishment, and deep, deep satisfaction and happiness. My relationship with God is just as vital and alive as it ever has been. I stay hungry for God.

For those who are sincere about their faith, religion also provides the motivation to live for the future rather than in the past. Prisons are a most unique environment filled with individuals seeking to overcome their life's failures not experienced in the wider society. Locked away from the mainstream, this quest to amend one's ways in life directly shapes how religion is portrayed as prisoners seek to ease the pain, shame, and guilt associated with offender status. Religion is a means through which those serving life in prison pin their hopes as they seek redemption and the opportunity to forgive and to be forgiven:

My religious beliefs help me in times of feeling trapped daily in negative prison life. It keeps me from the bondage of regret, anger, and bitterness. I just stay connected with God and tell him all. He gives me peace when I'm troubled, feeling self-pity. At first, I used religion more as a crutch to cope, but over time my faith deepened and I saw the big picture. My religion is now the foundation of how I live my life.

In an attempt to further explain the chain of events leading to their incarceration, some women put this experience in a broader "my being here is just a part of God's plan for me" religious context. For example:

I understand that God has a purpose in my life. That He intervened in my life by allowing me to make the decision I did and resulting in being incarcerated. I find peace in knowing that even now I can still be used, make something of my life.

Despite their past lives filled with the commission of crime and other ungodly behaviors, women lifers, in general, reported having overcome their initial disinterest in religious concerns to view God as watching over and protecting them while they served their respective sentences. Several women stressed they had reached phases in their lives where the presence of religious beliefs were essential for coping with the loss of freedom and autonomy that are central to the prison experience. Situated in an environment surrounded by the uncertainty of when they will ever again experience life as a law-abiding citizen, the use of religious principles to maintain a sense of hope is a crucial element in providing lifers the strength to carry on.

I am a believer in Christ and a woman of faith, otherwise I'm sure I would have ended it all years ago. It's not what I'd have chosen but God's agenda and I've gone through the "God is this what you've laid out for me?" I was honest with him about my desire to be free, and that desire is just as strong now as when I was jailed. Then I prayed that if it was his will that this be my earthly home, then please let the walls mean nothing to me.

Another woman who recognized participation in religious activities as providing her with a mental outlook that, unlike many other concerns in her life, could not be revoked shared:

Coping with prison life tests your religion. Imagine being forced to interact with others—some of whom are less than desirable company. The peace of my beliefs helps me to cope by being able to meditate and separate my thoughts from the chaos others tend to bring. Religion in all its forms and names brings faith. Faith and the hope of a freer tomorrow are what keep us all going.

Women lifers, in particular, highly praised their faith as helping them come to terms with, resolve, and overcome any feelings of hopelessness that routinely accompany isolation from the world at large. Given that life-sentenced offenders speak passionately about the states of despair they experience when estranged from family and friends, indifference by correctional staff, being misunderstood by their fellow offenders, the possibility of spending the remaining days of one's life in prison can be a huge burden to carry.[19] In the words of two women, it is through the grace of God they seek redemption:

> We all make tracks through some valley of failure! I am disappointed for so many, many different reasons yet I know only God holds a redeeming hand for any of us and the mess we make of our lives. So, I pray for grace abundantly and I know I'm not the only one looking to see what God is going to bring out of this or other concerns of my heart.

> Even though I'm in prison my basic needs are always met through God. And when things around me and my situation starts to feel hopeless and out of control, I know God still loves me and has my future mapped out and everything is going to be okay.

SUMMARY

We discovered that those who come to prison often confront religious questions for the first time in their lives. Religion very quickly becomes the saving grace for many who upon entry are experiencing tremendous pain and suffering. Not only are they grieving the losses from the outside world, but also may be experiencing pains of guilt and remorse as they contemplate their fate behind bars. The narratives shared here affirm the importance that religion plays in enriching the lives of this population of women serving long sentences. Additionally, these stories provide valuable insights into how this group of women used their strong faith as a resource to counteract the emotional distress that accompanies the painful experience of serving a life sentence. Locked away from loved ones and with nothing but time on their hands, it is apparent that most of the women while reflecting on their mistakes began searching for a new pathway that provides some sense of hope and redemption. This chapter confirmed that women lifers found participation in religious activities as new opportunities to establish supportive networks, which has reduced depression, anger, and aggression.[20]

Since the inception of the prison paradigm, religion has shown to serve many valuable functions, especially for women serving life sentences. Not only does religion provide a code of ethics by which these women live, it also provides a worldview that integrates the present with meaning and the future with a sense of hope. The women shared numerous stories of how their religious beliefs served as an important buffer to assist them in facing health deterioration, family losses, and other crises in their lives. But more importantly, the religion they professed served as a guiding hand getting them through "*one day at a time.*" For these women who have spent the majority of their adult lives behind bars, religion plays an important role in transforming their social world into a homelike setting. This community-based environment is made possible as those steeped in religious convention focus more intently on forgiveness, thankfulness, and the opportunity to show their love and support for each other. As the prison community awakens each day at the five o'clock headcount, hope rises simultaneously as these God-fearing women eagerly await a new day to discover and utilize their full potential.

NOTES

1. Clear and Sumter, "Prisoners, Prison and Religion."
2. Levitt and Loper, "The Influence of Religious Participation."
3. Kerley and Copes, "Keepin' My Mind Right."
4. Dye, Aday, Farney, and Raley, "The Rock I Cling To."
5. Maruna, Wilson, and Curran, "Why God Is Often Found behind Bars."
6. Kerley, *Religious Faith in Correctional Contexts.*
7. Turesky and Schultz, "Spirituality among Older Adults."
8. Aday, Krabill, and Deaton-Owens, "Religion in the Lives of Older Women Serving Life in Prison."
9. Leigey and Ryder, "The Pains of Permanent Imprisonment."
10. Aday, Krabill, and Deaton-Owens, "Religion in the Lives of Older Women."
11. Kerley, *Religious Faith in Correctional Contexts.*
12. Schneider and Feltey, "No Matter What Has Been Done Wrong."
13. George, *A Woman Doing Life.*
14. Maruna, Wilson, and Curran, "Why God Is Often Found behind Bars."
15. Aday and Krabill, *Women Aging in Prison.*
16. Deaton-Owens, Aday, and Wahidin, "The Effect of Health and Penal Harm on Aging Female Prisoners' Views of Dying in Prison."
17. Thomas and Zaitzow, "Conning or Conversion?"
18. George, *A Woman Doing Life.*
19. Johnson and McGunigall-Smith, "Life without Parole."
20. Levitt and Loper, "The Influence of Religious Participation."

Chapter 9

Life beyond Bars

Hopes, Expectations, and Fears for Release

"There is really no experience with the parole process. You are given a letter stating you are not ready for society."

"We are all struggling with the same issues. Mentally we try to grasp the concept that our lives are in 5 people's hands (the parole board) that don't know us at all. They read papers in a file and don't meet with us or talk with us at all . . . the amount of time that the board is asking a lifer to do, letting them get their hopes up when it's a parole hearing time, then denying the lifer 5 or 8 more years, that feels like mental abuse . . . and not allowing the lifer to take classes . . . a lifer is expected to rehabilitate themselves and don't know where to start."

When women initially receive their life sentence, many feel their lives are over and have no hope for parole or going home. One of the female lifers said she adjusted to prison with little trouble because she *"accepted the fact that I will most likely die here."* Others may expect lifers to die in prison, or think that they should, as the ultimate punishment for their crimes. This sentiment is clearly expressed in a June 1, 1998, news article which stated:

There's a popular misconception that life in prison doesn't mean all of one's natural life. In just the last year, there are 21 Georgia lifers who are no longer around to tell you otherwise. If they could, they'd let you know that parole for a life sentence is a rare commodity.[1]

When lifers do come up for parole, victim's families, prosecutors and judges, and the public often oppose a lifer's release. The reality is that most people serving sentences of life in prison with the possibility of parole will eventually be released back into society after serving between eighteen–twenty-nine years behind bars.[2] Estimates for those who are eligible for parole and release from U.S. prisons are as high as 70 percent of all "lifers."[3] One percent or fewer will commit a new offense after being released.[4]

In order to "adjust" to a life in prison and because of their disconnections to the outside world, lifers tend to focus on surviving what is inside the walls. Little attention, whether for self-preservation or lack of opportunities for lifers, is spent preparing lifers for getting out of prison. Instead, lifers are expected to wait or rehabilitate themselves. Indeed, lifers and long-term inmates relay accounts of change, redemption, and better selves/lives during and following their incarceration.[5]

While lifers may anxiously anticipate, hope, dream, and even feel ready for release, in what ways have/are they prepared? After serving such lengthy periods behind bars, what are their expectations and fears about life after prison? In this chapter, we detail these expectations and worries as women describe what their lives look like after their life sentence. We start with a discussion of the parole process in Georgia, continue with a description and explanation for women's barriers to reentry including housing, employment, stigma, health issues, family relationships and support, dealing with freedom, and a changed world that has passed them by, and conclude with a discussion of the ways the prison system and programs within prison do or do not prepare women lifers for life beyond bars.

THE PAROLE PROCESS: *"WHY AM I STILL HERE?"*

All of the women we surveyed were sentenced with the possibility of parole; thus, the parole process marks the first step for women lifers for a life beyond bars. Of the ninety-four women we interviewed at follow-up in 2018, all of whom had served at least fifteen years of their life sentence, seventy-four had been reviewed by the parole board. The majority of the women had been denied one to four times, with a smaller number having been denied parole five, six, and ten times. At the time of the follow-up survey, fewer than five of the women lifers had been granted parole and were waiting on release dates. Over the past eight years, between the initial survey and follow-up, approximately fifty women lifers had been released on parole, with more of these occurring in recent years. However, far more cases are denied than granted parole.[6] It is important to note that while more women lifers are "going home" than in the past, these releases are not on par with the numbers of new women receiving life sentences, which according to current law means no opportunity for parole until thirty years served.[7]

Although the state of Georgia outlines the basic procedure, the parole process applies differently to those with life sentences, and much is unknown about how the parole board makes decisions regarding lifers.[8] According to women lifers we surveyed, the process lacks transparency, and as one woman stated: *"There is no experience or process . . . it is a mystery."* Uncertainties, anxieties, and frustrations with the parole process and board are described as *"traumatic," "mental abuse,"* and like being in *"a sea of hopelessness."* Another described the process as *"just a mind game or roller coaster ride. You get your hopes up only to be let down. Even when you do all the things you can to better yourself . . . The crime never changes, but we grow and change, we grow up."* These ups and downs, and frustrations are felt in this woman's experience. Of the parole process she said:

> It has been very negative. My first parole eligibility was in 2012, after serving 20 years. I had an exceptional institutional conduct and my co-defendant had the complete opposite with gang membership and new violent charges he got in prison. We both got a 4-year set off in spite of our opposite conduct. The warden did a special parole consideration for me. I was granted parole Feb. 2, 2013. Then in May my parole was cancelled due to opposition by the victim's ex-wife. Then I got two more set offs in spite of my parent's pleas for help due to their health. My mom then died and my dad was forced into a nursing home because I am in prison.

One explanation for these feelings of frustration and hopelessness is that the entire process is "on paper" (now all electronic), and women never meet the parole board for face-to-face hearings. As these women explained:

> The parole process works with indiscriminate paper and there is no personal touches or even any real consideration. We get form letters denying our parole based on "due to the nature and circumstances of your charges" which could be a woman defending her life or some other "accident."

> A parole summary is done by a counselor confirming my parole address and groups completed with whatever comments needed by the counselor and faxed to the board. I have never had a face to face interview for parole when I come up. I have been denied parole on my summary that is sent down by the parole board.

Depersonalization defines the parole process. The whole of these women's lives is reduced to a summary of their crime and how "they are not ready for society." Denials take the same form, a very brief letter—approximately two sentences—which is delivered by mail or through a counselor. According to women's accounts, the process leaves them feeling like less than a human being. Many of the women seek only to be viewed as a person, not just a crime. They also want the chance to share their stories and be heard by the board members, who typically have more access to hear from the victim's families. This fifty-two-year old woman who had been denied parole twice said: *"The parole board doesn't know the person. I have done everything positive in 18 years but yet was turned down again. I think that the parole board need to know who we are, not just know who the victim's families are."* Another woman, similar in age and time served [fifty-nine-year-old, eighteen years served] made a similar comment: *"I would like to be looked at by the parole board as a person. See my changes and accomplishments. Circumstances of the crime will never change but I have."*

Women lifers desire more out of the parole process, including being able to talk to the parole board, meet with the members face to face, and have *"more interaction with the people who have a hand in deciding our fate."* This woman explained:

> I think it [parole board] would be more understanding on letting inmates return to society if someone would actually come and talk with the inmate and see the changes they have made instead of just going by a piece of paper that is submitted by a counselor who isn't even around us on a daily basis to see the changes.

Part of the mystery of the process is not knowing the real reasons for denial or what it takes to be granted parole. This woman stated: *"I find that the reason they give to everyone is always due to the severity of your crime your being denied. The severity of the crime will never change. So how will they ever find reason for parole?"* Quoting the language, "circumstances of the crime," which is given as rationale by the board for denying parole, women lifers emphasize how they cannot change the crime or the past. They work to change themselves, but feel the parole board is not set up to take these changes into account. A thirty-eight-year old Hispanic women, after serving sixteen years and receiving two denials, explained the following about lifers and parole:

> With the exception of few, we are regarded as the waiters. No matter what is offered, lifers can wait. Hey we got time, right? Regarding the few, as a whole, we are not seen. Most judgements are made individually; the fact that there are not written guidelines to complete for parole we are consistently denied parole due to the nature of our crime. The past cannot be changed but we as people can. The changes we make as people are ignored because of the past and we are robbed of a future.

Another woman questioned whether these changes even matter to the parole board:

> I would like to know if my conduct here, will it really make a difference to the parole board once I'm eligible for parole? Will they actually take this in or I'll

just be a #, instead of someone; they will say let's give her another chance, or deny me that chance?

Recently granted parole after twenty-five years in prison and three parole reviews, this woman shared a similar thought: *"It feels like the parole board uses a magic # as their voting process. After serving 20 years I received a 2-year set off. Then after serving 23 years I received a 1 year set off."*

The only real certainty that woman lifers have about the parole process is that set offs are the expectation. Set offs are denials of parole and the length of time before a woman is eligible for another parole review. These can be up to eight years for Georgia lifers. One woman who had served since 1993 told us how she received two eight-year denials followed by a third one-year denial. This pattern was common among women lifers who had experienced repeated denials:

The very first review was 2014, at which time, I was denied 3 years. I was reviewed the second time in 2018, at which time, I was denied 2 years. I know that it could have been a lot longer of a denial, so I am grateful. [served seventeen years of life sentence]

I expected a denial on my first parole and I was half way about the second one. Now this upcoming third parole, expect to make it. Still, lots of anxiety. [sentenced at age twenty-six, served twenty-seven years]

This same woman continued describing her experience, which reiterates many of the themes regarding lifers and parole:

This process gives much anxiety. I am an individual who has an excellent infraction record, have taken advantage of every opportunity and have created positive opportunities and outlets for others. Everything required of me I've done and went above but it seems the most impactful to the process is the victim's family.

The ups and downs, cycles of hope and despair, frustrations of denials, not being treated like people, and living with the opposition of victim's families are coupled with the knowledge that there is no support for them behind bars after being denied parole. Women lifers *"deal with this on our own which it affects us emotionally."* Another specifically mentioned how *"they don't have a group for dealing with being denied as I know of."* She added: *"It does something to you on the inside."*

Based on repeated reviews and fewer years set off, the women lifers tend to think "next time" their parole will be granted. Over 85 percent of the women lifers who have served fifteen years or more will be eligible for either a first or subsequent parole review within the next two years (2018–2020). Seeing the few women lifers granted parole and "going home" gives them hope that they will also get out. This hope is balanced by the worries about what their lives will look like after getting out of prison.

One of the more common worries women have after getting out also concerns parole—first, will they get it and then, can they meet the expectations to maintain parole. About half worry at least sometimes about these struggles with 22 percent having these worries often or always. Given the "parole paradox," women's concerns about maintaining parole are valid; when lifers do return to prison, it is most often for a technical violation of their parole conditions.[9] However, only about 5 percent of the women reported some worry about returning to prison. Many shared this thought, and other research supports these conclusions, that those who serve long-term sentences have a very low risk of recidivism. We heard this in the women's accounts:

> I hate to see a lifer return here but it is rarer than the average inmate who are in/out multiple times (life on the installment plan). Most lifers are family violence—we aren't criminals. Why degrade a human who is less likely ever to reoffend? We should be let out!

GOING HOME: *"I'M NOT TOO PROUD TO SAY 'I NEED HELP'"*

Women lifer's top concerns after parole involve their housing/living situation, meeting their and their family's financial needs and obtaining employment. The vast majority of women plan to live with family members—24.7 percent

CASE HISTORY 9.1: A KICK IN THE TEETH

"The first time I came up for parole was in 1999. They gave me a denial of 8 years." Since this time, Darlene, age forty-nine, has spent over twenty-five years in prison, and has been denied parole four additional times with set offs of 5, 3, 2, and then 1 year. In doing her best with her time, Darlene has taken numerous classes to improve herself and her chances for success if she gets out. For eighteen months she lived in the "Faith and Character Dorm" attending all mandatory and voluntary groups, graduated from the statewide lifer's support group, and obtained computer skills to a level where she became a teaching aide for the class. She is an avid reader, artist, painter, and writer, and mentor to other women lifers. With "glowing" reports for institutional conduct, repeated denials are hard to understand, and it is easy to give up hope. *"For some reason the parole board seems to think that people like me who do their best to stay out of trouble, not just because we want to go home, but because its who we choose to be, are just manipulating the system. It's kind of a kick in the teeth to find out that it doesn't matter to anyone though."*

with parents, 22.6 percent with siblings, 15.1 percent with children, 8.6 percent with a spouse, 10.8 percent with other family such as aunts/uncles and cousins, and 10.8 percent with friends. Relatively few of these women worry about reconnecting with family after getting out. They are satisfied with their family relationships and have maintained or increased contact with at least some of their family over time. The emphasis they place on the importance of family support (or lack of) for life after prison is clearly communicated.

One of the no-win situations women face with the parole process is the requirement for housing. Those who do not have family or places to live if released often will not receive parole. Currently facing this situation, the woman said: *"I would need an address—I have no housing or funds—so what scares me the most is maybe the parole board will not release me due to me not having anywhere to go."* Even among women with housing plans, they recognize this issue and note *"a lot of them* [lifers] *still here because they don't have no place to go."*

For women lifers, transitional housing programs are essential to getting out on parole, and for successful reentry. About 18 percent of the women plan to enter a transitional housing program. While not all women need (or have access to) a formal transitional program—12 percent indicate they will live alone when they get out of prison—for others this is their best chance to succeed after being cut off from society for such lengthy periods. As this woman stated:

Prior to receiving my parole papers in May 2018 I didn't much dwell on freedom. I felt it was too soon to think on it. Now I have a plan. . . . I'm not too proud to say that I need help. I believe once I do this 15-month program I'll be more prepared to reenter society.

Of her plans to go to a transitional center (T.C.), another women said: *"I know I'll have nothing and will have to work to build my life back up. . . . Without going to the T.C., I'd never have a chance."* These programs assist women in not only their housing needs, but also finding good employment, saving money before living on their own, transportation, and easing back into society which has changed.

Women with plans for transitional housing, unlike those who plan to live alone, have received more opportunities within prison to prepare for getting out. Based on their next parole hearing date, they will likely be out within the year. Unlike the majority of women, nearly 88 percent have participated in a reentry program. They are more likely to have taken college courses or earned a college degree while in prison. They are also more likely to rate their health and mental health as excellent or good compared to other women lifers.

Women lifers planning to enter transitional housing as well as those whose current plans are to live alone have family members who are still living, but connections with and supports from family are not available to them. One woman speaking about her family said: *"Once you are released most of your family is gone and you have nothing or nobody to help you back into society."* Over half of these women indicate that contact with family has become less frequent over time. Close to 90 percent of the women lifers who will not live with family after getting out are not satisfied with their family relationships. This is a very different experience compared to those who are satisfied with their family relationships and supports and plan to live with family after getting out of prison. As expressed by one of these women: *"I don't fear release, mainly because I have stability with family. But if I didn't have that, I would worry about everything."*

MAKING UP FOR LOST TIME

Regardless of the amount of family support, all of the women lifers voiced concerns about the importance of family in their adjustments to and transitions out of prison. Even among women with family support, their crimes, life sentences, and time separated from family have affected their relationships over time. As one woman described her situation: *"Many of my family members have placed their lives before my incarceration. Pretty much moved on with their lives."* For family members, life goes on. Among older women lifers who, after their release from prison, attempt to reconnect with their now grown children or remaining siblings, there are challenges and changes to these familial relationships. Now in her late fifties, and after twenty-three years behind bars, this one said: *"Life kind of stopped for me, not for them. They are very busy people."* For her and many other women, family support is not there when they are released. In other cases, after being insulated from the outside world and *"blocking it as being not real,"* upon release women must fully confront the emotions and realities of lost family members (i.e., death or distance) and changed people including themselves and their family.

On the other hand, women may celebrate and share in the excitement of meeting new additions to the family including their children's spouses, grandchildren, and great-grandchildren. Within existing and new relationships, some women after their life sentence expect a "new life" or "new beginning" with their families. This includes attempts to "make up for lost time" or "make the most of the remaining time" with grandparents and parents who have aged and may be in poor health or at the end of their lives as well as reconnecting with their now grown children. Incarcerated for life at the age of thirty-nine, this fifty-seven-year-old lifer shared her plans for reconnecting with family after getting out:

> My grandmother is 95 years old. I want to spend time with her along with sons and 17 grands and 4 great grands. And, enjoy my life. I own my house and have a place to go home to. Getting out of prison will be like a new beginning for me. I have done 19 years just wanting God to let me go home.

Another elaborated on a similar plan of how she hoped to get back time she had lost with her family and kids:

> My life after serving life looks beautiful to me. A beach and sand waiting surround me. My family and friends to welcome me, a career to establish me a new beginning. I'm full of hope. My base is set high. I've lost 20 years and I entered doing all that I can to create a wonderful life for myself and get back with my family and kid's [*sic*] the time we have lost. My life before prison was good, but being I was a spouse of domestic violence made it all became very bad. So I was happy to finally be free from it even if I was in prison at least I wasn't being hurt anymore. Not the way I would have hoped for to go out of it but you never know what someone else is thinking and their plans for you. I nearly died that day. So I'm thankful for every day I'm alive and try to live each day as if it is my last.

Despite the hope and excitement of celebrated reunions, there will also be old wounds and hurts felt by both the women and their family members that they must deal with after getting out of prison. Some hurts and damaged relationships existed prior to their incarceration, while some developed or were exacerbated by confinement and detachment from family. For these women, they feel they cannot *"get back the lost time"* or *"build a loving relationship."* One woman shared:

> In my case, the narrative my children were told concerning the circumstances that landed me in prison defines who they believe me to be. . . . This misconception has proven to be the wall that prevents my children and I the opportunity to build a loving relationship. No matter my efforts and accomplishments, my family, it seems do not see my positive change.

Another said:

> [My] children don't have anything to do with me—stepmother of my children turned my children away from me. [My] brother don't have anything to do with me. Both parents [are] dead. I can't give back all that precious time I was away.

Still hoping for that chance to build a relationship, one woman added: *"My sons are still not communicating* [with me]*, but God will heal this in His time* [smiley face]. *"*

Complicating these existing relationship problems as well as their ability to reconnect with family after release is the fact that many women are from out of state or have most of their family support from members who are out of state. Physical and the accompanying emotional distance from family is attributed to several sources by the women. For example, one woman shared: *"I got married at 18 and moved to Georgia. My family disowned me."* In another context, a woman described her move to Georgia: *"I'm from Ohio. I fled an abusive relationship to come live with friends and start over with my 3-year-old."* Although not "disowned" by her family, this woman shared her experience with family distance: *"My family in Miami has distanced themselves from me. I've come to terms with this. It's hard but we must go on."* A final example is also of a woman from Ohio. She said: *"I am from Ohio. I felt suffocated and needed to get away. Rebellion caused me to leave. The problem after leaving prison is that being separated for so long we are now strangers to each other which causes conflict that may have difficulty being resolved."*

As these women describe, the emotional distance can be as difficult to overcome as the physical distance. Being separated from families for such lengthy periods of time, women lifers question the ways can they relate to their family members after getting out of prison. Of her parents and sibling, one woman lifer said: *"It's been 24 ½ years now. They don't know me anymore."* In one of her letters, one woman told us: *"I will not fit in at all with family though they are going to try to welcome me with open arms. Other than blood, we have no common frame of reference."* She added: *"That goes for my high school and college friends who write . . . my community will be the people I've come to love during my incarceration, but I can't live with them according to the Parole Board."* Even with family support, there are barriers to building relationships with family who will never be able to understand the experiences of life behind bars. This is especially true for juvenile lifers who *"grew up"* in prison.

The unfortunate thing is that I have been in here longer than I have been free, so this has become my home in my memories so much more than my real home when I was free. In essence, I feel that this is all I know in terms of life experience. . . . Getting out of prison after serving life, I imagine is a difficult transition especially in adjusting to be reintegrated back into the family and other social relationships. . . . It is difficult to connect with my family when they come to visit just because I feel so far removed being in here and this is a totally different world from the one out there. I hope that it doesn't take long to shed that and feel welcome and accepted back into society.

Women like her, who were sentenced at age fifteen, have family support now, but prison life is all they have known. For over twenty years, interactions with their families have been as an incarcerated person. Now as an adult, relationship dynamics between parents and children have changed and are very different than they were as a pre-incarceration teen.

Whether mothering as they would have hoped or having a stable, violence-free intimate relationship, many of the women lifers, regardless of their age at sentence, missed important milestones in their life-course including having children and getting married. Is it too late for them to experience these major life events? Are they too old once they are released after a life sentence in prison? For juvenile lifers and younger women who entered prison before becoming mothers, they may never have a chance to have biological children as all of their childbearing years were spent behind bars. As these women shared, their *"new beginnings"* involve questions, hopes, and plans for getting married and being a *"great mother,"* and are another way they envision making up for lost time:

> My life to me looks good. I have my kids and grandkids who are waiting on me, and they have been my biggest supports. I am blessed to have a job waiting on me. My concern is I've never been married, and I think I'm too old to get married, but I do want to get married.

> I would love to get out of prison and start a new life for myself and be a great mother and grandmother and friend to my family. I thank God for keeping me alive to see that day.

> Life after prison? Easy freedom to do what I want without permission. Having a stable job, getting married, have a life without feeling like I'm always falling on eggshells and slipping on glass. Freedom means a new journey to establish myself after looking in the mirror of my past self for so long.

Although these women voiced hopes for marriage, mothering, and other *"new journeys,"* many women who experienced domestic abuse do not hold these same expectations. While some may be able to recognize *"red flags"* now, others are *"still angry"* and *"still do not trust men."*

GETTING A JOB: *"I'M NO LONGER THAT GIRL"* AND *"WHAT ARE MY OPTIONS?"*

While admitting there will be difficulties living in society after being incarcerated for a long period of time, the overall message from women lifers when asked about their life after a life sentence is one of survival and success. In fact, one woman stated: *"This has been a hard journey, but I know that I have a purpose. I have survived prison."* Expressions of excitement and determination are more pronounced as they relay their plans than are their fears or worry. A dominant reason given for their anticipated successes beyond prison was their perceptions of personal transformation—*"I am a better person now"* or *"I am not longer that girl."* This is particularly the case when women feel prepared for careers and employment after prison, as clearly articulated by this woman:

> My life after prison will be full of hard work determination in obtaining my goals. I plan to use what I've learned as a vet assistant to further my career in that field. I hope to one day own my own chain of doggie daycares to be a success for me and my daughters. As before coming to prison I had not accomplished nothing by dropping out of school and getting pregnant, and getting into trouble, but now I have a positive outlook for my future and the home life I want to have. I have family and friends support with anything I may need upon release. I plan to work hard achieving what I need to be productive. I've grown into a mature woman. I'm no long that girl without goals and dreams of her own.

Besides working with animals, others mentioned specific plans for employment whether regaining pre-sentence careers or ones they have trained for while in prison. These include continuing in the nursing field; landscaping businesses; cleaning businesses; writing and publishing books, stories, and poems they have written while in prison; and opening/working in agencies to help others such as at-risk youth, homeless, domestic violence survivors, and others transitioning out of prison.

Only a few of the women lifers were willing to share with us their thoughts how these *"enthusiastic goals and future plans"* may not match their realities when (and if) they get out of prison. It was clear that these were goals and future plans that the parole board expected to hear, not their fears and worries about getting out. However, amid these varied goals and pursuits, two themes are evident. Many realize the struggles they face as an "ex" and anticipate/avoid this stigma by planning to own their own businesses—for example, doggie daycare/groomers or cleaning businesses—or working to "pay it forward" helping other stigmatized groups. Speaking about both themes, one woman described her expectations:

> I expect to put in very long days working and catching up, paying bills, and also more importantly "paying forward" to make the world not only a better place but make sure that no one ever has to go through what I have been through. I wish to work with veterans and their families. There are precious few support organizations for female veterans and/or female felons. I wish to change

this. There is to be expected stigma related to be a felon. This will have to be overcome as well as my sixty-six years of age. I intend to go to work even if I have to start up my own business. I have to have investment funds to start my own businesses. Employers will have to take a leap of faith to employ this older disabled veteran. I am in vocation school upgrading my computer skills to make sure employers get the most for dollars that they invest in me.

In addition to the worry they *"will be overlooked because of* [their] *prison history,"* women lifers, especially those in their mid- to late forties, are concerned about their ability to work and provide for themselves financially when they are released. Missed milestones of career and saving for retirement are common concerns. A forty-five-year-old woman lifer who is a certified dog trainer as well as warehouse and forklift certified said:

I will work in anything to support myself and create a positive life to be proud of for myself and society. [I worry] that I've been incarcerated so long and have nothing, and that I don't have enough time before I'm too old to build a life and savings for old age.

Another woman shared similar worries:

I have a good support system so I feel confident about my re-entry for the most part. I worry that I was just 22 when I came and I'll be 49 this year. I have no retirement plan and I worry about my quality of life after 50 and into old age.

Older women also mentioned health worries including arthritis and mobility issues as specific barriers to employment. Imagining her life after prison, this seventy-year-old woman questioned her options:

I can only imagine. After 21 years in prison, I believe that I will enjoy a true sense of freedom, being 70 years old. I can sit back and rest which I never did before my being brought to prison at 50 years old . . . but yet I consider myself as being . . . BLESSED. And to speak truthfully, health issues are our biggest concern. My family and social relationships were limited before this confinement. I worked all the time, so I really can't explain what is essential. I'm a maid. I'm good at it even at my age—my health is an issue . . . what are my options?

As detailed in the chapter on health issues, women lifers face chronic and age-related health problems which affect their quality of life and physical abilities. Once released from prison, women carry these problems with them, which compounds reentry concerns and their likelihood of success. Some lack resources or proper medical care, access to important medications, and ability to work. A forty-three-year-old woman who was in excellent health asked:

When they [DOC] hold them for more than 20 years, what type of health are they in when they leave? What kind of job can they do? How can parole expect them to be productive in the world when they are leaving old in wheel chairs, in walkers, with health issues. This concerns me.

One personal example of these types of concerns is shared by this forty-nine-year-old in poor health:

My concern at this present time is my health. About 1 year ago I was deathly ill. I had a 47 lb. mass removed from my stomach and I have to wear this hernia truss because they cut me so deep I continue to blow holes in my stomach walls (hernias). So once I am released it will be hard to obtain a job. Right now, I'm medically unassigned and have lifting profiles, etc. . . . Upon my release, I would have to consider SS disability.

While none of the women lifers we interviewed had plans to go from prison to a nursing home, those in poor health, with disabilities, or advanced age will not be able to work, provide for themselves financially, and will have to depend on support from family, if able, or governmental assistance. Most will have no retirement income or any sort of financial safety net.

A WORLD THAT'S PASSED US BY

Prison friendships are very important to women lifers, but worries about missing friendships and prison life after getting out of prison, fitting in with those on the outside, or dealing with regained freedom—between 7–10 percent mention worry about these issues—are not emphasized by them. However, they do worry about being out of touch with the world and dealing with the changes in society since they were first incarcerated: *"I've never seen a cell phone, the Internet, debit cards, things people take for granted. We'll be thrown out into a world that's passed us by."*

A woman lifer, sixteen years old at her sentence, considered her reentry *"an exciting journey"* but said, *"I have a lot to learn and experience."* Elaborating on how much there is to learn, this woman explained: *"I was 15 when I came in so I don't know how to drive or live on my own in the world. I will be basically starting from that frame of mind in age and I will have a lot of obstacles to overcome."* She was not worried as much about new technology because she had taken courses and worked with computers, keeping up with these changes. Most women lifers do not have these opportunities and do feel the world has passed them by. Fears about the world outside of prison, whether technology or freedom, often reside alongside with their plans for release. As one woman shared:

Life after a life sentence just starts a new section of our sentence. We've been gone so long so much has changed. Most of us grew up here. There is no world outside the barbed wire. Any world wide web or streaming doesn't exist. When released we come as newborns from a cave to a modern city. Think Fred Flintstone dropped into the Jetson's house.

A few of the women who are approaching their actual release dates noted in their plans/preparations secured access to clothing and food vouchers. However, women's reentry worries include *"small stuff"* such as clothing and shopping. Other than commissary orders, women lifers have not purchased clothing, hygiene, or food products of their own choosing. For twenty or more years, they have been told what to wear on their bodies, what to use to clean and care for their bodies, and what food to eat. These initial "free-world" losses become new worries for reentry. In dealing with freedom, choice, and lack of structure, women lifers worry about "overindulging" in free-world food at one extreme and living frugally at the other. Aware of these struggles, this women said: *"I know there will be a lot of readjusting from being within a structured environment for so long but being aware of this will help me to prepare for that."* Other women lifers, though, are not aware and not prepared for this type of freedom.

READINESS FOR RELEASE: *"THERE'S NOT A LOT OF HELP"*

An additional theme central to women's expectations and fears about getting out of prison is their tendency to recognize these struggles, whether with housing, family relationships, employment, or a changed world, for other women lifers, but not for themselves. This woman's statement is one example:

I think a lot of women with life sentences have to deal with lack of family support. Many of them have lost loved ones. Also, many of them become institutionalized where this becomes their home.

Other women preface their responses with phrases such as *"I've been lucky"* or *"I have family support"* but others do not. Implied is the perception that "those" women have something to worry about.

I've been lucky to have people and a support system out there but most people I feel are being set up for failure because there's not a lot of help in or out.

I'm lucky, I've been able to participate in a lot, but generally long-term offenders are not able to avail themselves to a lot of programs due to their time. They

are putting long-term offenders at a disadvantage because they're not being
trained to hold down a job in this new world we'll enter.

These comparisons with "others" are interesting because many of the women
lifers felt that they could not compare their experience to those of other inmates, or they do not wish to compare themselves. It is the case, however, and
the aim of this book, to demonstrate that women lifers are different than other
women in prison, not just in their pathways or sentences but in the struggles
that will face them if they get out.

On the one hand, compared to other women in prison, women lifers felt
that *"we are treated all the same—BAD."* They are *"just numbers"* or inmates to staff, and they are all expected to follow the rules and directives of
those with authority. In contrast, a few women lifers felt that they are treated
better than short-time inmates because they are more reliable and responsible.
They represent stability for the institution as they work assigned details,
maintain the facility, and carry the collective institutional memory from year
to year. Many have survived policy and administrative changes over decades
behind bars. With high rates of staff turnover, women lifers have more years
of prison work experience than most staff. While this history may be beneficial for the prison, women lifers' institutional presence is taken for granted.

However, the most common comparison to other women in prison we
heard from women lifers was: *"We are treated worse because of our time."*
In their own words: *"Treat us like we are the lowest of the lowest"* and *"People with life sentences feel like nobody cares about them. They're just here
to rot . . . put on the back burner."* Whether intentional, indicative of penal
harm, or a practical solution to the large numbers of incarcerated persons and
limited programming, women lifers are left with a lot of time and few opportunities, especially in educational, vocational training, and therapy programs.
They often hear *"you've not allowed"* programs until you have two years or
less left on your sentence. For a woman lifer, this could be more than twenty
years. Because of their indeterminate sentences, most do not know when they
have two years left. In addition to the "less than 2-year rule," *"They* [prison
officials/state] *don't want to allow lifers to take trades to better themselves.
They tell lifers that they got to have their first denial* [parole] *before taking
a vocational trade."* Based on these "rules" women lifers are internalizing
the message from prison administrators that educating or bettering their lives
in prison and beyond is a waste of time. In response, one woman lifer said:
*"Don't look at our time and feel that educating us more would be a waste of
time."* After serving eighteen years this fifty-year-old lifer agreed:

They don't like to educate "lifers" b/c of our time—they feel it is a waste of time
since we don't know when we'll get out. But it leaves us feeling left behind. I've

never seen the internet, cell phones, email, etc. Things people take for granted and are used in everyday life. Re-entering a world that's left us behind can be challenging and fearful.

Another woman added:

Allow us to get in any academic trade just like everybody else. If we want to learn and better ourselves, why not? I have my GED and would love to learn graphic arts or customer service, but I can't because of the time I'm serving.

Education and Vocational Programs

Among the women we interviewed who served over fifteen years in prison, about 15 percent still do not have their GED; some cannot read or write. Obtaining a GED, however, is the most common type of education training offered to women lifers.

A small percentage are able to take college courses by correspondence. On-site at one of the women's prisons, Life University now offers a full associate's degree in Positive Human Development and Social Change.

Right now, I am enrolled in Life University through the Chillon Project. This degree has changed my life in so many ways and opened my mind to a world of possibilities in creating change within myself as well as in the world. I know that most people out there probably feel that inmates should not receive an education, but we are still human and desire for opportunities to prove we are worthy of another chance as productive members of society.

A very selective and competitive application process,[10] the program is not limited to only women with life sentences. In 2016, approximately one-third of the fifteen-seat cohort accepted into the program were women lifers.

In general, though, because of their time, women lifers lack opportunities for education. About 40 percent indicated they have not participated in education programs—they already have a degree, or they are not eligible—even after fifteen years behind bars. Even fewer women lifers—about half—have participated in vocational programs as these are reserved for those with shorter sentences who are re-entering society. With time, women lifers petition to participate in these programs. Some do, but most do not. In addition, the types of vocational training are limited to programs in cosmetology, computer programming, and customer service.

Particularly important for reentry after serving lengthy sentences are computer courses. Over 70 percent have not had computer skills or technology classes. More often than not *"Lifers aren't allowed computer programming."* One woman recognized the problem with this, saying: *"But that's basically*

**CASE HISTORY 9.2: I CAN'T WAIT TO GET OUT
AND FINALLY SEE THE INTERNET**

Married at age sixteen, a child by age nineteen, and a life sentence at age twenty-two, Jackie entered prison with her GED. She was always inquisitive and sought knowledge whether asking tons of questions of her parents or reading every book she could *"from psychology to quantum theory to U.S. world wars."* While incarcerated she was one of the few women lifers who completed a class, "Computer Technology and Customer Service," where she learned Microsoft Office (Word, Excel, Access, and PowerPoint). Her skills were so well developed that she worked as an aide in the class for many years. Using these skills, she learned to manage data, compose memos, work with spreadsheets, and write reports. She read about developing business plans and taught other students. She often worked to repair computers when they were down. Despite this knowledge and skills, Jackie says after twenty-five years or more in prison, *"I will leave here with absolutely nothing. I'm going to need to know as much as I can to find a job out there and get somewhere in life. I can't wait to get out and finally see the Internet."*

---

running the world now so we leave today we're lost, no skills at all." It is not the case that the prison does not offer computer or graphic art; one of the women's prisons has an exceptional program and instructor, but limited resources, space, and time are often the issue. With demand for programs high, lifers with time go to the back of the line.

For women lifers, if you can find your way and be selected for one of these educational or vocational programs, then you have options and a list of classes, activities, and programs to enjoy. For example, in the "Faith and Character Dorm," which is a selective group (i.e., application process, interview, wait, and acceptance), women have mandatory groups, but also access to groups such as Tabeo, Spanish, sign language, advanced fitness, yoga, arts and crafts, creative writing, public speaking, and dance. Special and exclusive programs such as beekeeping and training service dogs are also available, but dependent on volunteer interests and time:

I'm not a typical inmate—I'm educated, had an independent nature and artistic career. In March 2016, BEEKEEPING was made available to lifers. I have to thank our volunteers, both master beekeepers. Meeting these two smart (liberal) women was the best thing to happen to me in 10 years.

These types of programs can be useful for jobs after getting out of prisons, but they are usually "enrichments" and ways women lifers pass time, and how volunteers "give back" to their communities and "help" those behind bars. Most women lifers, especially early in their sentence, are not selected for a program, and *"it seems like you are just taking up space."* In addition, once you finish a program, likely fifteen–eighteen months' duration, you move back into general population where your time still stretches out *"with appalling length."*

More common than educational, vocational training, and special groups are work details which provide "free" labor for the institution. Women are not paid for their labor, but they spend most hours of the day working in the prison—kitchen, landscaping, dorm, and medical orderlies. While many take pride in these details, they also petition for "good" long-term details and have many complaints about changes, removal, or lack of details/work assignments. For some of the women, these details provide skills that will transfer outside of prison to employment. Others are overqualified for these jobs, and despite being *"mind-numbing"* tasks such as cleaning the dorms, the details offer a way to stay busy. *"Cleaning is not real stimulating for my mind. I just put my headphones on and I'm lost in another world."*

Reentry programs

Reentry has emerged as a key policy initiative in the last decade. As Nellis[11] and others[12] note, these efforts have "largely ignored persons serving life sentences." Reentry programs are available, but it is unclear how relevant these are for women lifers. Primarily designed for short-timers and aimed at reducing recidivism, some of the women lifers feel that the programs *"are really not geared toward re-entry"* or at least are not *"a program that is set up for lifer's reentry."* Most would like a reentry program that is *"not just a 'catch-up.'"* Of the programs that are available, the focus is on job interviewing, résumés, and budgets.

As they accumulate years, women do engage in more programs, including those preparing them for reentry; however, it is surprising that of the women lifers with more than fifteen years served, 23 percent have not engaged in a reentry program. Much of the "reentry" comes too late, and women do not ease back to society. Like their entries into prison which are sudden and overwhelming, their exits out of prison are rather sudden and full of unknowns. As already mentioned, transitional housing provides a much-needed place to settle in and steady themselves. These programs are typically fifteen months. Given their lengthy sentences, some of the women do not think this is enough time. Sentenced at age fifteen and having served twenty years, this woman shared her thoughts:

> We are more reliable and responsible than the short-term inmates. Sometimes inmates look to us for help or advice because we've been around a while. . . .
> We deserve a chance at life and lifers usually do well once they are released, but they bring us in young and we leave out old.

She continued describing her health and healthcare issues, reflecting on how short life is and how much time she and those like her have in prison, missing the family support she has and mourning for herself and others the family support she has lost over time. But she also articulated recommendations that she (and others) think would benefit women lifers:

> I think life would be improved here if they allowed lifers to be a part of more than the prison has to offer. We are usually put off because they feel that we have plenty of time to do whatever. Also, I feel like they should have more space in transitional programs and less space in prison, overcrowding the prison space. More lifers should have the chance to prove themselves within a reasonable amount of time—I suggest to allow us to participate in long-term and work release programs and quit setting people back constantly. After 15 years or more what else can we possibility accomplish that we haven't already.

One of the relatively new programs that only a few of the women lifers know about and even fewer have participated in is a victim-offender dialogue initiative. Offered for all inmates in Georgia, victim's families must agree to participate, which for some is not likely for lifers because of the continued struggle with anger, pain, and loss. The program could be extremely important for women lifers because victims' families are an influential part of the parole/denial decision process.

Overall, when women lifers are eligible to participate in programs, whether for vocational training and skills or support groups, they do find them helpful. However, most of these women at one point were *"waiters"* for these programs and recognize that not every woman has these same opportunities in prison:

> Being part of a program is a link to information that can be transforming. Being in here for so long, 22 years for me, so much has changed especially technology. Personally, I have all this knowledge but it's not available to everyone.

After completing these programs, in theory, women lifers should be *"ready to be put back into society":*

> These programs have allowed me to keep growing as I'm able to educate myself, stay abreast of and interactions with others keeps me connected. I'm not the same person I was 21 years ago. I've matured and grown in every aspect of my life. I admit my choices in the past caused hurt and harm to others. I take full responsibility. I do deserve another chance and I'm willing to keep pushing forward, doing all I can to redeem and rehabilitate myself.

In practice, these personal transformations are not enough for the parole board to let them out.

SUMMARY

Women lifers are often treated differently than other women in prison because of their sentence, to their disadvantage. In other ways, they are treated the same as other women in prison regardless of their sentence, again to their disadvantage. While women lifers want to the treated the same—access to programs—regardless of their sentence and want to be treated different—support, parole decisions, and reentry needs—because of their sentence, prisons do not operate this way. Many are left in no-win situations including parole and their unique reentry needs.

We know from the women lifers' accounts that the parole process is frustrating and characterized by ups and downs, setoffs, and lack of transparency or consideration of circumstances of personal change.[13] However, most women lifers will get out of prison. If they have an address to parole out, they will start in transitional centers, and for those who have family support they likely will live with family as they start their new beginning beyond bars. They will try to make up for lost time, but this will be complicated by family matters and the fact that they all have changed over time while separated by prison walls. Some will be in old age with few options given their health, age, and stigma.

Much discussion among women lifers and those responsible for their care and release rests on women's bad choices. While there is some merit in this type of discussion, it can be frustrating and fruitless in the long run if policies and public sentiments remain stacked against women serving/having served a life sentence behind bars. Often policies do not reflect the low risk of recidivism for these women, and are instead based on the "circumstances of the crime" and impact on victims.[14] In addition, some may question whether narratives of personal transformation and goals for success are manipulations of the system. We question if their *"enthusiastic goals and future plans"* will match up with the realities they face upon release.

NOTES

1. Quote from the Georgia State Board of Pardons and Parole in 1998, cited in Mauer, King, and Young, *The Meaning of Life: Long Prison Sentences in Context*, 2.

2. Mauer, "Changing the Knowledge Base and Public Perception of Long-Term Prisoners"; Liem, *After Life Imprisonment.*

3. Nellis, *Life Goes On.*

4. Liem, *After Life Imprisonment*; Kazemian and Travis, "Imperative for Inclusion of Long Termers and Lifers in Research and Policy."

5. Toch, "'I Am Not Now Who I Used to Be Then': Risk Assessment and the Maturation of Long-Term Prison Inmates"; Herbert, "Inside or Outside? Expanding the Narratives about Life-Sentenced Prisoners."

6. State Board of Pardon and Parole, *Annual Report Fiscal Year 2017*, 20. https://pap.georgia.gov/sites/pap.georgia.gov/files/Annual_Reports/PAP_AnnualReport -Final_WEB.pdf

7. See State Board of Pardon and Paroles website. https://pap.georgia.gov/life -sentences.

8. Southern Center for Human Rights, *Parole Handbook*. https://pap.georgia .gov/sites/pap.georgia.gov/files/Reentry/Parole%20Handbook%202015.pdf

9. Liem, "Desistance after Life Imprisonment."

10. Fabisiak, "The Chillon Project at Life University." For more information on the program see: http://www.compassion.life.edu/wp-content/uploads/Chillon-Project-Brochure-August-2017.pdf.

11. Nellis, *Life Goes On.*

12. Kazemian and Travis, "Imperative for Inclusion of Long Termers and Lifers in Research and Policy."

13. Schneider, *Battered Women Doing Time.*

14. Some state courts (e.g., California) have clarified parole decision making, and ruled that "the Board must grant parole unless it concludes that the inmate is still dangerous. . . . The Board cannot use the circumstances of the crime, standing alone, as a basis to deny parole." See Weisberg, Mukamal, and Segall, *Life in Limbo*, 10. Georgia does not use this type of risk assessment for those with life sentences.

Chapter 10

Challenging the Existing Narrative about Women Lifers

This book has offered a rare glimpse into the lives of women lifers. It is a privilege for us to share their stories. They have affected our lives and our hope is that we can affect change in policy for them and women like them. Their stories are all unique. Each woman could (and might) write an entire book about their own pathways, experiences within prison, and getting out after a life sentence. But they share many experiences as well, and we have attempted to document those experiences using as many of their voices as possible. We have learned that these women are from all walks of life, ranging from those who, when incarcerated, were living in dire poverty to those who owned multiple homes and drove a Mercedes-Benz. They entered prison at different points in their life with some in their mid-teens to others who were in their sixties and seventies. A disproportionate number were black, and although we did not make their story about racial disparities that often have been documented in the prison system, we feel these are important to address. However, we focused on the similarities and differences in the ways this group of women adjust to their lengthy stay behind bars. With the growing number of women lifers, we think it is important that the public at large better understand the unique circumstances that brought these women to prison and the major challenges they face in carving out a successful life in prison and beyond.

In many ways we found that the story of women lifers is a story of the "haves" and the "have nots." Similar to life on the outside, those who find themselves among the "haves" ascribed position typically have better opportunities that come their way including programs and prized work details. For example, the "haves" included those women who entered prison with a considerable amount of social capital. Such resources included those with strong family and friendship ties with the financial capabilities to make more frequent visits to prison as well as offering financial support to the women on a regular basis. This latter gesture enables some women to live a more entitled life with opportunities to purchase food and other commodities from the commissary or co-payments for health care access. Being incarcerated in a state that does not reimburse prisoners for their daily work serves as an important liability for those without any external financial support. Likewise, individuals without family support or with families living a great distance from prison and who are unable to visit have a much different prison experience. They will more likely suffer from depression, feel forgotten and alone in a world surrounded by strangers. The "have nots" will also continue to have barriers in their lives when it comes time for reentry as they seek a caring community on the outside.

Regardless of ethnicity, class, age, or sexual orientation, most women lifers perceive themselves as a forgotten group and one that is invisible— meaning their special needs are rarely given consideration in the day-to-day scheme of prison life. Early on, they feel excluded from many of the programs because being lifers they have to wait their turn, which may be years later. Most lifers also encounter the sudden shock of incarceration with 95 percent entering prison for the first time in their lives. This is a fate they had never considered, and walking an emotional tightrope becomes a common theme in the lives of all women serving life from the first day in prison to their very last. They feel forgotten by society, by prison officials, and, in some cases, by their very own families. Women lifers also feel misunderstood by the public and the policy makers. They feel the term "lifer" carries such a negative stigma, and this label is a very heavy cross to bear, since it is applied directly to the very nature of their character. Women lifers also hold similar concerns such as fears associated with their declining health or how their children and other families are doing. They wonder about their invisible parole date or why the criminal justice system let them down. The sharing of these individual yet common realities provides these women with a sense of community and togetherness.

We found the women thankful for considering them as a special category of people and eager to share their stories with the hopes that their "words of wisdom" will help others take a different path. This group was willing to reach down into their souls and share painful stories from their past, often shedding tears along the way, because they wanted to "pay their experience forward" to help others both in and out of prison. In an attempt to make a difference, many of the women engage in mentoring younger women to steer them back on course. By sharing their lived experiences, they also want people to know that besides being separated by a wall or a tall fence, they are still first and foremost mothers, grandmothers, sisters, nieces, aunts, daughters, and in some cases wives who, for a lack of a better explanation, were at the wrong place at the wrong time. Some got caught up in situations of violence or had no control over the crime committed. The overwhelming majority lean on their faith daily and remain highly devoted and sincere about the role of religion in their lives. They have been battered and bruised and continue to suffer from those wounds, but are doing their very best to heal and reclaim their voice. This is the face this group of lifers would have you see. They would like for you to know that they are not evil persons or hardened killers often portrayed in the media, but good persons seeking a second chance. Life-sentenced individuals normally come to a pragmatic assessment of their appalling and often permanent situation. They reluctantly come to accept the fact prison will be their involuntary home for the foreseeable future and that other fellow lifers will become an important part of their new makeshift family.[1]

For some women, incarceration provides a respite from a tumultuous life on the outside, a structured community, and a new lease on life. With pre-prison conditions filled with trauma and chaos, landing in prison can have a personal bearing on health and safety. Not only did we hear stories about intense pain and suffering, but also about transformation of their old self into a person filled with confidence and hope. For most, their faith provided the women with a framework that added important meaning to their current situation and contributed to the formation of a positive self-identity. As a whole, the women lifers avoided trouble and made the most of the opportunities be it work, education, and any rehabilitative programs that might be available to them. The women were very eager to pursue any and all programming that might prepare them for a successful reentry back into society.

WOMEN LIFERS AND THE STATE OF CORRECTIONS

Over the past thirty years, the trend toward mass incarceration has literally changed the landscape in the U.S. prison system, raising questions on how to best manage this tremendous influx and exit of prisoners. With the massive increase in prison capacity, the severe curtailment of discretionary early release and the introduction of truth in sentencing laws, women have been thrust into the criminal justice system at alarming rates. The U.S. women's incarceration rate is small compared to men, but it is still the highest rate for women in the world.[2] While only 4 percent of the world's female population resides in the United States, our country accounts for over 30 percent of the world's incarcerated women. Even with many of the women's legitimate pathways to prison highly questionable, states have chosen the punitive approach, offering harsh sentences to women without giving any consideration whatsoever to devastating social conditions that brought them to prison in the first place.[3]

The trend to hold on to prisoners, despite the fact that they have served the suggested number of years provided at sentencing, has become the norm. This chronic condition of social incapacitation has led to severe restrictions infringing on prisoner rights and opportunities before, during, and after release.[4] There is an unspoken rule among parole boards that "it would be a miscarriage of justice" if a woman serving life was released the first time when coming up for parole—even when recommended by all concerned parties. When prisoners no longer pose a public safety risk and have already served their defined sentence, continued incarceration may constitute a violation of their right to a just and proportionate punishment. By rendering excessively long sentences, inflexible parole board gatekeepers can be counterproductive when considering public safety guidelines. Keeping people locked up for years well beyond an eligible parole date serves little purpose other than extending retribution.

From a human rights perspective, a prison sentence can be considered cruel and inhumane punishment if excessively long relative to the crime and the culpability of the person committing the crime. While assuming responsibility for committing a violent act, scholars have argued that consideration should be given to those with histories of interpersonal violence and childhood physical and sexual abuse.[5] Vulnerable women are more likely to commit crimes while in a state of mental anguish or, in some cases, may only be a party to a crime through no fault of their own. In numerous cases, the women we interviewed were obviously threatened with their lives or forced to engage in illegal behaviors by overpowering and controlling men. They were used for economic gain and, in some rare cases, offered as sex workers to obtain drug money for the man in their life. When various elements of the criminal justice system fail to help protect these battered victims, they are often left deciding between their own lives and the lives of their violent partner. Yet these brave women who have endured like any ordinary prisoner of war are still perceived as villains by those on the outside as well other nonlifers.

When battered women kill, most do so in self-defense but are still treated harshly within the legal system. Time and time again, the women in our sample shared stories about how they made every conceivable attempt to escape their life-threatening situation, but to no avail. Even with the legal recognition of battered woman syndrome in the courts, a large majority of abused women charged with killing their partners accepted plea bargains and were given long sentences at the encouragement of either incompetent or uninterested court-appointed legal representation. Often these women never get the opportunity to tell their side of the story, and once sentenced they soon learn that no one else is interested, either. The opportunity to appear in person before the parole board to make their case is nonexistent, and so they must rely on making their case with a socially distant written brief. Also lacking is a clear pathway toward redemption. When women lifers conform perfectly to the system's rules or seek a new way of life going forward often through their religious faith, they find themselves labeled as a con or a manipulator. With sincere motives unfairly questioned by prison officials or parole board members, frustration with a perceived gender-biased system is understandable.

When considering future policy issues, some consideration must be given to the rapidly growing number of older women. The recent growth of this population can be linked to new sentencing laws as well as the failure of correctional and parole systems to activate existing release apparatuses such as parole and compassionate release for those where incarceration no longer makes sense. We found that the average age for women lifers entering the prison was twenty-nine years of age. This figure includes 16 percent of women who entered prison as delinquents (< age eighteen). By our calculation, the overwhelming majority of women serving life will be at least sixty years old before becoming eligible for parole. Given the fact that most are put off several years more, an increasing number will reach old age behind bars. The number of incarcerated lifers held in Georgia has increased by 25 percent since we gathered our initial baseline data eight years ago. If sentencing trends continue, housing such a large number of geriatric women will prove challenging, especially with the current strains of overcrowding and resources already drastically stretched.

The rapid growth of women's incarceration has resulted in the realization that recent criminal justice reforms have not addressed the special health needs of incarcerated women. We found that survivors of childhood and adult sexual and physical abuse were particularly vulnerable to a variety of mental and physical health issues. Given their extensive histories of toxic stress, it is not surprising that women serving life reported high rates of depression, anxiety, interpersonal insensitivity, symptoms of PTSD, and substance abuse. Recognizing the negative health consequences of these importation experiences and how these factors are often exacerbated by the deprivations of prison, more persistent and careful screening is necessary to ensure that health needs are addressed in a timely fashion. However, on numerous occasions the women indicated that they are experiencing just the opposite. Rather than being proactive in managing healthcare needs through screening and chronic care clinics, those responsible for healthcare delivery may delay treatment or fail to provide a proper drug regimen. To discourage medical requests, a co-payment has been instituted which, according to women lifers, prohibited them from seeking health interventions. While some states require as much as a $15 co-pay, without any compensation for prison labor, many prisoners simply feel they cannot afford medical treatment.[6] While the implementation of these policies was introduced to prevent overutilization of medical services, such practice could be viewed as discriminatory. Such practices may prove, in the long run, ineffective especially when medical treatment is delayed and health conditions become more acute.[7]

Correctional officials have several choices as they consider accommodating the increasing number of lifers in the criminal justice system. Since the 1980s, imprisonment has become the major solution for correcting those who make unlawful decisions and has, for the most part, ruled out alternative sentencing strategies, even for those with special circumstances. Another solution is to consider pathways to assist those who have served their time and have obtained a low-risk assessment for reoffending. It should be noted that once released from prison, the vast majority of older lifers do not return. In fact, the return rate for long-termers convicted of murder (most likely prisoners of advanced age) is less than 1 percent for women serving life.[8] Some states are now reviewing a person's medical state rather than focusing exclusively on the crime committed. While some states have laws in place for governors to grant clemency to older, sick prisoners, this policy is rarely implemented. Rather, most states like Georgia, have opted for taking a firm stand toward incapacitation even for prisoners who are now considered "patients." This "lock them up and throw away the key" approach means that states will now be required to add additional services for an elderly population including end-of-life care such as hospice and special units for those with dementia. This lack of mercy and a "second chance" is already placing a tremendous burden on not only those charged with the care of long-termers, but the general public who must fund the emerging assisted-living facilities behind bars.

PATHWAYS TOWARD REENTRY

Keeping people beyond a time when they can no longer function independently has proven to be costly to the system. Old and sick inmates are often difficult to place and, at the same time, are taking up bed space for others entering the system. Those in favor of recent reentry policies also have suggested that parole boards often fail to recognize a person's capacity for change. Parole boards frequently make their decision based on the nature of the crime and victims' reactions toward parole. They continue to deny parole based on the initial crime of conviction regardless of how many years ago it was committed as well as failing to seek any evidence that the person charged for the crime has changed for the better.[9] Perhaps it is time to look beyond the crime that was committed and have respect for the human dignity and good found in every person. Such a regard for personal dignity involves the opportunity for the formerly incarcerated to reintegrate back into society, a chance for atonement, and an opportunity to demonstrate to the criminal justice system that through personal growth *"they are no longer the girl they used to be."*

The lengthy transformation process has not been an easy task and often begins upon immediate entry to prison. With histories of cumulative trauma experienced both outside and inside prison, lingering subjective distress continues to challenge women lifers trying to make the best of a bad situation. Toxic events from childhood and across the life-course still influence their current state of health and mental well-being. Despite these negative experiences associated with long-term incarceration, these women with the help of their undying faith continue to seek a pathway to redemption. With their involvement in prison programs and desire to change a destructive mind-set, a transformation process occurs with hopes of a better future in the new world, and *"an opportunity to rebuild a life after the punishment and correction phase."* With their faith growing stronger year by year, the rebirthing into a new transformed person continues as time drags on. Serving thirty years to life, they will need to mark the calendar over ten thousand times before even becoming eligible for parole. The journey is a long one traveled within the throes of their mind as the body remains stuck alongside countless others serving life. Many of the women have found themselves in a better place strengthened by their time separated from the community. Having survived a turbulent past, they are now anxious to emerge from prison, ready to renew ties with their families, ready to show that they can be trusted, and ready to prove their self-worth.

ALTERNATIVE PROGRAMMING AND POLICIES

We found that women in our study held similar beliefs about programming as lifers elsewhere.[10] Many felt that they were being denied entrance into specific programs due their lifer status. Placed at the bottom of the list can be frustrating for those eager to get started with what is perceived to be activities and programming that would help make their case for reentry. The question of course is: When is the optimum time to be selected for these specialized programs? With over four hundred women now in various stages of their sentence, early entry into these prize programs is rare. Since the lifers are now expected to serve thirty years, many of the current reentry programs could very likely be outdated. With rapid changes in technology expected in the coming decades, it will be even more challenging to prepare those individuals who will be able to return to society in mid-life. Others will be retirement age and beyond and their preparation needs will be entirely different. The administration with limited funds and limited space has not made education and programming for lifers a priority although women lifers are considered the most dedicated for bettering themselves academically and vocationally.[11]

If life-serving women are not immediately eligible for specific dedicated programs to that cause, perhaps considerations should be given for opportunities to improve other aspects of their lives. Research has found that women's correctional facilities operate most effectively with an appropriate level of structure. While that structure is easily applied to the body, a wondering unstructured mind attempting to make valid use of endless "time" often goes lacking. Of course, many women fill this void with religious activities, but what about other enrichment programs that would be most useful in helping these long-termers become more self-actualized. With such diversity among this population, special attention should be given to accommodating their life cycle experiences. The following serve as a few suggested recommendations that might make a difference in rebuilding the lives of those who make prison their home for a substantial part of their lives. In comparison to those women who come and go, those serving life have the most invested and by making them stronger, in turn, makes the entire prison environment a better place to live and to work.

Women lifers lack support at the initial stages of their life sentence. Support groups on separation anxiety, grief and loss, legal issues, identity management, self-esteem, friendship selection, environmental stress, loneliness, fears and desires, maintaining connections to family, parenting from prison, and abuse survivors are examples of added support for recent entry. This may also include a "lifers" dorm so that younger, new women lifers first come into their assigned prison/dorm surrounded by those "like them." This housing arrangement could be disadvantageous—little interaction with short-time inmates may produce an "us versus them" culture and may perpetuate stereotypes about mad or evil women who kill. However, it would be easier for lifers to find one another and find needed support. Support starts day one. While these support programs could be voluntary, they would be a way to offer structured support within the initial chaos of a life sentence in prison. Such a program could be led by other women lifers, a way to give back and pay forward. For most women lifers, just having someone who understands and will acknowledge them makes a difference.

Additional groups are needed for age or health-related supports that focus on life transitions, ageism, energy level changes, living with chronic illnesses, grandparenting from prison, death of family and friends, and reminiscing about life. Recreational or exercise groups have been found to work well in women's prisons, and with older women. For all women, health and mental health needs are sources of concern while in prison. Policies and practices in place require women to have a mental health case in order to see a therapist. These services are not open to everyone, but instead the responsibility to address emotional, mental, or psychological distress rests with unit counselors who have no training as "psychologists" or "psychiatrists."

Gender-specific training that stresses fairness and humane treatment and a basic understanding of the major issues presented in this book that serve as obstacles to prison adjustment would prove beneficial for those who work in direct contact with women lifers. Those who work on a daily basis with those serving life sentences should have a better understanding of the special needs of this growing, unique group. There should be a basic understanding of the lifer's abusive pasts and the consequences of the physical, sexual, or emotional trauma they have encountered prior to incarceration. There should also be an understanding of the consequences of losing contact with the outside world, especially their children. Other troubling issues include lack of privacy, coping with acute and/or chronic health issues that undermine their well-being. Training that also includes a fundamental knowledge of the various physical, cognitive, social, and emotional changes that accompany the aging process is important. Recognizing the decline in gait and motor ability, senses related to hearing and sight may prevent older women from responding in an appropriate manner to correctional officers. Being able to show empathy and treat this population with respect goes a long way in how women will respond positively in such a confined state. At a system level, prison administrators must also recognize the differences in access to services, rules, programs, and support groups between prisons and over time. Women lifers see the differences, as they are transferred between prisons over time, and perceive these as unfair. Location matters and culture of the institution matters in women lifers' adjustment to prison, including their ability to find redemption and personal transformation.

Also at a system level, we must address the massive prison industrial complex and what it is doing to those incarcerated and their families. Nearly every facet of the prison environment "costs," whether food on weekends, sick calls, or contact with family. More opportunities are needed for women lifers to connect with their family, and this means fewer barriers to maintaining family contact. Eliminating for-profit management of phones and items approved for packages and purchase are a couple of examples. Women lifers can see who is really benefited by these programs—it is not the lifers, and it is not their families.

Challenging the narrative of women lifers includes reentry needs. This begins with changes to the parole decision-making process, including:

1. Provide more transparency into the parole process (i.e., how do the guidelines and risk level predictors apply to lifers?).
2. Provide clear check points and goals for meeting parole expectations (e.g., once women lifers complete this goal or this program, then parole is granted).
3. Institute face-to-face meetings with women lifers by representatives of the parole board (not the prison) with decisions face-to-face rather than form letter.
4. Allow supporters to speak on behalf of the women lifers, not only the victim's family/supporters.
5. Eliminate perspective of prosecutor, investigators, and judges in parole decisions.
6. Utilize risk assessment for lifers. Reprioritize decisions so that they are not based on circumstances of the crime, but risk to society.
7. Address number of set offs including no minimum number and a maximum number of set offs before is parole granted.
8. Address the problems of the parole paradox where a vast majority who return to prison do so for parole violations rather than new crimes. Some of the unique reentry needs of women lifers make the parole paradox even more relevant as they continue to face no-win situations.

In addition to changes to the parole experience, reentry planning needs to start earlier and should be connected to current real-life reentry (microdynamics) barriers and successes. This includes more reliance on transitional housing, but for a longer time period, and work-release programs for lifers. Upon early reentry planning women lifers will also need assistance reconnecting with family members. If more support and fewer barriers to family connections were the norm from the initial entry into prison, some of the problems with reconnecting with family could be addressed. Because religion plays such a prominent role in women's time behind bars, it may be wise to draw on these strengths. Religious groups and churches offer support and transition as women lifers' reentry society, but these changes cannot rest solely with faith-based initiatives. Communities as a whole must challenge the narratives and respond as well.

A commitment to reentry, all efforts should be framed by the unique experiences of women lifers including their lives before (pathways informed reentry planning and care), the long amount of time they have been cut off from society, and the challenges of being "older," "a felon," and "starting over" after serving a life sentence. As we have heard from women lifers, this is not their experience within prison or in getting out. Mentor programs for lifers after release—as they have relied on these inside prison—could be beneficial. Dealing with "freedom" and continued "loss," "successful" lifers who have reentered society could return to speak to groups of other women lifers about their struggles and successes in their "first days out" (i.e., in the prison or in the transitional housing). Currently, policies prevent this type of contact between "felons," and a major issue throughout the system is a silencing of incarcerated women's perspectives and voices by policy makers.

A final takeaway and recommendation regarding women lifers at all stages is that we recognize the diversity of women lifers going in and coming out of prison after decades behind bars. Younger women (forties and fifties) and those entering "old age" (seventies and eighties) have different reentry needs including family, work, financial supports; ability to embrace a changed world; health needs/problems; time remaining in this life to be free/outside of prison. We must acknowledge how the current policies regarding parole for women lifers are futile if there comes a point where there is no reentry plan for older women held in prison for so long. Their only alternative will be a sentence of death in prison. For those who are released on parole, advanced reentry planning should focus on continuity of care (physical and mental), including establishing new doctor, pharmacy, and ways to obtain both physical (transportation issues, mail order, etc.) and financial health needs. By keeping lifers into old age, states have great difficulty in placing those in need of a healthcare setting. Some may need home healthcare services or appropriate long-term care.

CONCLUSION

Women serving life sentences often come to prison as broken people searching for an opportunity to gain control over their lives. It has been the aim of this book to provide policy makers, prison officials, and the public with a better understanding of the lived experiences of this voiceless group of prisoners. It has been acknowledged that women who have been repeatedly victimized are highly vulnerable to the harshness of prisons, hindering their coping ability. With the passage of time, lifers tend to become better adjusted to the prison environment, showing more empathy toward themselves and others.[12] With more thoughtfulness toward others, some of the older women indicated that they do their very best to mentor the "younger ones," helping them refrain from making careless mistakes. In effect, the women in their later years of incarceration take pride in their growth process. Over the years as they mature and began to gain a sense of self-worth, the ability to adapt to the prison environment becomes more apparent. This is not to say that life is without disappointments and occasional feelings of despair. They have learned that adjustment to lifelong confinement remains an ongoing process and not one for the fainthearted. Having endured a life filled with turmoil and loss, women serving life are some of the strongest and most resilient people you will ever meet.

NOTES

1. Johnson and Dobrzanska, "Mature Coping among Life-Sentenced Inmates."
2. Kajstura, "States of Women's Incarceration."
3. Ajinkya, "Rethinking How to Address the Growing Female Prison Population."
4. Drucker, *A Plague of Prisons: The Epidemiology of Mass Incarceration in America.*
5. Messina and Grella, "Childhood Trauma and Women's Health Outcomes in a California Prison Population."
6. Aday and Krabill, *Women Aging in Prison.*
7. Ahalt, Trestman, Rich, Greifinger, and Williams, "Paying the Price: The Pressing Need for Quality, Costs, and Outcomes Data to Improve Correctional Health Care for Older Prisoners."
8. Kazemian and Travis, "Imperative for Inclusion of Long Termers and Lifers in Research and Policy."
9. Fellner, "Old behind Bars: The Aging Prison Population in the United States."
10. Lempert, *Women Doing Life.*
11. George, *A Woman Doing Life.*
12. Johnson and Dobrzanska, "Mature Coping among Life-Sentenced Inmates."

Bibliography

"2010 Georgia Code." Justia. Accessed October 7, 2018. https://law.justia.com /codes/georgia/2010/title-16/chapter-2/article-2/16-2-20/

"Crime in the United States." Federal Bureau of Investigation, 2017. https://ucr.fbi .gov/crime-in-the-u.s/2017/crime-in-the-u.s.-2017

"Inmate Statistical Profile: Active Lifers." Georgia Department of Corrections, July 2010. http://www.dcor.state.ga.us/sites/all/files/pdf/Research/Monthly/Profile_lif ers_2010_06.pdf

"Three Supreme Court Cases That Have Shaped Juvenile Justice." PBS, 2014. http:// www.pbs.org/pov/15tolife/supreme-court-cases/

Aday, Ronald H. *Aging Prisoners: Crisis in American Corrections.* Westport, CT: Praeger, 2003.

Aday, Ronald H., Meredith Huey Dye, and Amanda K. Kaiser. "Examining the Traumatic Effects of Sexual Victimization on the Health of Incarcerated Women." *Women and Criminal Justice* 24, no. 4 (2014): 341–61.

Aday, Ronald, and Lori Farney. "Malign Neglect: Assessing Older Women's Health Care Experiences in Prison." *Journal of Bioethics* 11, no. 3 (2014): 359–72.

Aday, Ronald, and Jennifer Krabill. "Grief and Loss: The Silenced Emotion behind Bars." In *Social Justice Perspectives on Loss and Grief*, edited by Tashel Bordere and Darcy Harris, 87–105. New York: Routledge Publishing Company, 2015.

Aday, Ronald, and Jennifer Krabill. *Women Aging in Prison: A Neglected Population in the Correctional System.* Boulder, CO: Lynne Rienner, 2011.

Aday, Ronald, Jennifer Krabill, and Dayron Deaton-Owens. "Religion in the Lives of Older Women Serving Life in Prison." *Journal of Women and Aging* 26, no. 3 (2014): 238–56.

Ahalt, Cyrus, Robert Trestman, Josiah Rich, Robert Greifinger, and Brie Williams. "Paying the Price: The Pressing Need for Quality, Costs, and Outcomes Data to Improve Correctional Health Care for Older Prisoners." *Journal of the American Geriatrics Society* 61, no. 11 (2013): 2013–19.

Ajinkya, Julie. 2018. "Rethinking How to Address the Growing Female Prison Population." Center for American Progress, 2013. https://www.americanprogress.org/issues/women/news/2013/03/08/55787/rethinking-how-to-address-the-growing-female-prison-population/

Banning, Jan. *Pulaski Women's Prison, 2013*. http://www.janbanning.com/pulaski/

Beattie, L. Elisabeth, and Mary Angela Shaughnessy. *Sisters in Pain: Battered Women Fight Back*. Lexington: University of Kentucky Press, 2000.

Belknap, Joanne. *The Invisible Woman: Gender, Crime, and Justice*, Fourth edition. Stamford, CT: Cengage Learning, 2015.

Braithwaite, Ronald, Kimberly Jacob Arriola, and Cassandra Newkirk. *Health Issues among Incarcerated Women*. New Brunswick, NJ: Rutgers University Press, 2006.

Brennen, Tim, Markus Breitenbach, William Dieterich, Emily J. Salisbury, and Patricia Van Voorhis. "Women's Pathways to Serious and Habitual Crime: A Person-Centered Analysis Incorporating Gender Responsive Factors." *Criminal Justice and Behavior* 39, no. 11 (2012): 1481–1508.

Bright, Charlotte, and Sharon Bowland. "Assessing Interpersonal Trauma in Older Adult Women." *Journal of Loss and Trauma* 13, no. 4 (2008): 373–93.

Bronson, Jennifer, Jessica Stroop, Stephanie Zimmer, and Marcus Berzofzy. *Drug Use, Dependence, and Abuse among State Prisoners and Jail Inmates, 2007–2009*. Bureau of Justice Statistics. Washington, DC: U.S. Department of Justice, 2017. https://www.bjs.gov/content/pub/pdf/dudaspji0709

Byock, Ira. "Dying Well in Corrections: Why Should We Care?" *Journal of Correctional Health Care* 9, no. 2 (2002): 102–17.

Carceral, K. C. *Prison, Inc.: A Convict Exposes Life inside a Private Prison.* New York: New York University Press, 2006.

Carson, E. Ann. *Prisoners in 2016*. Washington, DC: U.S. Department of Justice, Office of Justice Programs, 2018. https://www.bjs.gov/content/pub/pdf/p16.pdf

Casey-Acevedo, Karen, and Tim Bakken. "Visiting Women in Prison: Who Visits and Who Cares?" *Journal of Offender Rehabilitation* 34, no. 3 (2002): 67–83.

Celinska, Katarzyna, and Jane Siegel. "Mothers in Trouble: Coping with Actual or Pending Separation from Children Due to Incarceration." *The Prison Journal* 90, no. 4 (2010): 447–74.

Chesney-Lind, Meda. "Patriarchy, Crime and Justice: Feminist Criminology in an Era of Backlash." *Feminist Criminology* 1 (2016): 6–26.

Chesney-Lind, Meda, and Noelie Rodriguez. "Women under Lock and Key: A View from the Inside." In *Girls, Women, and Crime: Selected Readings*, edited by Meda Chesney-Lind and Lisa Pasko, 187–98. Second edition. Los Angeles: Sage, 2013.

Christian, Johnna, Jeff Mellow, and Shenique Thomas. "Social and Economic Implications of Family Connections to Prisoners." *Journal of Criminal Justice* 34, no. 4 (2006): 443–52.

Clear, Todd R., and Natasha A. Frost. *The Punishment Imperative: The Rise and Failure of Mass Incarceration in America*. New York: New York University Press, 2014.

Clear, Todd, and Melvina Sumter. "Prisoners, Prison and Religion: Religion and Adjustment to Prison." *Journal of Offender Rehabilitation* 35, no. 3–4 (2002): 127–59.

Cochran, Joshua. "The Ties That Bind or the Ties That Break: Examining the Relationship between Visitation and Prisoner Misconduct." *Journal of Criminal Justice* 40, no. 5 (2012): 433–40.

Conklin, Jack. *Criminology*. Boston: Pearson, 2004.

Crewe, Ben, Susie Hulley, and Serena Wright. "The Gendered Pains of Life Imprisonment." *British Journal of Criminology* 57, no. 9 (2017): 1359–78.

Daly, Kathleen. *Gender, Crime, and Punishment*. New Haven, CT: Yale University Press, 1994.

Deaton-Owens, Dayron, Ronald H. Aday, and Azrini Wahidin. "The Effect of Health and Penal Harm on Aging Female Prisoners' Views of Dying in Prison." *OMEGA — Journal of Death and Dying* 60, no. 1 (2010): 51–70.

DeHart, Dana D. "Pathways to Prison: Impact of Victimization in the Lives of Incarcerated Women." *Violence against Women* 14, no. 12 (2008): 1362–81.

DeHart, Dana, Shannon Lynch, Joanne Belknap, Priscilla Dass-Brailsford, and Bonnie Green. "Life History Models of Female Offending: The Roles of Serious Mental Illness and Trauma in Women's Pathways to Jail." *Psychology of Women Quarterly* 38, no. 1 (2013): 138–51.

Derogatis, Leonard R. *Brief Symptom Inventory (BSI): Administration, Scoring, and Procedures Manual*, Third edition. Minneapolis, MN: National Computer Systems, 1993.

Doka, Kenneth. *Disenfranchised Grief: Recognizing Hidden Sorrow*. Lanham, MD: Lexington Books, 1989.

Drucker, Earnest. *A Plague of Prisons: The Epidemiology of Mass Incarceration in America*. New York: The New Press, 2013.

Dutton, Donald. *The Abusive Personality: Violence and Control in Intimate Relationships*. New York: The Guilford Press, 1999.

Dutton, Donald. *Rethinking Domestic Violence*. Vancouver: University of British Columbia Press, 2007.

Dye, Meredith, and Ron Aday. "'I Just Wanted to Die': Pre-prison and Current Suicide Ideation among Women Serving Life Sentences." *Criminal Justice and Behavior* 40, no. 8 (2013): 832–49.

Dye, Meredith, Ronald Aday, Lori Farney, and Jordon Raley. "'The Rock I Cling To': Religious Engagement in the Lives of Life-Sentenced Women." *The Prison Journal* 94, no. 3 (2014): 388–408.

Fabisiak, Thomas. "The Chillon Project at Life University." Marietta, GA: Life University, 2017. http://www.compassion.life.edu/wp-content/uploads/Chillon-Project-Brochure-August-2017.pdf

Fearn, Noelle E., and Kelly Parker. "Health Care for Women Inmates: Issues, Perceptions, and Policy Considerations." *California Journal of Health Promotion* 3, no. 2 (2005): 1–22.

Fedock, Gina. "Life before 'I Killed the Man That Raped Me': Pre-Prison Life Experiences of Incarcerated Women with Life Sentences and Subsequent Treatment Needs." *Women and Criminal Justice* 28, no. 1 (2017) 63–80.

Fellner, Jamie. "Old behind Bars: The Aging Prison Population in the United States." Human Rights Watch, 2012. https://www.hrw.org/sites/default/files/reports/uspris ons0112webwcover_0.pdf.

Ferraro, Kathleen. "Battered Women: Strategies for Survival." In *Violence between Intimate Partners: Patterns, Causes, and Effects*, edited by Albert Cardarelli, 127. Boston: Allyn and Bacon, 1997.

Fox, James, and Emma Fridel. "Gender Differences in Patterns and Trends in U.S. Homicide, 1976–2015." *Violence and Gender* 4, no. 2 (2017): 37–43.

Genders, Elaine, and Elaine Player. "Women Lifers: Assessing the Experience." *The Prison Journal* 70, no. 1 (1990): 46–57.

George, Erin. *A Woman Doing Life: Notes from a Prison for Women.* New York: Oxford, 2010.

George, Erin. *A Woman Doing Life: Notes from a Prison for Women.* Second edition. New York: Oxford University Press, 2015.

Gillum, Tameka, Cris Sullivan, and Deborah Bybee. "The Importance of Spirituality in the Lives of Domestic Violence Survivors." *Violence against Women* 12, no. 3 (2006): 240–50.

Girshick, Lori B. *No Safe Haven: Stories of Women in Prison.* Boston: Northeastern University Press, 1999.

Goffman, Erving. *Asylums: Essays on the Social Situation of Mental Patients and Other Inmates.* Garden City, NY: Anchor Books, 1961.

Granse, Barbara. "Why Should We Care? Hospice Social Work Practice in a Prison Setting." *Smith College Studies in Social Work* 73, no. 3 (2003): 359–75.

Greer, Kimberly R. "The Changing Nature of Interpersonal Relationships in a Women's Prison." *The Prison Journal* 80, no. 4 (2000): 442–68.

Haney, Craig. *Reforming Punishment: Psychological Limits to the Pains of Imprisonment.* Washington, DC: American Psychological Association, 2006.

Hansson, Robert, and Margaret Stroebe. *Bereavement in Late Life: Coping, Adaptation, and Developmental Influences.* Washington, DC: American Psychological Association, 2007.

Harner, Holly M., Patricia M. Hentz, and Maria Carmela Evangelista. "Grief Interrupted: The Experiences of Loss among Incarcerated Women." *Qualitative Health Research* 21, no. 4 (2011): 454–64.

Herbert, Steve. "Inside or Outside? Expanding the Narratives about Life-Sentenced Prisoners." *Punishment and Society* (online) (2017): https://doiorg/10.1177 /1462474517737048

Hoffman, Heath C., George E. Dickinson, and Chelsea L. Dunn. "Communication Policy Changes in State Adult Correctional Facilities from 1971 to 2005." *Criminal Justice Review* 32, no. 1 (2007): 47–64.

Irwin, John, and Donald Cressey. "Thieves, Convicts and the Inmate Culture." *Social Problems* 10, no. 2 (1962): 142–55.

Jewkes, Yvonne. "Loss, Liminality, and the Life Sentence: Managing Identity through a Disrupted Lifecourse." In *The Effects of Imprisonment*, edited by Alison Liebling and Shadd Maruna, 366–88. Portland, OR: Willan Publishing, 2005.

Jiang, Shanhe and Marianne Fisher-Giorlando. "Inmate Misconduct: A Test of the Deprivation, Importation, and Situational Models." *The Prison Journal* 82, no. 3 (2002): 335–58.

Johnson, Byron R., David B. Larson, and Timothy C. Pitts. "Religious Programs, Institutional Adjustment, and Recidivism among Former Inmates in Prison Fellowship Programs." *Justice Quarterly* 14 (1997): 145–66.

Johnston, Jeffrey. "Party to the Crime: Don't Be Caught with the Wrong Crowd." 2014. https://www.jeffreyjohnstonlaw.com/blog/2014/10/party-to-a-crime.shtml

Johnson, Robert, and Ania Dobrzanska. "Mature Coping among Life-Sentenced Inmates: An Exploratory Study of Adjustment Dynamics." *Corrections Compendium* 30, no. 6 (2005): 8–38.

Johnson, Robert, and Sandra McGunigall-Smith. "Life without Parole, America's Other Death Penalty: Notes on Life under Sentence of Death by Incarceration." *The Prison Journal* 88, no. 2 (2008): 328–46.

Jones, Sandra J., and Elizabeth Beck. "Disenfranchised Grief and Nonfinite Loss as Experienced by the Families of Death Row Inmates." *OMEGA—Journal of Death and Dying* 54, no. 4 (2007): 281–99.

Jose-Kamper, Christina. "Coming to Terms with Existential Death: An Analysis of Women's Adaption to Life in Prison." *Social Justice* 17 (1990): 110–25.

Kajstura, Aleks. "States of Women's Incarceration: The Global Context 2018." Prison Policy Initiative, 2013. https://www.prisonpolicy.org/global/women/2018.html

Kazemian, Lila, and Jeremy Travis. "Imperative for Inclusion of Long Termers and Lifers in Research and Policy." *Criminology and Public Policy* 14 (2015): 355–95.

Kerley, Kent. *Religious Faith in Correctional Contexts*. Boulder, CO: FirstForumPress, 2014.

Kerley, Kent, and Heith Copes. "Keepin' My Mind Right: Identity, Maintenance and Religious Social Support in the Prison Context." *International Journal of Offender Therapy and Comparative Criminology* 53, no. 2 (2009): 228–44.

Krabill, Jennifer, and Ronald Aday. "Exploring the Social World of Aging Female Prisoners." *Women and Criminal Justice* 17, no. 1 (2005): 27–54.

Kruttschnitt, Candace, Rosemary Gartner, and Amy Miller. "Doing Her Own Time? Women's Responses to Prison in the Context of the Old and the New Penology." *Criminology* 38, no. 3 (2000): 681–718.

Kubiak, Sheryl, Julia Hanna, and Marianne Balton. "'I Came to Prison to Do My Time—Not to Get Raped': Coping within the Institutional Setting." *Stress, Trauma, and Crisis* 8, no. 2–3 (2005): 157–77.

Labelle, Deborah, and Sheryl Kubiak. "Balancing Gender Equity for Women Prisoners." *Feminist Studies* 30, no. 2 (2004): 416–26.

Lalive d'Epinay, Christian J., Stefano Cavalli, and Luc A. Guillet. "Bereavement in Very Old Age: Impact on Health and Relationships of the Loss of a Spouse, a Child, a Sibling, or a Close Friend." *OMEGA — Journal of Death and Dying* 60, no. 4 (2010): 301–25.

Leigey, Margaret. *The Forgotten Men: Serving a Life without Parole Sentence*. New Brunswick, NJ: Rutgers University Press, 2015.

Leigey, Margaret, and Katie Reed. "A Women's Life before Serving Life: Examining the Negative Pre-Incarceration Life Events of Female Life Sentenced Inmates." *Women and Criminal Justice* 20, no. 4 (2010): 302–22.

Leigey, Margaret, and Michael Ryder. "The Pains of Permanent Imprisonment: Examining Perceptions of Confinement among Older Life without Parole Inmates." *International Journal of Offender Therapy and Comparative Criminology* 59, no. 7, (2014): 726–742.

Lempert, Lora Bex. *Women Doing Life: Gender, Punishment, and the Struggle for Identity.* New York: New York University Press, 2016.

Leonard, Elizabeth Dermody. *Convicted Survivors: The Imprisonment of Battered Women Who Kill.* Albany: State University of New York Press, 2002.

Levitt, Heidi M., and Kimberly Ware. "Religious Leaders' Perspectives on Marriage, Divorce, and Intimate Partner Violence." *Quarterly Journal of Women* 30, no. 2 (2006): 212–22.

Levitt, Lacey, and Ann Loper. "The Influence of Religious Participation on the Adjustment of Female Inmates." *American Journal of Orthopsychiatry* 79, no. 1 (2009): 1–7.

Liem, Marieke. *After Life Imprisonment: Reentry in the Era of Mass Incarceration.* New York: New York University Press, 2016.

Liem, Marieke, "Desistance after Life Imprisonment." In *New Perspectives on Desistance: Theoretical and Empirical Developments,* edited by E. L. Hart and E. F. J. C. van Ginneken, 85–108. London: Palgrave Macmillan, 2017.

Liu, Liu, and Wing Hong Chui. "Social Support and Chinese Female Offenders' Prison Adjustment." *Prison Journal* 94, no. 1 (2014): 30–51.

Loper, Ann Booker, and Jennifer Whitney Gildea. "Social Support and Anger Expression among Incarcerated Women." *Journal of Offender Rehabilitation* 38, no. 4 (2004): 27–50.

Lurigio, Arthur J. "People with Serious Mental Illness in the Criminal Justice System: Causes, Consequences, and Correctives." *The Prison Journal* 91, no. 3 (2011): 66S–86S.

Lynch, Shannon M., Dana D. Dehart, Joanne E. Belknap, Bonnie L. Green, Priscilla Dass-Brailsford, Kristine A. Johnson, and Elizabeth Whaley. "A Multisite Study of the Prevalence of Serious Mental Illness, PTSD, and Substance Use Disorders of Women in Jail." *Psychiatric Services* 65, no. 5 (2014): 670–74.

MacKenzie, Doris Layton, and Lynne I. Goodstein. "Long-Term Incarceration Impacts and Characteristics of Long-Term Offenders: An Empirical Analysis." *Criminal Justice and Behavior* 12 (1985): 395–414.

Maeve, M. Katherine, and Michael S. Vaughn. "Nursing with Prisoners: The Practice of Caring, Forensic Nursing or Penal Harm Nursing?" *Advances in Nursing Science* 24, no. 2 (2001): 47–64.

Mancini, Christina, Thomas Baker, Karla Sainju, Kristin Golden, Laura Bedard, and Marc Gertz. "Examining External Support Received in Prison and Concerns about Reentry among Incarcerated Women." *Feminist Criminology* 11, no. 2 (2016): 163–90.

Maruna, Shadd, Louise Wilson, and Kathryn Curran. "Why God Is Often Found behind Bars: Prison Conversions and the Crisis of Self-Narrative." *Research in Human Development* 3, no. 2 (2006): 161–84.

Maschi, Tina, Keith Morgen, Kristen Zgoba, Deborah Courtney, and Jennifer Ristow. "Age, Cumulative Trauma and Stressful Life Events, and Post-Traumatic Stress Symptoms among Older Adults in Prison: Do Subjective Impressions Matter?" *The Gerontologist* 57, no. 5 (2011): 675–86.

Mauer, Marc, "Changing the Knowledge Base and Public Perception of Long-Term Prisoners." *Criminology and Public Policy* 14, no. 2 (2015): 351–53.

Mauer, Marc. *Race to Incarcerate*, Second edition. New York: The New Press, 2006.

Mauer, Marc, and Meda Chesney-Lind. *Invisible Punishment: The Collateral Consequences of Mass Imprisonment.* New York: The New Press, 2002.

Mauer, Marc, Ryan King, and Malcolm Young. *The Meaning of Life: Long Prison Sentences in Context.* Washington, DC: The Sentencing Project, May 2004. https://www.sentencingproject.org/publications/the-meaning-of-life-long-prison-sentences-in-context/.

McDaniel Lowry, Jodi. *Jan: The Youngest Woman Sentenced to Georgia's Death Row.* Parker, CO: Outskirts Press, 2017.

Messina, Nena, and Kristine Grella. "Childhood Trauma and Women's Health Outcomes in a California Prison Population." *American Journal of Public Health* 96, no. 10 (2005): 1842–48.

Meyer, Cheryl, and Michelle Oberman. *Mothers Who Kill Their Children: Understanding the Acts of Moms from Susan Smith to the "Prom Mom."* New York: New York University Press, 2001.

Mignon, Sylvia, and Paige Ransford. "Mothers in Prison: Maintaining Connections with Children." *Social Work in Public Health* 27, no. 1–2 (2012): 69–88.

Nash, Shondrah Tarrezz, and Latonya Hesterberg. "Biblical Framings of and Responses to Spousal Violence in the Narratives of Abused Christian Women." *Violence against Women* 15, no. 3 (2009): 340–61.

Nellis, Ashley. "Throw Away the Key: The Expansion of Life without Parole Sentences in the United States." *Federal Sentencing Reporter* 23, no. 1 (2010): 27–32.

Nellis, Ashley. *Life Goes On: The Historic Rise in Life Sentences in America.* Washington, DC: The Sentencing Project, September 2013. sentencingproject.org/wp-content/uploads/2015/12/Life-Goes-On.pdf

Nellis, Ashley. *Still Life: America's Increasing Use of Life and Long-term Sentences.* Washington, DC: The Sentencing Project, May 2017. https://www.sentencingproject.org/wp-content/uploads/2017/05/Still-Life.pdf

Nuytiens, An, and Jenneke Christiaens. "Female Pathways to Crime and Prison: Challenging the (US) Gendered Pathways Perspective." *European Journal of Criminology* 13, no. 2 (2016): 195–213.

Owen, Barbara. *"In the Mix": Struggle and Survival in a Women's Prison.* Albany, NY: Springer Publishing, 1998.

Poehlmann, Julie. "Representations of Attachment Relationships in Children of Incarcerated Mothers." *Child Development* 76, no. 3 (2005): 679–96.

Quina, Kathryn, Ann Varna Garis, John Stevenson, Maria Garrido, Jody Brown, Roberta Richman, Jeffrey Renzi, Judith Fox, and Kimberly Mitchell. "Through the Bullet-Proof Glass: Conducting Research in Prison Settings." *Journal of Trauma and Disassociation* 8, no. 2 (2007): 123–39.

Rold, William. "Thirty Years after *Estelle v. Gamble*: A Legal Retrospective." *Journal of Correctional Health Care* 14, no. 1 (2008): 11–20.

Roscher, Sherri. "The Development of Coping Strategies in Female Inmates with Life Sentences." PhD dissertation, Wright State University, 2005.

Rovner, Josh. *Juvenile Life without Parole: An Overview*. Washington, DC: The Sentencing Project, October 2017. Accessed October 7, 2018. http://www.sentencingproject.org/publications/juvenile-life-without-parole/

Sawyer, Wendy. "Food for Thought: Prison Food Is a Public Health Problem." Prison Policy Institute, 2017. https://www.prisonpolicy.org/blog/2017/03/03/prison-food/

Schneider, Rachel. *Battered Women Doing Time: Injustice in the Criminal Justice System*. Boulder, CO: First Forum Press/Lynne Rienner, 2014.

Schneider, Rachel, and Katryn Feltey. "No Matter What Has Been Done Wrong Can Always Be Redone Right: Spirituality in the Lives of Imprisoned Battered Women." *Violence against Women* 15, no. 4 (2009): 443–59.

The Sentencing Project. "Women in the Justice System." Accessed October 7, 2018. http://www.sentencingproject.org/template/page.cfm?id=138

Severance, Theresa. "'You Know Who You Can Go To': Cooperation and Exchange between Incarcerated Women." *Prison Journal* 85, no. 3 (2005): 343–67.

Silver, Eric. "Understanding the Relationship between Mental Disorder and Violence: The Need for a Criminological Perspective." *Law and Human Behavior* 30, (2006): 685–706.

Solinger, Rickie, Paula C. Johnson, Martha L. Raimon, Tina Reynolds, and Ruby Tapia. *Interrupted Life: Experiences of Incarcerated Women in the United States*. Berkeley: University of California Press, 2010.

Southern Center for Human Rights. *Parole Handbook: A Guide to the Parole Consideration Process for People in Georgia Prisons*, Fourth edition. Atlanta, GA: Author, 2015.

State Board of Pardons and Paroles. *Annual Report Fiscal Year 2017*. Atlanta, GA: Author, 2017. https://pap.georgia.gov/sites/pap.georgia.gov/files/Annual_Reports/PAP_AnnualReport-Final_WEB.pdf/.

Stevenson, Robert G., and Raymond McCutchen. "When Meaning Has Lost Its Way: Life and Loss 'Behind Bars.'" *Illness, Crisis and Loss* 14, no. 2 (2006): 103–19.

Stoller, Nancy. "Space, Place, and Movement as Aspects of Health Care in Women's Prisons." *Social Science and Medicine* 56, no. 11 (2003): 2263–75.

Sykes, Gresham M. *The Society of Captives: A Study of a Maximum-Security Prison*. Princeton, NJ: Princeton University Press, 1958.

Templer, Donald. "The Construction and Validation of a Death Anxiety Scale." *Journal of General Psychology* 82, no. 2 (1970): 165–77.

Thomas, Jim, and Barbara Zaitzow. "Conning or Conversion: The Role of Religion in Prison Coping." *The Prison Journal* 86, no. 2 (2006): 242–59.

Toch, Hans. "'I Am Not Now Who I Used to Be Then': Risk Assessment and the Maturation of Long-Term Prison Inmates." *The Prison Journal* 90, no. 1 (2010): 4–11.

Tracy, Steven. "Patriarchy and Domestic Violence: Challenging Common Misconceptions." *Journal of Evangelical Theological Society* 50, no. 3 (2007): 580–83.

Travis, Jeremy, Elizabeth C. McBride, and Amy L. Solomon. *Families Left Behind: The Hidden Costs of Incarceration and Reentry.* Washington, DC: Urban Institute, 2005. Accessed July 22, 2017. https://www.urban.org/research/publication /families-left-behind

Turesky, Derek, and Jessica Schultz. "Spirituality among Older Adults: An Exploration of the Development Context, Impact on Mental and Physical Health, and Integration into Counseling." *Journal of Religion, Spirituality, and Aging* 22, no. 2 (2010): 162–79.

Van Tongeren, Daryl R., and Kelli J. Klebe. "Reconceptualizing Prison Adjustment: A Multidimensional Approach Exploring Female Offenders' Adjustment to Prison Life." *The Prison Journal* 90, no. 1 (2010): 48–68.

Vaughn, Michael, and Sue Collins. "Medical Malpractice in Correctional Facilities: State Tort Remedies for Inappropriate and Inadequate Health Care Administered to Prisoners." *The Prison Journal* 83, no. 4 (2004): 505–34.

Wahidin, Azrini. *Older Women in the Criminal Justice System: Running Out of Time.* London: Jessica Kingsley Publishers, 2004.

Wahidin, Azrini, and Sharon Tate. "Prison (E)scapes and Body Tropes: Older Women in the Prison Time Machine." *Journal of Body and Society* 11, no. 3 (2005): 59–79.

Wallace, Paul Harvey, and Cliff Roberson. *Family Violence: Legal, Medical, and Social Perspectives.* New York: Routledge, 2017.

Webb, Sallie Glover, and Donna L. Hubbard. "Voices of Incarcerated and Formerly Incarcerated Women." In *Health Issues among Incarcerated Women,* edited by Ronald Braithwaite, Kimberly Jacob Arriola, and Cassandra Newkirk, 32–46. New Brunswick, NJ: Rutgers University Press, 2006.

Weisberg, Robert, Debbie Mukamal, and Jordon Segall. *Life in Limbo.* Stanford, CA: Stanford Criminal Justice Center/Law School, 2011.

Whiteley, Kathryn. "'I Am More Than a Crime': Interviews with Women Who Kill." In *Demystifying the Big House: Exploring Prison Experience and Media Representations,* edited by Katie Foss, 211–27. Carbondale: Southern Illinois University Press, 2018.

Wolf, Marsha, Uyen Ly, Margaret Hobart, and Mary Kernic. "Barriers to Seeking Police Help for Intimate Partner Violence." *Journal of Family Violence* 18, no. 2 (2003): 121–29.

Wright, Kevin. "A Study of Individual, Environmental, and Interactive Effects in Explaining Adjustment to Prison." *Justice Quarterly* 8, no. 2 (1991): 217–42.

Zamble, Edward, and Frank J. Porporino. *Coping, Behavior, and Adaptation in Prison Inmates.* New York: Springer, 1988.

Zosky, Diane. "The Application of Object Relations Theory to Domestic Violence." *Clinical Social Work Journal* 27, no. 1 (1999): 66–69.

Index

broken bones, 39, 51, 53
bunking assignments, 117

cancer, 91, 113, 119-120
careers (occupational), 32, 188
cellphones, 39, 190, 193
Chillon Project, 193
chivalry hypothesis, 2
Christian sects, 165
chronic illnesses, 111-12, 122, 142, 150,
    206
cognitive challenges, 207
computer programming, 193
coping:
    with a life sentence, 7-8, 129, 134,
        158, 166;
    death of loved one, 142-43, 148;
    declining health, 85, 142, 207;
    loss of freedom, 173
correctional officers. *See* staff.
courts and sentencing, 17, 23, 26-27, 61,
    129, 202
crazy, 20, 28, 50, 65, 71
crime, circumstances of, 180
cycle of violence, 50-51

Daly, Kathleen, 17
death anxiety, 150-51
death related losses, 142
death penalty, 25, 60, 160
death with dignity, 152
demographic profile, 7
dental, 11, 121, 142
depersonalization, 179
depression, 11, 124-30;
    abuse history, 53, 111;
    adjustment to prison, 57, 73, 82, 99,
        134, 136;
    drug use, 30;
    grief, 153;
    reentry, 203;
    religion, 161, 174.
    See also mental health

deprivation, 11, 25, 47, 70, 110, 123,
    135, 137, 158, 260, 203
disciplinary infraction, 53, 57
disenfranchised grief, 145
divorce, 10, 38, 40-41, 45-48, 52, 85,
    89, 97, 134, 136, 141
drug addiction, 30, 52, 110, 134
dying in prison, 12, 49, 64, 150-53

early release, 177, 201
end-of-life care, 152, 169, 204
education, 9-12;
    access to, 192-95, 206;
    GED, 9, 19, 73, 193-94;
    lack of, 5, 19, 24-25, 102, 165, 192;
    improvements in, 57, 71, 73-74, 78,
        201;
    vocational, 73, 188, 193-196
Estelle v. Gamble, 123-124
evil woman hypothesis, 2
exercise in prison, 113-15, 117, 207

Faith and Character-Based Program, 73
family:
    aging, 91, 100;
    contact, 90, 100;
    drugs, 19;
    living members, 9, 90;
    loss of, 59-60, 72;
    prison adjustment, 86;
    satisfaction with, 98;
    supports, 1, 12, 15, 45, 56, 57, 75,
        85, 87;
    violence, 20, 40, 41, 47, 74;
    worries of, 67
fear of:
    being forgotten, 12, 101, 105, 140;
    dying in prison, 151, 162, 169;
    getting out, 62, 193;
    growing old in prison, 148-50, 190;
    physical violence, 20, 45;
    the unknown, 65, 125
functional health, 116, 148